WHITE RULE IN SOUTH AFRICA
1830-1910

WHITE RULE IN SOUTH AFRICA
1830-1910

VARIETIES IN GOVERNMENTAL POLICIES AFFECTING AFRICANS

by

Edgar H. Brookes

M.A., D.LITT., LL.D.

PIETERMARITZBURG
UNIVERSITY OF NATAL PRESS
1974

© UNIVERSITY OF NATAL PRESS

ISBN 0 86980 031 0

This book is an extensive revision of 'The History of Native Policy in South Africa' which first appeared in 1924. A second revised edition was published in 1927.

Printed in the Republic of South Africa
INTERPRINT (PTY) LTD . DURBAN

Table of Contents

Preface 7

CHAPTER

I	Introductory	9
II	Early Cape Policy	15
III	Early Voortrekker Policy	35
IV	Natal: The Shepstone Policy I	41
V	Natal: The Shepstone Policy II	59
VI	The Evolution of the Transkeian Policy	73
VII	The Transkeian Council System (continued) . . .	87
VIII	Transvaal and Orange Free State Policies . . .	97
IX	African Customary Law	111
X	The Recognition and Codification of African Customary Law	129
XI	Local Administration	153
XII	Land Distribution and Land Tenure	159
XIII	Agriculture	175
XIV	Industry	189
XV	Religion and Education	195
XVI	Addendum: South Africa since 1910	203
Index	. . . .	211

70403

Preface

In 1924, at the ripe age of twenty-seven, I published a book entitled 'The History of Native Policy in South Africa'. A second and revised edition was published in 1927.

This book was ambivalent. As a history it has, on the whole, stood the test of time very well. But it was also a political treatise and in general supported, with moderation but decisively, the doctrine of differentiation or separate development, which is the basis of present-day Governmental policy in South Africa.

Between the years 1927 and 1929 my views on these matters changed radically. At a public conference at Fort Hare in 1930 I recanted my earlier views before a large and representative gathering of students. Since then I have moved steadily in the direction of a policy of equal rights in a united South Africa, and I was National Chairman of the South African Liberal Party when it was compelled to dissolve itself in the face of legislation prohibiting multi-racial political parties.

My political views are now well-known both inside and outside South Africa. Thus there has never been a third edition of my 'History of Native Policy'.

But because of the value of its historical content my book, long out of print, is still being quoted in high schools and universities and students are being referred to library copies for study. It would be a help to them to be able to get their own copies of the accurate history divorced from the questionable political comment.

This is precisely what this book sets out to provide. I have not replaced my earlier political remarks with later and (as I would feel) better ones, but have as far as possible confined myself to an objective history of the period from 1830, when Africans first came under white rule, to 1910, the date of formation of the Union of South Africa. A concluding chapter indicates the main lines of policy after 1910.

The writing of this book has been made possible by a research grant from the South African Institute of Race Relations, and I desire to express my thanks to the Institute, its Director and its Research Officers for this help.

EDGAR H. BROOKES

CHAPTER I

Introductory

It is advisable to indicate right from the beginning the scope and limitations of this study. It is not a work of social anthropology, and takes for granted some knowledge of the African 'tribal' past. The subject before us is a study of institutions, a research into the way in which the white governments of South Africa, colonial or republican, attempted to govern the Africans who had come under their rule. Not without some hesitation the year 1830 has been taken as the starting-point of this study, for this is the year when the Cape Government – at that time the only white Government in South Africa – first had to make provision for the government of Africans within its borders.

The reason for hesitation was the fact that other indigenous groups had come within the colonial boundaries earlier. The 'Bushmen' and 'Hottentots'* were with the Dutch East India Company from the moment of Van Riebeeck's landing in 1652. No white government effectively controlled the Bushmen during the period covered by this book. As regards the Hottentots, as W. M. Macmillan in his 'The Cape Colour Question'[1] (the first of a trilogy which revolutionised South African historical study) and more recently, Sheila Patterson in her 'Colour and Culture in South Africa',[2] have pointed out, the Hottentots were outside the law, as if they were an independent and distinct people.

'It was not,' writes Professor Macmillan,[3] 'that the Company or its officials were willingly countenancing injustices. Often they punished white colonists for offences against Hottentots. Once, at least, they cancelled a grant of land on the ground of the prior occupational rights of one Wild-Schat, a Hottentot captain on the outskirts of Stellenbosch. But without administrative machinery, and without police to make protection effective, it was the rule of a Company rather than of a State, and the definition of the legal status of the Hottentots was left a thorny legacy to the Company's successors.'

British legislation of 1809 brought the Hottentots fully within the ambit of the Colonial Courts and at the same time subjected them to a Pass Law. But by the famous 'Fiftieth Ordinance' of 1828, they, with

---

* I use the earlier and better-known unscientific terms throughout this Chapter, but not in any pejorative sense.

all 'free persons of colour', were exempted from nearly all discriminatory legislation, and thus the way was open for a society *legally* (if not always practically) free from colour discrimination. The non-racial franchise introduced by the Cape of Good Hope Constitution Ordinance of 1852 was a logical extension of these principles. Africans coming under Cape rule before the annexation of the Transkeian Territories, benefited to a considerable extent from this. It was only after the episode of the Cape rule of Lesotho and the extensive Transkeian annexations that the white leaders of the Cape took fright and attempted to build up a separate and parallel system of administration, which was fully developed in the Transkei.

The emancipation of the slaves in 1834 accelerated the process by which the Hottentots were absorbed in the larger and somewhat amorphous mass of the 'Cape Coloured People'. The Hottentots as an independent and defined group have virtually ceased to exist in the Cape, and that is why this study starts with the first incorporation of Africans in 1830.

Nevertheless the years between 1652 and 1830 left certain important legacies, good and bad, to those who began to rule Africans. First was the very widespread feeling that colour was a mark of inferiority, a characteristic of all slave societies. Second was the conception of a legally non-racial society which influenced Cape policy very greatly in the nineteenth century, until the era of extensive annexations caused Cape politicians to take fright at the prospect of being 'overwhelmed' by a large black majority.

It is at this point that we may pass to the crucial date of 1830. Before doing so a brief note on Sources should be made.

Sources

The research on which this book is based was almost entirely directed to primary sources, of which the quantity is simply bewildering, and which in the early 1920's had hardly been touched. This has involved an amount of labour which can better be imagined than described. To read – as the writer had to do – through every scrap of printed matter in the Archives relating to Native Affairs in the Cape is in itself a Herculean task, especially when one recollects the arid tracts in that vast expanse, reminiscent of nothing so much as of Chaucer's Poor Parson's Tale. To wade, again, through the quaint spelling, and more than quaint writing, of the Archives of the Republic of Lydenburg is in itself a liberal education. But the general content and distribution of the various Archives are sufficiently well-known to historical students to render it unnecessary to mention in more detail more than a few specially interesting sources.

The Archives of the Province of the Transvaal (1877-81) are of special value to any investigator of the Shepstone system, as showing the Shepstones (Sir Theophilus and Mr. Henrique) with a free hand deliberately and consciously introducing that system into the

Transvaal. No study of Natal records can be complete without them.

Light is thrown on both the Transvaal and Natal by a study of the Archives of the New Republic (1884-7). They are better arranged (and better written) than other early Republican documents; and throw much light on the cross-currents of Transvaal-Natal-Zululand policy in a very obscure and confused period. The writer cannot refrain from mentioning that among these documents he found a neatly-written memorandum accompanying a map drawn to illustrate the New Republic-Zululand boundary question (1884). In the bottom lefthand corner of the map is the familiar and honoured signature 'Louis Botha' – probably among the first of many official documents bearing that name.

The Archives of Lydenburg, of the 'Province of the Transvaal' (1877-81) and of the New Republic are all to be found in the Central Archives at Pretoria.

In the Cape and Natal there is, for part of the period, a series of publications to which no parallel exists in the other Provinces. The Cape Native Blue Books were commenced in 1874 as the result of a resolution of the Cape House of Assembly of 10th June 1873, and the Natal Native Blue Books at the instance of Governor Sir Henry Bulwer in 1878. From 1890 both sets tend to become the typical Government Blue Book, than which perhaps no more need be said. Up to that date they furnish not only a most valuable but also a most interesting and easily accessible source. Containing the original reports of the Magistrates of the two most thickly-populated Native areas in South Africa over a considerable period of years, they are invaluable. In the earlier years, too, Magistrates 'spread themselves' in a quaint but interesting way, even to the extent of quoting Horace – an anfractuosity perhaps less common now than then.

As regards Natal, the writer had the additional advantage of the loan (through the courtesy of Mrs. S. O. Samuelson and Mrs. H. S. Walker) of a large quantity of official and personal papers of the late Mr. S. O. Samuelson, Under Secretary for Native Affairs in Natal from 1893 to 1909 – material of the very highest historical value, and hitherto inaccessible to researchers.

The Transvaal offered no such adventitious aids. Here it was a case of written documents not merely first or last, but all the time. For the benefit of subsequent researchers, the author would mention that the State Attorney's papers may, with advantage, be consulted in addition to those of the Superintendent of Natives.

Reference must be made here to Commission Reports. The most valuable and interesting are those of the Commons Select Committees of 1836 and 1851, the Cape Native Laws and Customs Commission of 1883, the historic Natal Commissions of 1846-7, 1852-3, 1881-2 and 1905-7 and the South African Native Laws and Customs Commission of 1903-5.

A brief Bibliography of some of the more important secondary sources is given in an Appendix to this Chapter.

NOTES TO CHAPTER I

1 Macmillan, W. M.: "The Cape Colour Question: A Historical Survey" (London, Faber & Gwyer, 1927)
2 Patterson, Sheila: "Colour and Culture in South Africa" (London, Routledge and Kegan Paul, 1953)
3 Macmillan: *op. cit.* p. 35

SELECTED BIBLIOGRAPHY

The list below does not claim to be a complete bibliography of the rule of blacks by whites from 1830 to 1910. It is simply an indication of some of the more outstanding books on the subject since the first publication in 1924 of the volume of which this is a revision.

AGAR-HAMILTON, J. A. I.: The Native Policy of the Voortrekkers (Cape Town, Maskew Miller, 1928).
BINNS, C. T.: The Last Zulu King (London, Longmans, Green & Co., 1963).
—, C. T.: Dinuzulu (London, Longmans, Green & Co., 1968).
BROOKE, A.: Robert Gray (Cape Town, Oxford University Press, 1947).
BROOKES, E. H. and WEBB, C. DE B.: A History of Natal (Pietermaritzburg, Natal University Press, 1965).
—, E. H. and HURWITZ, N.: The Native Reserves of Natal (Vol. VII of Natal Regional Survey. Cape Town, Oxford University Press, 1955).
CAMPBELL, W. B.: The South African Frontier 1865-85: A Study in Expansion (S.A. Archives Year-Book, Vol. 22, 1889).
DAVENPORT, T.: The Afrikaner Bond (Cape Town, Oxford University Press, 1966).
DE KIEWIET C. W.: The Imperial Factor in South African Politics (Cambridge, University Press, 1937).
DU TOIT, A. E.: The Cape Frontier 1847-1866 (Archives Year Book for South African History, 1954 Vol. I, Government Printer, Elsies River, 1954).
EMANUELSON, O. E.: History of Native Education in Natal 1835-1927 (Unpublished Thesis in University of Natal Library).
GALBRAITH, J. L. S.: Reluctant Empire: British Policy on the South African Frontier 1836-54 (Berkeley, University of California Press, 1963).
GORDON, R. E.: Shepstone (Cape Town, A. A. Balkema, 1968).
HERD, N.: 1922: The Revolt on the Rand (Johannesburg, Blue Crane Books, 1966).
HINCHLIFF, P. B.: John William Colenso, Bishop of Natal (London, Nelson, 1969).
HOERNLÉ, R. F. A.: South African Native Policy and the Liberal Spirit (Cape Town, University of Cape Town Press, 1939).
HORTON-DAVIES and SHEPHERD, R. H. W.: South African Missions 1800-1950 (London, Nelson, 1954).
HOUGHTON, D. H.: Life in the Ciskei: the Keiskamma Hoek Survey 1947-51 (Johannesburg, S.A. Institute of Race Relations, 1955).
HORWITZ, R.: The Political Economy of South Africa (London, Weidenveld & Nicholson, 1967).
HUNTER, MONICA: Reaction to Conquest (London, Oxford University Press, 1966).
LORAM, C. T.: The Education of the South African Native (London, Longmans, Green & Co. 1927).
MACMILLAN, W. M.: The Cape Coloured Question (London, Faber & Gwyer, 1927).
—, W. M.: Bantu, Boer and Briton (Revised Edition) (London, Oxford University Press, 1963).
—, W. M.: Complex South Africa (London, Faber & Faber, 1936).

PATTERSON, SHEILA: Colour and Culture in South Africa (London, Routledge & Kegan Paul, 1963).
REES, W.: Colenso Letters from Natal (Pietermaritzburg, Shuter & Shooter, 1958).
ROGERS, H.: Native Administration in the Union of South Africa (Pretoria, Government Printer, 1948).
RUTHERFORD, J.: Sir George Grey: A Study in Colonial Government (London, Cassell, 1961).
SCHAPERA, I.: Tribal Innovators (London, Athlone Press, 1970).
SHEPHERD, R. H. W.: Lovedale, South Africa: The Story of a Century (Lovedale, Lovedale Press, 1942).
SULLIVAN, J.: The Native Policy of Sir T. Shepstone (Johannesburg, Coulter Marshall, 1928).
SUNDKLER, B.: Bantu Prophets (London, Camelot Press, 1948).
TATZ, C. M.: Shadow and Substance in South Africa: A Study in Land and Franchise Policies affecting Africans 1910-1960 (Pietermaritzburg, University of Natal Press, 1962).
THOMPSON, L. M.: African Societies in Southern Africa (London, Heineman, 1969).
TYLDEN, G.: The Rise of the Basuto (Cape Town, Juta, 1957).
VAN DER HORST, S. T.: Native Labour in South Africa (London, Cassell, 1970).
VILAKAZI, A.: Zulu Transformations (Pietermaritzburg, University of Natal Press, 1962).
WELSH, D.: The Roots of Segregation: Native Policy in Natal 1845-1910 (Cape Town, Oxford University Press, 1971).
WOLFSON, F.: Some Aspects of Native Administration in Natal under Sir Theophilus Shepstone (Unpublished Thesis, University of the Witwatersrand 1946).
WILLIAMS, D.: When Races Meet (Johannesburg, A.P.R. Publishers, 1967).

CHAPTER II

Early Cape Policy

It is a matter of great difficulty to fix on a date which marks the beginnings of the permanent submission of Bantu tribes in appreciable numbers to white Governments. But probably we shall be near enough to accuracy if we take the despatch of Sir Lowry Cole dated 2nd January 1830, and the reply of the Colonial Secretary, Sir George Murray, dated 6th May of the same year, as a suitable starting point. Sir George Murray's despatch is so important and illuminating that it deserves to be quoted *in extenso*:

'I have received your despatch of the 2nd January last, in which you report the results of your recent visit to the eastern frontier of the Colony under your government, and I am happy to learn that all serious apprehension of an invasion from Caffraria has subsided.

'I concur with you however in regretting that a portion of the ceded Territory continues to be occupied by bodies of Caffres, whose numbers I collect, from the tenor of your despatch, to be very considerable. This is undoubtedly a great evil; for while on the one hand it is not to be expected that these people will ever voluntarily evacuate the Colonial territory, I am not, on the other hand, prepared to authorise you to expel them by force of arms from the land of their birth.

'At the same time it is clear that, without entirely abandoning the policy which sought to set up a bar of separation between the Caffres and the Colonists, the former cannot be allowed to remain as owners of the soil in permanent occupation of the Colonial territory. That policy which embraces the interest of the Caffres themselves should not be lost sight of. It was a wise measure to remove them from temptations which must attach to their close proximity to the borders of the Colony; and it would be not only sacrificing the ultimate hope of their civilisation, but the immediate welfare of an extensive district of the colony, to allow the Caffres to retain their present locations without some effectual guarantee that they will not abuse the temporary indulgence which you have felt yourself induced to continue to them. That guarantee should be their peaceable conduct; and it must be fully understood that every attempt which they shall make to plunder the farms or property of the colonists, will, as in the case of Makomo, be visited by the immediate expulsion of the whole tribe to which the plunderers shall belong. I confess I see no other course which can be followed, consistently with the safety of the Colony, for leading these people to adopt the habits of civilised life; and this should be not only fully explained to them, but arrangements should be made and promulgated by proclamation for enforcing their expulsion from the Colony simultaneously with the occurrence of any gross misconduct on their part.

'I need not, of course, impress upon you the necessity of taking effectual measures for preventing any of the tribes beyond the boundary from locating themselves in the Ceded Territory.'

It will be noticed that the British Government approached the problem of ruling Africans with extreme distaste. The history of the next seventeen years in the Cape is merely a record of the efforts of Great Britain to evade all responsibility in this direction; and it is not until the closing weeks of the year 1847 that we find this hesitating policy ended by the masterful hand of Sir Harry Smith.

Combined with the distaste for ruling Africans directly was a strong wish to control the tribes through treaties with their Chiefs.

The beginnings of the Treaty System are to be observed as early as 1833. On 27th November of that year, a Colonial Office despatch was addressed to Sir Benjamin D'Urban calling his attention to the propriety of 'cultivating an intercourse with the Chiefs of the Caffre tribes' by stationing 'prudent and intelligent' men among them as Government Agents. The Colonial Secretary expressed the view that many, if not all, of these chiefs might be gradually induced, in return for small annual presents, to become responsible for the peaceable conduct of their clans. In accordance with these instructions, Sir Benjamin D'Urban concluded the first of a series of treaties – that with the Griqua Captain Andries Waterboer – on the 11th December, 1834.

The reply of the Colonial Office[1] was almost embarrassingly cordial: 'I not only approve in the fullest manner,' wrote Lord Aberdeen, 'of the object and terms of this agreement, but I am desirous of expressing the high satisfaction which it has afforded to His Majesty's Government to learn that you have, even in one instance, succeeded so completely to realise the view which the King's Government entertain of the only policy which it becomes this country to observe and steadfastly to pursue in regard to the native tribes by which the colony under your Government is in a great measure encompassed.'

It must be perfectly clear that the policy of the British Government was definitely laid down in unmistakeable terms before the conclusion of the Sixth Frontier War, and before the accession of Lord Glenelg to office. That policy was (1) to avoid assuming the direct rule of African tribes, (2) to enter into treaties with the various African chiefs on the basis of their independent sovereignty. Lord Glenelg in 1836 introduced no new policy; he simply carried out the previously defined policies of his predecessors. It is most unfair to associate his name exclusively with the treaty system and its failures.

Not Lord Glenelg, but Sir Benjamin D'Urban, was the apostle of change. Before the commencement of the Sixth Frontier War he had informed Mr. Spring Rice, then Colonial Secretary, that 'a complete and effectual reformation of our system of dealing with the native tribes (if that may be called a system which seems to have been guided by no fixed principle, certainly by no just one) has become absolutely necessary.' His criticism was as unfair as his own earlier policy was conspicuously lacking in constructive elements. Unjust or unwise the Colonial Office policy may have been: unprincipled it certainly was not.

In the last weeks of the year 1834 broke out, as is well known, the Sixth Frontier War. Into its romantic details and stirring military history it is no part of the plan of this work to enter.

On 10th May 1835, the tract of land between the Keiskama and the Kei Rivers was proclaimed British Territory under the designation of the 'Province of Queen Adelaide'. This proclamation which may be assumed to reflect Sir Benjamin D'Urban's own unbiassed policy did not, as is often incorrectly assumed, involve the proclamation of direct British sovereignty over the tribes previously resident in that area. On the contrary it declared that 'Tyali, Macomo, Eno, Botma, T'Slambie, Dushanie,* etc.,' were 'forever expelled' from the Territory of Queen Adelaide and would be treated as enemies if found therein. At the same time the intention was to treat these chiefs, even in their new homes beyond the Kei, as British subjects.

Had Sir Benjamin D'Urban's policy been carried out, the only result would have been furious intestine wars between the tribes thus thrust back over the Kei and those at that time occupying land in the Transkeian districts. These conflicts would have resulted inevitably in a further inroad into the European area – an area which would have been more sparsely populated than that which the Bantu had just overrun. The only argument in favour of the change was that the Kei was a better military frontier than the Keiskama. It will be argued that Sir Benjamin D'Urban was well-meaning. But so was Lord Glenelg. A modern novelist has told us that, short of grave moral crime, the accusation of being well-meaning is the worst that can be brought against a man in a position of responsibility.

We shall see, in a moment, that Sir Benjamin D'Urban, in the concluding months of 1835, entirely reversed his previous policy; but the news of this reversal had not reached Lord Glenelg when he penned his notorious despatch of 26th December 1835. In the circumstances it is difficult to maintain that Sir Benjamin D'Urban was entirely in the right or Lord Glenelg entirely in the wrong. The issues have been so confused by the commencement of the Great Trek immediately after the retrocession of Queen Adelaide, that it is difficult to see the problem in its proper perspective as a minor incident of frontier policy. More eloquent misrepresentation – from both sides – has been wasted on the Glenelg Despatch and the Treaty System than on any other part

---

* I follow the spelling of the proclamation.

of South African frontier policy. It has been claimed[2] that Dr. Philip was in favour of the retrocession of Queen Adelaide. As a matter of fact Dr. Philip's own evidence on the subject, given before the Commons Select Committee on 4th July 1836, was as follows:[3]

'I think it will be a matter to be regretted if the new province shall be again dissevered from the Colony. Had I been consulted before the Caffre war on the propriety of annexing the country between the Keiskama and the Kye [sic] to the Colony, I should have said, let the Caffres alone, the work of civilisation is going forward among them, and in a little time what you wish for will come about of itself without any violent means being necessary to bring it about; but, now that the thing has been done, there are many considerations which make it desirable that the recent treaty, with such modifications as may be deemed necessary, should be confirmed by the British Government.'

Dr. Philip refers to the 'recent treaty'. What was this treaty? It becomes necessary to go back and explain that Sir Benjamin D'Urban's proclamation of 10th May 1835 never became fully operative, one excellent reason being that the 'expelled' tribes refused to cross the Kei, and it was found that immense loss of life and heavy expenditure would have to be incurred to shift them. Accordingly on the 17th September a treaty was signed with the leading chiefs concerned, by which they agreed to become British subjects and, while retaining their own laws and customs, to come generally under the control of the Cape Government. This was a far more satisfactory solution than the expulsion of the tribes over the new boundary line. By this arrangement approximately 72 000 Africans came under European rule. The Governor proceeded to appoint an Agent-General and tribal agents to supervise the subject tribes. For these two points – the extension of civilised control to the Africans, and the beginning of European administration among them – Sir Benjamin D'Urban must be held responsible.

Unfortunately his despatches announcing the treaty and these appointments crossed Lord Glenelg's despatch of the 26th December. There can be no doubt that Lord Glenelg's plain duty, on receiving the new information, would have been to cancel his previous despatch and to make further inquiries. In any case, he might have waited until the Commons Select Committee, which had begun to take evidence early in 1836, had issued its report. The arrangements for the retrocession were, however, proceeded with and concluded at King William's Town on the 5th December 1836.

Looking at these events with our present knowledge of the problems involved, it is easy to see that Sir Benjamin D'Urban's later policy was right, and that his own earlier policy and Lord Glenelg's policy throughout were both wrong. But, when we consider that Lord Glenelg was simply carrying on a policy of some years' standing, the policy of predecessors of both parties at the Colonial Office, and that he had the strong support not merely of missionaries like Dr. Philip but of a South African born administrator lately resident in the Eastern Districts –

Andries Stockenström – it is impossible to censure him. To judge a man's actions by their results is, surely, unfair. Had there been no Great Trek – a thing which no individual could possibly have foreseen – Lord Glenelg's despatch of 1836 would have appeared no more and no less foolish than Sir Harry Smith's solemn exhortation to the chiefs at King William's Town on 7th January 1848 to 'abolish the sin of buying wives' and 'to acknowledge no chiefs but the Queen of England and her representatives'.

Mention has been made of the Commons Select Committee of 1836-7. It consisted of Mr. Fowell Buxton (Chairman), Sir Rufane Donkin, Sir George Grey, Colonel Thompson and Messrs. Hawes, Bagshaw, Holland, Lushington, Pease, Baines, Johnston, Hindley, Plumptre, Wilson and Hardy, the last-named being subsequently replaced by Mr. W. E. Gladstone. Of these gentlemen only Sir Rufane Donkin, Mr. Bagshaw, Mr. Holland and Mr. Gladstone manifested any open sympathy with the Colonists. So far as Sir George Grey was not a mere silent voter, his sympathies appear to have been with the Chairman's party.

Many of the incidents of the evidence led before this Committee, and a few points in its report, are well known to the student of South African history in the pages of Theal. What we are chiefly concerned with here are the conclusions which had a practical effect in the shaping of South African policy. It is commonly supposed that the Committee reported wholeheartedly in favour of the treaty system. On the contrary, the Committee speaks with a double voice. In theory it is against treaties: in practice it recommends for the Cape a series of treaties embracing most of the tribes then known to Europeans.

On page 80 of the Committee's report we read:

'Treaties with Natives inexpedient

'As a general rule . . . it is inexpedient that treaties should be frequently entered into between the local Government and the tribes in their vicinity. Compacts between parties negotiating on terms of such entire disparity are rather the preparatives and the apology for disputes than securities for peace: as often as the resentment or cupidity of the more powerful body may be excited, a ready pretext for complaint will be found in the ambiguity of the language in which these agreements must be drawn up, and in the superior sagacity which the Europeans will exercise in framing, in interpreting and in evading them. The safety and welfare of an uncivilised race require that their relations with their more cultivated neighbours should be diminished rather than multiplied.'

But on page 81 we find the following:

'Cape of Good Hope

'It may be concluded that the territory called Adelaide has in fact been surrendered to the Caffres and that Lieutenant-Governor Stockenström is proceeding to execute Lord Glenelg's instructions. Your Committee will therefore transcribe them in this place . . .

'1. A treaty, fixing the boundaries of the Colony, must be made in writing, in English and in the Caffre language, and, being explained to each border Chief, must be signed or attested by each. Copies of this treaty must be delivered to each of the contracting Chiefs.

'2. A separate treaty must be made in the English and in the Native languages, with the Chief of every tribe to which a portion of territory is assigned within the British Dominions: defining the limits of his allocation, the degree of his responsibility, and the nature of his relations with the British Government, and all other matters admitting of specification. A copy of this treaty in the native tongue must be preserved by the Chief.

'3. A separate treaty must be made in the Native and English languages with the Chief of every tribe in alliance with us, or in any degree under our protection, defining also in each case all that can be specified in such an instrument. A copy of the treaty must be preserved by each Chief.

'Your Committee would strongly impress upon His Majesty's Government the propriety of a strict adherence to these Regulations.'

Thus ambiguously fortified, the Colonial Office proceeded to work out its previously adopted treaty system more fully. Treaties were signed with Mzilikazi (Moselekatse) on 3rd March 1836; with the Fingo captains Umhlambiso and Jokweni on 10th December 1836; with the emigrant Tembu chief Mapasa on 18th January 1837 and on 28th January 1841; with the Gunukwebe clans on 19th June 1838; with the Gaika clans on 2nd December 1840; with the Mdlambe clans on 31st December 1840; with Mpande on 15th October 1843; with Adam Kok in November 1843 and in February 1846; with Moshesh on 13th December 1843; with Faku on 7th October 1844;* with Kreli on 4th November 1844; with the Rarabe and Fingo chiefs in January 1845.[4] (The spelling used in the Treaties is followed here.)

By a series of coincidences unfortunate for British reputation, while many of these treaties were repudiated when Britain subsequently came into collision with the tribes concerned and while the treaty system in general was publicly repudiated by Sir Harry Smith in 1847, the engagements with Faku were made the basis of the attack on the Republic of Natal, the treaty with Moshoeshoe (Moshesh) was used as an argument for the annexation of Basutoland (Lesotho) at the expense of the Orange Free State and the treaty with Andries Waterboer was employed in a very questionable way for the annexation of the

---

* Informal engagements were entered into in 1839 and 1841.

Kimberley diamond fields. It is advisable to mention this chain of unfortunate circumstances as explaining to some extent the strong criticisms subsequently made of the treaty system. But it should be noted that the policy of the very Voortrekkers who began to quit the eastern Cape as the treaty system came into effect was marked by certain very famous treaties.

The Government of the new Province of Queen Adelaide, now renamed British Kaffraria, showed from the very first signs of a greater reliance on the European magistrate and a more definite attempt to civilize than the contemporary Natal policy. The chiefs still ruled their people according to Native customary law, but their decisions were liable to be reviewed by the magistrate, and if found 'inconsistent with justice and humanity' they might be reversed.[5]

Roman-Dutch common law was clearly inapplicable, and the idea of recognising Native Law as such was not entertained: so for some years the territory was kept under martial law and the magistrates adjudicated as martial law officers, being thus left free to use their discretion.[6] The failure to recognise Native Law can apparently be explained only by Sir Harry Smith's absence in the Orange River Sovereignty and Natal: for Sir Harry Smith had been one of the first men in South Africa to advocate a Code of Native Law.[7]

In this confused and difficult situation there broke out the Seventh Frontier War (commonly known as the War of the Axe). The result of this sanguinary conflict was the complete reversal of the previous official policy, and a return to the later policy of Sir Benjamin D'Urban, and this we owe almost entirely to one man – Sir Harry Smith. Though Sir Harry only assumed duty as Governor on the 1st December 1847, he proceeded with his usual sanguine and impetuous haste to the settlement of the whole boundary question and to the dictating of terms of peace to the already defeated clans within a few weeks. The territory between the Keiskama and the Kei Rivers, nearly but not quite identical with the old Province of Queen Adelaide, was annexed, not to the Cape Colony but to Great Britain direct, under the name of British Kaffraria. Further north round the headwaters of the Keiskama River the Colonial boundary itself was pushed eastward. British Kaffraria was to be regarded as a reserve for the African people, over whom the High Commissioner was to assume the position of a Paramount Chief. Able officials, among whom Captain (later Colonel) Maclean and Mr. Charles Brownlee should receive special mention, were appointed to office in the province.

On the 7th January 1848 a great meeting of chiefs and others was called to hear what their new position would be as subjects of the Queen. It is necessary, if we are to understand the foundations of Cape African policy, to follow the terms of this settlement. Unfortunately for the subsequent historian, Dr. Theal has described this historic meeting so vividly that it seems almost a duty to quote him rather than refer to the original documents:[12]

'After a prayer by the reverend Mr. Dugmore, Wesleyan Missionary, Sir Harry Smith addressed the Kaffirs upon their position. The Chiefs then made oath:

1. To obey the laws and commands of the high Commissioner, as great chief and representative of the Queen of England;

2. To compel their people to do the same;

3. To disbelieve in and cease to tolerate or practise witchcraft in any shape;

4. To prevent the violation of women;

5. To abhor murder, and to put to death every murderer;

6. To make their people honest and peaceable, and never to rob from the colony or from one another;

7. To acknowledge that their lands were held from the Queen of England;

8. To acknowledge no chief but the Queen of England and her representatives;

9. To abolish the sin of buying wives;

10. To listen to the missionaries and make their people do so;

11. On every anniversary of that day to bring to King William's Town a fat ox in acknowledgement of holding their lands from the Queen.

'Some of these conditions were subversive of the whole framework of the Kaffir society,[13] nevertheless the chiefs took the oath in the name of the Great Spirit without any compunction. Few of them had any intention of keeping it.

'Sandile and Kona represented that the ground on which their people were then living was too limited in extent for their needs, and wanted the high commissioner to give them also the territory between the Keiskama and Fish Rivers. They were informed that there was plenty of vacant land towards the Kei on which they could build kraals and make gardens. None of the others had any request to make; and all were profuse of thanks.

'Sir Harry Smith then addressed them again, telling them what would happen if they were not faithful. "Look at that wagon," he said, pointing to one at a distance which had been prepared for an explosion, "and hear me give the word 'Fire!'" The train was lit and the wagon was sent skyward in a thousand pieces. "That is what I shall do for you," he continued, "if you do not behave yourselves." Taking a sheet of paper in his hand: "Do you see this?" said he. Tearing it and throwing the pieces to the wind, "There go the treaties," he exclaimed. "Do you hear? No more treaties!"'

In this dramatic manner the policy of 1830-47 in the Cape went sky-high with Sir Harry Smith's wagon. Circumstances had proved too strong for abstract reasonings. When the British Government ratified the new arrangements on the 31st March 1848 it could be said definitely that white South Africa had begun that long process of governing black South Africa which it is the object of this volume to examine.

Immediately adjoining British Kaffraria was the recently constituted magisterial division of Victoria East. In this area it was proposed to settle in locations a large number of the Mfengu who had assisted the Government in the War of the Axe. This important duty was entrusted to the Rev. Henry Calderwood, who was nominated Civil Commissioner for the Division. The scheme of settlement for which Mr. Calderwood was chiefly responsible, but which owed its success very largely to Sir Harry Smith's prompt and generous support, was not only highly successful in itself, but also the precursor of many similar schemes in the Ciskei and Transkei.

The Africans were placed in locations and allocated individual holdings on which a quit-rent of £1 per annum (reduced for the first year to 10/-) was payable. No difficulty was found in collecting this money from the Mfengu – who, indeed, were better off than they had ever been in their lives – and in the very first year, while the scheme was still in an experimental stage, a revenue of £475 10s. 0d. (being 951 quit-rents at 10/- each) was collected. Thus, from the very beginning, the Cape aimed at making its native population self-supporting. We may compare this with the early Natal hut tax introduced and collected without difficulty by Shepstone. The quit-rent however (so it was argued) was an inducement to industry and tended to tie the Native down to his plot and prevent vagrancy. From the very beginning the money collected from the locations was ear-marked for expenditure on them.

The superintendence of the locations was made extremely simple, they being managed principally by Native headmen under the direction of white superintendents, who corresponded with the Government through Mr. Calderwood in his capacity of Civil Commissioner.

Mfengu and others, found in the Division, not attached to any location, were made liable to punishment: and any incipient vagrancy was thus nipped in the bud.

Prizes were offered for the best and largest quantity of cultivated ground, the best fencing, the best crop of wheat or other 'European produce' and the best stock of poultry in each location. Under this inducement, and aided by the zealous and able supervision of Mr. Calderwood, the Mfengu progressed rapidly in civilization and material wealth, and the Government was able definitely to use them as a civilizing agency by transplanting some of them to the Transkei in 1865. Among African peoples the Mfengu have proved easily adaptable to European methods and very amenable to the influences of civilization.[8]

In British Kaffraria itself, Sir Harry Smith instituted the practice of distributing presents amongst chiefs, increasing the quantity and value for good conduct and reducing, or in aggravated cases entirely suspending, them for misconduct. Sir Harry designedly used this system as a civilizing agency by introducing agricultural and other implements among the presents. For the year 1849 the gifts included cloth and moleskin jackets, corduroy and moleskin trousers, check shirts, neckerchiefs, Glengarry caps, 'female dresses', shawls, blankets, saddles, bridles, spades, sickles, files, steel polled axes, felling axes, pick-axes, cooking pots, 'basting spoons', hand-saws, ploughs, sledge-hammers, crowbars, augurs, adzes, drawing knives, gimlets, vices and bags of nails. The Aborigines Protection Society contributed one hundred spades and twelve ploughs.[9]

Unfortunately, in British Kaffraria as elsewhere, Sir Harry Smith's sanguine and impetuous temperament made him proceed with the walls before the foundations were properly laid. The great meeting of 7th January 1848 had been spectacular and impressive for the moment: but the chiefs were very far from being thoroughly subdued. On Christmas Eve 1850 broke out what is usually known as the Eighth Kaffir War, a desperate struggle which was prolonged to the autumn of 1853. In the course of the war, Sir Harry Smith was recalled, by the irony of fate on the pretext that his prosecution of hostilities was not vigorous enough! He was replaced early in 1852 by Sir George Cathcart.

With the new Governor came a new policy. Under the terms of settlement of 1853 the people were to be governed by their own chiefs according to their existing laws and usages in regard to matters of internal discipline. Magistrates ceased to have any administrative or judicial authority and became 'political agents'.[10] So strongly was this new system adhered to that the Governor would not even intervene to prevent judicial murders for alleged witchcraft.

The territorial reconstruction of 1853 involved the reservation of land for Africans as purely Native territory under the rule of the chiefs. This was not a reaction towards what is generally called the Glenelg policy for the chiefs were definitely treated as subjects of the Crown and not as independent potentates.

It is only fair to say that Sir George Cathcart himself did not at first advocate this scheme of segregation as a general Native policy but merely as an expedient, by precluding European colonization, for placing a barrier between the Colony and the tribes beyond the Kei.[11] As regards others, however, the case is different. There can be little doubt that the whole scheme represents the considered and deliberate policy of Earl Grey. For in essence it was the contemporaneous Shepstone policy applied to the Cape, and the Shepstone policy had been approved by Earl Grey with almost embarrassing cordiality.[12] That policy had been advocated before the Commons Select Committee[13] of 1851 by Sir George Napier, and the conflicting recommendations of Sir Peregrine Maitland[14] had not been able to remove the impression made by the concrete success of the policy of recognising the chiefs in Natal. When we consider the way in which Sir George Cathcart dealt with Moshoeshoe (Moshesh) and the Basotho problem, we are forced to the conclusion that a year or two's experience had converted him to the Colonial Office's views.

The system of 1853 never had time to work itself out. Before any results, good or bad, could be seen, it came under the control of a great constructive statesman who did not hesitate to 'scrap' it and return to a more skilful elaboration of the policy of Sir Harry Smith. There may have been wiser South African statesmen than Sir George Grey, but none with a more singlehearted devotion to the interests of his people, or with a more active philanthropy. He assumed duty on the 5th December 1854. Less than three weeks later he was writing[15] to his namesake at the Colonial Office as follows:

'The plan I propose to pursue . . . is to attempt to gain an influence over all the tribes included between the present north-eastern boundary of this Colony and Natal by employing them upon public works which will tend to open up their country; by establishing institutions for the education of their children and the relief of their sick; by introducing among them institutions of a civil character suited to their present condition; and by these and other means to attempt gradually to win them to civilization and Christianity, and thus to change by degrees our at present unconquered and apparently irreclaimable foes into friends who may have common interests with ourselves.'

The direction thus given to the Native policy of the Cape towards its eastern territories has determined its course ever since. Less of a great man than Shepstone, Grey was more of a good man. With less permanence of tenure, he had, while he was in office, funds not entirely inadequate for his schemes. A less striking personality, he was content to create a system and to delegate freely to others: thus, when he was withdrawn, his policy survived him.

It will be noticed from the passage quoted above that Sir George Grey had definitely decided no longer to treat the question of African rule as a mere problem of frontiers. He had definitely decided to extend European rule, in the interests of the Africans themselves, to all the tribes of South Africa as occasion permitted. It is not without a certain dramatic justice that the first public announcement of the new policy was made in the Speech from the Throne to the first Parliament of the Cape Colony on the 15th March 1855. From that date the gradual process of annexation continued until in March 1894 the Governor's dream was realised, and the Cape reached, at all points, the southern frontiers of Natal.

Sir George Grey had contemplated the introduction among the Africans of 'institutions of a civil character suited to their present condition'. The meaning of this phrase soon became apparent. The chief was to be gradually replaced by the white magistrate[16]– a complete reversal of the policy pursued under Sir George Cathcart. The first tentative steps in this direction were made in 1855.

Sir George Grey rightly saw that the great obstacle to the introduction of a European judicature was the fact that the fines levied by the chief's court formed a major portion of his revenue. If the chiefs could only be assured that they would not be material losers, the initiation of a new order of things would not be so formidable a task after all. The cattle-sickness prevailing in the year 1855, by drying up the source from which fines might be levied, furnished an excellent opportunity for a change.

An estimate was therefore made of the approximate annual value of the fines received by the several chiefs under the existing system, taking into account the uncertain nature of the revenue raised from such a source, the difficulty and unpopularity of levying it, and other similar circumstances; the chiefs were then offered a monthly stipend, at an equivalent rate, payable by the Government, together with an allowance of so much a head for so many councillors to be paid to the individuals performing the duties of that office, at the stipulated rate, for the number of days they performed such duties.

'Under such a plan,' Sir George Grey himself writes, 'the worst part of the Kaffir policy is broken down. Every Chief of importance will receive a certain regular income, for which he will be dependent upon the Government of the Country and will therefore have the strongest interest in its maintenance and success. European laws will, by imperceptible degrees, take the place of their own barbarous customs, and any Kaffir Chief of importance will be daily brought into contact with a talented and honourable European gentleman, who will hourly interest himself in the advance and improvement of the entire tribe, and must in process of time gain an influence over the Native races which will produce very beneficial effects.'

It will be gathered that the introduction of the magisterial system took the form of magistrates being selected to 'assist' the chiefs. An illustration of the manner in which they acted will be seen from the subjoined report of Captain J. Reeve, 73rd Regiment, Special Magistrate with Chief Kama, dated Middledrift, 7th March 1856:

'It is with the greatest satisfaction that I have to acquaint you that the system of His Excellency with regard to this district seems to have given general satisfaction both to the Chief and his people.

'In all cases which have been brought before Kama, I have been present, and have done my utmost to keep in view His Excellency's wish as to my position as adviser and assessor with the Chief-in-Council.

'I have found in every case in which I have expressed an opinion, or asked a question, that the greatest respect has been shown me respecting it.

'I have carefully explained to Kama that I have to act as his friend and *not* as the Chief of his tribe, and I am convinced that he sees that now in its proper light, and feel sure that this feeling will soon obtain throughout the tribe, though I am aware, from some of the questions asked me by headmen whom I have visited, that a general feeling obtained among the people at first, that it was the intention of the Government to give them white men as Chiefs. I need scarcely say that I have laboured to correct this impression.

'I am confident that Kama and those of his people with whom I have been much in contact, look upon me as their friend, as they have, on several occasions, come to me for advice and assistance when misunderstood by white men, and I am glad on several occasions to have removed difficulties, and corrected errors to the satisfaction of both parties.

'I have succeeded on one occasion in levying a fine in money by the decision of Kama and his Council: it was a trifling case, and the fine at my request was small, but I conceived that his Excellency would desire to have money fines to be gradually introduced, as it seems to have many advantages on the old system. In this instance the fine was paid at once to me in the presence of the Chief and Council, its justice acknowledged, and being small, thankfully paid.'

Utilising consummate cunning, or aided by extraordinary luck, Sir George Grey had struck a vital blow at the power of the chiefs under the mask of these innocuous regulations. For, while the chief was legally entitled to be present at all trials, he no longer had any pecuniary interest in the bulk of them. His subsidy came in monthly, whether he did much or whether he did little. It is not surprising, then, that in a very few years the Ciskeian chiefs had ceased to adjudicate in criminal cases, being replaced entirely by the magistrates. In civil cases, however, they continued for many years to arbitrate privately, although they had no legal power to enforce their decisions, and this action was generally popular with the people.

There is no doubt that Sir George Grey is entitled personally to the whole credit for the conception of this scheme. Colonel Maclean, the Commissioner for British Kaffraria, was much averse to its being put into execution and wrote at length against it. Both he and the Governor felt that the embers of war were still smouldering in British Kaffraria – a belief confirmed by the strange episode of Mhlakaza and Nongqase (1857) and the self-destruction of so many thousands of the Xhosa people by starvation. After this terrible time, however, peace reigned in Kaffraria; and the situation was such that the Colonial Office confirmed all that Grey had done and definitely took over British Kaffraria (1860) as a separate dependency of the Crown.

Doubtless the fact that the Grey system was financially self-supporting weighed heavily in its favour at the Colonial Office. The payments to chiefs and headmen were met out of the annual hut tax levied in imitation of the similar impost in Natal. A 'horse tax' of 2/- per animal was suggested in 1861, but never actually levied. The financial autonomy of the 'Native Territories' was not the least important feature of the Grey policy.[17]

The Courts constituted in British Kaffraria were at a loss to know exactly what system of law to administer. It was many years before proper arrangements were made. For a short while during the year 1860 the courts actually refused to take cognisance of *ikazi* (*ukulobola*) cases, but this attitude was reversed in the same year.

Grey was, as Governor, interested not only in the African but in the white settlement of the Ciskei (British Kaffraria). Valuable research has been done in recent years on this part of his work, but it is of course only indirectly related to our main theme. Grey's white settlement plans did at least mean that, as in the case of Natal but even more so, black and white areas were inextricably mixed up, and a policy such as was afterwards applied to the more homogeneous Transkei was rendered impossible.

While these political, legal and other changes were taking place, attention was also paid to the amelioration of African life. Medical treatment and hospitals were provided. As early as 1856 it was estimated that, in one quarter, 1 679 Xhosa, 495 Mfengu and 204 Hottentots received treatment in British Kaffraria.[18] The splendid work of Dr. J. P. Fitzgerald at the King William's Town Hospital must never be forgotten. An early instance of the gratitude felt for this treatment is evidenced by a letter to Queen Victoria dated King William's Town, 23rd June 1856, and dictated by one Mahlati Zikali through Lot Hrayi, the hospital interpreter. Mahlati Zikali had been cured, by operation, at the King William's Town Hospital of blindness after sixteen years:

'I am very thankful to you, dearest Queen Victoria, because you have sent for me a good doctor, a clever man. I was sixteen years blind, Mother and Queen, now I see perfectly. I see everything. I can see the stars, and the moon, and the sun. I used to be led before, but now, Mother O Queen, I am able to walk myself. Let God bless you as long as you live on earth. Let God bless Mother. Thou must not be tired to bear our infirmities, O Queen Victoria.'

It must not be thought that tribalism was destroyed during the few years of Sir George Grey's rule. The chiefs retained their old influence for a time almost as strongly as ever[19] but, while something of their political power had gone, the communal spirit was still to a large extent undisturbed.

On 17th April 1866, British Kaffraria was definitely annexed to the Cape Colony – in spite of bitter opposition to the annexing Act (No. 3 of 1865). It is an extraordinary thing – as we shall see later in our examination of the Basutoland episode – how the people of the Cape and their political leaders time after time evaded the responsibility (as it was then thought to be) of ruling the Africans around them. They wished to throw this responsibility on Great Britain, yet they vehemently resented British interference in their internal affairs.

Against their will, then, and only as a direct result of the Governor's personal pressure, the electorate of the Cape – including a few Africans already[20] – became responsible for the government of British Kaffraria. The Ciskei, as this area came to be called, became an integral part of the Colony. Colonial law applied to it, though the magistrates shrank from the absurdity of applying it to many civil cases, and without any legal authority continued to be guided by tribal law in these.²¹ The autonomous system of the Transkei, described in a later chapter, was not at this date thought of.

On 28th November 1872 the Constitution Ordinance Amendment Act (No. 1 of 1872) received the Royal Assent. By this Act the Cape Colony received full responsible government and was thus for the first time mistress of her own fortunes and unfettered ruler of large numbers of Africans.²²

It will be our duty later to examine how she fulfilled her trust, both in the Colony proper and in the semi-autonomous Transkeian Territories.

NOTES TO CHAPTER II

1 Despatch of Lord Aberdeen dated 11th April 1835.
2 Theal: History of South Africa since 1795, Chapter XXVII (London: George Allen & Unwin, 4th edition 1915).
3 Commons Select Committee on Aborigines (British Settlements) 1836, p. 625.
4 Most of these treaties and several additional ones are to be found in Blue Book 'Pattern of Copies or Extracts of any Engagements subsisting between this Country and any States or Native Tribes in South Africa' presented to the House of Lords by Lord Carnarvon and ordered to be printed 25th March 1884.
5 Report of Native Laws and Customs Commission (Cape) 1883, p. 16.
6 Governor Sir Geo. Cathcart to Sir G. A. Pakington, Despatch No. 3 of 20th May 1862.
7 Col. Harry Smith to Sir Benjamin D'Urban, 18th April 1836.
8 For the Smith-Calderwood Location Scheme see Sir Harry Smith to Earl Grey, 15th March 1849 and 24th May 1849. Blue Book 'Correspondence relative to Kafir Tribes' 1850 *passim*. The locations were thoroughly inspected and reported on by Calderwood on 22nd January 1855.
9 Blue Book – Eastern Frontier Kafir Tribes, 1850-51, p. 7.
10 Report of Native Laws and Customs Commission (Cape) 1883, p. 16.
11 Sir George Cathcart to Sir G. A. Pakington, 20th May 1852.
12 See his Despatches Nos. 566 and 567 of 7th and 11th January 1851.
13 Evidence, p. 213.
14 Evidence, p. 359.
15 Governor Sir George Grey to the Right Hon. Sir George Grey, Bart., December 22nd, 1854.
16 Report of Native Laws and Customs Commission (Cape) 1883. Where no other reference is made in the succeeding paragraphs, my authority is Sir George Grey's Despatch No. 46 to Sir William Molesworth and the latter's reply No. 45 of 20th March 1856.
17 Duke of Newcastle to Sir George Grey, 4th May 1861.
18 Sir George Grey to the Right Hon. H. Labouchere, 18th August 1956.
19 For some striking instances of this see the Evidence of Sir Walter Currie before the Select Committee of the Cape Legislative Council on Kaffir Passes, 1862, p. 6.
20 As is well known, the Cape of Good Hope Constitution Ordinance (1852) contained no political colour bar.
21 Report of Native Laws and Customs Commission (Cape) 1883, p. 17.
22 Including the Basotho, annexed in 1871. *Vide infra*.

APPENDIX TO CHAPTER II – THE TREATY SYSTEM

Copies of the Treaties with Mzilikazi (Moselekatse)
Mpande (Panda) and Moshoeshoe (Moshesh)

A

Articles of Agreement between the Governor of the Colony of the Cape of Good Hope, on the one part, and Umsiligas (by his representative and Chief Councillor Um'nonbate, specially appointed for the purpose of treating) on the other part.

1. The King of the Abaqua Zooloo or Qua Machaban, Umsiligas, engages to be a faithful friend and ally of the Colony.

2. He engages to preserve order in his territory and to abstain from war unless forced thereto in self-defence.

3. He engages to protect all white men who may visit his country, and to defend and treat in a friendly manner, all missionaries or other persons who may, with his consent, settle and reside in his territory so long as they act in accordance with justice.

4. He engages to defend and assist all travellers or traders who may reach his country either with the object of extending knowledge or otherwise benefiting mankind.

5. He engages not to interfere with the remnants of tribes, resident in the vicinity of his country, unless in self-defence, and promises to permit them to enjoy, undisturbed, the advantages of religious instructors, should any such be disposed to settle among them.

6. And generally, he engages to cultivate and encourage peace, and apprise the Colonial Government of any intended or actual hostile movements in the interior, and to act in concert with the said government in subduing whatever may be calculated to disturb the general peace, or retard the civilisation and prosperity of the native tribes of South Africa.

In consequence of the above engagements the Governor, upon his part, engages:

1. That he will regard Umsiligas and his subjects as friends, and will receive any of them as such when they visit the Colony.

2. That he will grant, in the first instance, as presents for Umsiligas, a variety of articles suitable to his present condition, and will continue supplies of this kind from time to time so long as the terms agreed upon should be strictly observed.

And in order to facilitate intercourse hereafter, between Umsiligas and the Colony, the Governor will duly consider the request made for an individual of the Colony to be resident with the Abaqua Zooloo or Qua Machaban, and endeavour to obtain a missionary for that purpose, who will be most calculated, under circumstances, to forward the views of the contracting parties.

Thus done at the Government House in Cape Town this third day of March, in the year of Our Lord One thousand eight hundred and thirty-six.

            B. D'URBAN, Governor (L.S.)
            UM'NOMBATE his X mark (L.S.)

Signed and sealed in our presence:
ANDREW SMITH, M.D.
JAS. EDW. ALEXANDER, A.D.C.

B

Articles of a Treaty made and entered into between and Signed by the undersigned PANDA, King of the Zoolah Nation, on the one part, and the undersigned, the Honourable HENRY CLOETE, Esq., L.L., LL.D., in his capacity as Her Majesty's Commissioner for the Territory of Natal, on the other part.

Article 1. There shall be henceforth and forever peace and friendship between the undersigned King Panda and his subjects, and Her Majesty Queen Victoria, and all her Majesty's subjects.

Article 2. It is hereby agreed between the undersigned that the respective boundaries between the Territory of Natal and the Zoolah Nation, shall be defined at the sea-line by the mouth of the River Tugela, and from thence upwards until the junction of that stream with the river Umsinyatee (or Buffalo River), from thence upwards by the said river Umsinyatee (or Buffalo River); or such other boundary line along or near its banks, as may, at any time hereafter, be fixed upon by the undersigned, Her Majesty's Commissioner for the Territory of Natal, or such other Commissioner as Her Majesty may appoint, and by any two Indunas or Commissioners, whom the undersigned Panda, King of the Zoolah nation, may appoint for that purpose, and from thence northward to the foot of the Quathlamba (or Drakensberg) Mountains.

Article 3. The undersigned Panda, King of the Zoolah nation, hereby agrees and binds himself to direct Koedoe, the captain of certain kraals placed by the late King Dingaan on the right bank of the Tugela, and all such other captains or Chiefs of kraals as may be found to come within the boundaries of the territory of Natal, hereby fixed and determined, to be removed from their respective stations.

The undersigned, Her Majesty's Commissioner, for and on behalf of Her Majesty hereby agreeing and consenting to allow them to remain until their crops shall have been reaped, and then to take with them all their effects and lawful property.

Thus done and agreed upon and confirmed by the signature and marks of the undersigned King Panda, and the undersigned, Her Majesty's Commissioner, at the chief town of Elapeen, on this the 5th day of October, 1843, in the presence of the undermentioned witnesses:

This is the mark of the King X.
Panda, made by himself.
This is the mark of the Induna X.
Umsinhlaan, made by himself.
This is the mark of the Induna X
Umkondasi, made by himself.
H. Cloete, L.L.
Her Majesty's High Commissioner.

Witnesses:

D. C. TOOKEY

C. J. BUISSINE

This document has been faithfully interpreted from word to word by me, to the King Panda, who declared fully to understand and approve of the contents thereof.

J. KIRKMAN

I, the undersigned, Chief and King of the Zoolah nation, do hereby declare to cede all right and title, which I heretofore had to the mouth of the River Umvolosi, and to the bay there situate, to, and in favour of Her Majesty Queen Victoria, or the lawful sovereign of Great Britain for the time being, for ever, with full liberty to visit, land upon, and occupy, the shores along the said bay, and mouth of the said River Umvolosi, the undersigned hereby agreeing and consenting to appoint whenever he shall be thereto requested, two indunas or Commissioners for the purpose of defining, and proving the limits and extent, of the sea shore so ceded and given up to Her Majesty Queen Victoria, or the lawful sovereign of Great Britain for the time being.

In witness hereof I have hereto affixed my mark at my chief town of Elapeen, on the 5th day of October, 1843, in the presence of the undersigned witnesses:

This is the mark of King PANDA X made by himself.

X the mark of the Induna UMVANKLAMA.

X the mark of the Induna UMKONDANE.

Witnesses:

D. C. TOOKEY

C. J. BUISSINE

This document has been faithfully interpreted from word to word by me, to the King Panda, who declared fully to understand and approve of the contents thereof.

J. KIRKMAN

C

Articles of Treaty and Agreement between the Governor of the Colony of the Cape of Good Hope, on the one part, and Moshesh, Chief of the Basutos, on the other part.

1. The Chief of the Basutos engages to be the faithful friend and ally of the Colony.

2. He engages to preserve order in his territory, to restrain and punish any attempt to violate the peace of the frontier of the Colony by any people being within his country, or by any people from the interior who may attempt to pass through the territory for that purpose; and to seize, and send back to the Colonial authorities, any criminals or fugitives from the Colony.

3. The territory of the chief Moshesh is bounded from the west, from the junction of the Caledon with the Gariep Rivers, by the Gariep river from the junction aforesaid; and the north, by a line extending from about 25 to 30 miles north of the Caledon River, excepting near to its source, and at its junction with the Gariep, where the lands of Bethulia and the territory of Sikonyella come close upon its northern bank.

4. He also engages to assist the colonial authorities in any enterprise which they may find it necessary to undertake for the recovery of property, or the apprehension of banditti, who, having been pursued from the Colony, may have taken refuge in any part of the Country under his jurisdiction.

5. And, generally, he engages to apprise the Colonial authorities of any intended predatory or hostile attempt against the Colony which may come to his knowledge, and to co-operate, cordially and in all good faith, with the Colonial

Government, in preserving peace and extending civilisation among the native tribes.

In consequence of the above agreement, the Governor, upon his part, engages:
To make the chief a present from the colonial treasury of not less than £75 annually, either in money or in arms and ammunition, as the Chief may desire.

And in order to facilitate a due observance of these mutual engagements, and to secure the benefits which they are intended to afford to both parties, the Chief Moshesh will correspond direct with the Government on all subjects mutually concerning his territory and the Colony; and he also engages to receive and protect any agent whom the Government, in course of time, may think necessary to appoint, at his residence, and confidentially communicate with such agent upon all matters concerning his territory and the Colony.

Thus done at Government House in Cape Town, this fifth day of October in the year of our Lord, one thousand eight hundred and forty-three.

(L.S.) GEO. NAPIER,
Governor.

Signed and sealed in our presence:
JOHN MONTAGU, Secretary to Government.
JOHN PHILIP, D.D.

Thus done at Thaba Bossi, on the 13th day of December, in the year of our Lord one thousand eight hundred and forty-three.

(L.S.) mark of X MOSHESH

Signed and sealed in our presence:
T. E. CASSALIS
JEAN THOMAS ARBOUSSET
JAMES WALKER
PAULUS MANTATEE, Mark O of
JOSHUA MAKOANYANE, Mark X of
HAMILTON MOORE DYKE

CHAPTER III

Early Voortrekker Policy

The causes of the Great Trek have often been examined, but it seems desirable to pass them briefly in review before examining the beginnings of Voortrekker policies towards the Africans.

In a way every compelling cause of the Trek had something to do with attitudes towards Africans, but some were only indirectly connected with this. It has been said that the Great Trek was a revolt of the eighteenth century against the nineteenth. It has also been said, and with equal truth, that the feeling of the Trekkers was not so much against the British Government as against government as such. Law and order had caught up with frontiersmen accustomed to deal vigorously and directly with their own problems. South Africa's 'wild east' can be compared in this respect with America's 'wild west'.

One reason often given for the Trek is the emancipation of slaves. But that this was a very minor reason can be seen from the fact that the bulk of the slaves were in the western Cape and the bulk of the Trekkers came from the eastern Cape.[1]

That the moving cause of the Great Trek lay in the field of race relations and colour policies[2] cannot be doubted. This is not a matter in which critical moral judgments are called for. Even if they were, they could not concentrate all the blame on one side. Were the English or the Scots more to blame for sixteenth century border raids? On the Cape's eastern frontier, Xhosa cattle thieves were numerous. Vengeful and acquisitive commandoes exacted not a tooth for a tooth, but two teeth for a tooth. The British frontier authorities tried to hold the balances even, but this was an attitude not approved by the Trekkers, any more than American frontiersmen appreciated federal intervention to protect the Indians. Those who trekked away from the Cape Colony felt that the first duty of a white government was to protect white colonists. They were prepared to fight their own battles, as they had been compelled to do under the rule of the Dutch East India Company. If they were to have troops and government officials on the frontier, these ought to be there as protectors not as impartial arbiters. Changes of policy, unforeseen and inexplicable, followed from Cabinet changes in Britain. Colonial Secretaries followed one another in rapid succession. It could not be expected that embattled frontiersmen should even understand these changes, let alone accept them. The frontier farmers felt that they 'understood the Native' and that officials and missionaries were dangerous theorists, reasoning from unchecked first principles, and not from practical experience.

Such feelings as these impelled the heroic first Trekkers to leave their homes and their accustomed way of life for a pathless wilderness, and, incidentally, to found three of the four divisions of South Africa. They knew that they were going into an area populated by African nations and tribes. The way in which they handled these is, in view of their objection to British methods, of intense interest.

In the earlier years of the Trek, any study of policies towards Africans must concentrate largely on the Republic of Natalia. There was much left to be desired in this policy, but a careful reading of the relative Archives leaves us in no doubt as to the superiority of the Republic of Natalia over the Republic of Lydenburg, the South African Republic prior to 1877, the much later New Republic and the Orange Free State. In concentrating on the policies of Natal, we are therefore seeing Voortrekker policy at its most coherent.

The mere fact that depopulated Natal was selected as the first Voortrekker territory is in itself significant. The Trekkers were not animated by a lust for conquest, but by a passion for land and for security. In the end this passion could not be fully satisfied, and shortly after 1840 even empty Natal soon had 25 000 African refugees from Zulu rule[3] and by 1845 there were 100 000.

Largely depopulated Natal was certainly subject to the Zulu military monarchy and Retief, as the Trekker leader, hastened to conclude a treaty with its head, Dingane. The Treaty was found on Retief's dead body after the Battle of Blood River, and the whole sequence of events may well have led the surviving Voortrekker leaders to think that Retief had been too magnanimous and too trustful.

Nevertheless when Dingane's younger brother Mpande revolted against him, the Republic of Natalia entered into treaty relations with the rebellious prince. The treaty, however, was of a very different nature from that between Retief and Dingane, which was a pact between equals. Mpande, recognised as the king of the Zulus, was definitely to rule as the vassal of the Republic. He had to pay a vast indemnity of 40 000 head of cattle[4] and to cede to the Republic all the land between the Thukela and the Black Mfolozi,[5] approximately half of Zululand.

This unashamed acquisitiveness for land appears again and again in Voortrekker history, and sometimes forged or unreliable documents of cession were produced to justify it.[6] As it happened, the Republic was unable to stake out farms in southern Zululand before the British annexation, and in 1843 the British Administration restored the Thukela boundary.[7] Our study must therefore concentrate on the way in which the Republic of Natalia dealt with its own African subjects within its own restricted boundaries.

From the commencement of 1840 scarcely a session of the Volksraad of Natalia passed without a discussion of this subject, and members were repeatedly urged to effectual action.

It must be pointed out that the emancipation of these tribes, until recently under the, to them, grievous bondage of the Zulu monarchy, and the relatively mild nature of the White Government's rule, rendered the Africans concerned exceedingly amenable to control, at any rate for many years.[8] They were submissive, orderly and respectful towards the white population.[9] Proposals to move them, provided they were not sent back to Zululand, would probably not have been resisted by force.

In dealing with the problems of the African influx, the government was much assisted by its independent position which enabled it to act with promptitude and decision in every emergency without the necessity of applying to a distant authority.

Generally speaking the policy of the Republic was to mark off an area for predominantly white occupation, to retain sufficient Africans therein for agricultural labour purposes, to secure an equitable distribution of this labour supply, to segregate the remaining part of the African population, and to rule such Africans as remained in the white area paternally, justly and kindly, but retaining them in a position of entire subordination – social, religious, political and economic. There was to be no attempt to break down the tribal system except so far as the families living on farms were concerned. It was not intended to force Africans to stay within the white area and work – not intended, because it was not necessary. The Africans wanted to remain within the white areas. Those who were refugees had temporarily broken away from tribal ties, and, if the Volksraad's policy were right, the opportunity of securing labour before the tribal system should be resuscitated was a golden one. This only must be said – that the members of the Volksraad, like Shepstone a few years later, were suiting a practical policy to practical ends. Like him, they were not concerned whether their system would be a satisfactory one for a South Africa embracing all the African tribes more than a century ahead. Unlike him, they deliberately shirked the problem of how to govern an overwhelming African population at the time.

A 'Plakkers Wet' (Squatters' Law) was passed in 1839 and on the 5th August 1840 the Volksraad passed a resolution[10] to the effect that the Commandant-General alone should be permitted to have more than five families of 'Zolas' on his farm.[11] The objects of this legislation appear to have been, first to limit the total number of natives in the white area, second to secure an equitable distribution of the labour supply, and third to prevent the practice of 'kaffir-farming'. On the 3rd January 1842 another resolution was passed authorising the Commandants to supervise distribution 'according to law'. On the 4th September 1843 the original law was confirmed, the general limitation to five families being expressly mentioned.

In August 1841 was passed the famous resolution which proposed to dispose of the surplus African population by placing it on a tract of land between the Mtamvuna and Mzimvubu Rivers, to the south of the Republic – a proposal repeated more than once afterwards. It was this resolution, and the complaints of Chief Faku regarding it, which gave the British Government a pretext for definitely interfering in the Republic's affairs once again. The Volksraad was never actually able to carry it out, though it was confirmed in the above-mentioned resolution of 4th September 1843.

On 10th May 1843 Natal was formally annexed to the British Empire, the Volksraad giving its formal consent in the following August. But for the next two years and a half the territory was in a curious state of transition. The Cape Government was represented during part of this time by the Commissioner, Dr. Henry Cloete; and a small garrison under Major Smith held Durban. Meanwhile the Volksraad continued to function at Pietermaritzburg and pass resolutions of some importance. It was not until December 1845 that the future government of Natal was settled, the Volksraad abolished, and a number of new officials unacquainted with the language[12] and traditions of the Voortrekker settlers took office.

It is at this stage that we must leave the Voortrekkers, for what follows is the development of the 'Shepstone system' in the Colony of Natal. The later Voortrekker policies will be considered when we pass to the study of the Transvaal and Orange Free State. It is not without hesitation that we sum up from imperfect records over a short period, the early Voortrekker policies here, but it is submitted that what follows is a reasonable and not unduly critical conclusion from the available facts.

(1) The Voortrekkers were willing to enter into treaty relations with African rulers as sovereign princes.

(2) They, however, much preferred to have them as vassals of the white states.

(3) The question of encouraging tribalism among their direct African subjects did not become an urgent practical one during the period 1838 to 1845.

(4) Nor did the question of slavery or 'apprenticeship' become important, although it did later in the Transvaal (*vide infra*).

(5) The African subjects of the Voortrekkers were considered mainly as a source of farm labour, and efforts were made to ensure its equitable distribution among the white farmers.

(6) First steps were taken towards the segregation of the 'surplus' population in a vassal state, but it was impossible to do this in the time available before the British annexation.

(7) No instances of gross cruelty can be found in the early Republican state.

NOTES TO CHAPTER III

1 Agar-Hamilton, J. A. I.: The Native Policy of the Voortrekkers (Cape Town, Maskew Miller, 1928) pp. 9-10. All historians of this period are deeply indebted to Dr. Agar Hamilton for this fine piece of research.
2 *Ibid.* pp. 12-14.
3 Report of Natal Native Affairs Commission 1852-3, p. 8.
4 P. H. Zietsman's journal, certified correct by Chief Commandant A. W. J. Pretorius and printed in Bird, J.: Annals of Natal (Pietermaritzburg, P. Davis & Sons, 1888). Vol. I, pp. 576-99.
5 *Ibid.* p. 895 (Pretorius's Proclamation).
6 See *inter alia*, Brookes, E. H. and Webb, C. de B.: A History of Natal (Pietermaritzburg, University of Natal Press, 1965) Chapter XIII.
7 Bird, J.: Annals of Natal (Pietermaritzburg, P. Davis & Sons, 1888) Vol. II, pp. 299-300.
8 See remarks of C. Brownlee in Cape Native Blue Book 1875, p. 123.
9 Report of Natal Native Commission 1852-3, pp. 8-9.
10 In Volume A 1/2 in Union Archives, Pretoria.
11 We find this limitation to five families later in the Orange Free State and in the South African Republic.
12 Shepstone was an exception: 'Hij spraak het platte Afrikaansche Hollandsch." (Jorissen: Transvaalsche Herrinneringen, 1897) p. 23.

CHAPTER IV

Natal: The Shepstone Policy I

The transition period between the submission of the Volksraad (1843) and the arrival of the British officials (1845) had very important effects bearing on the future policy of Natal towards its African population.

The spectacle, first of white men fighting among themselves, and second of two weak governments functioning in the same territory, served to convince the discontented Africans in Zululand – most of them, it is true, sons of those who had resided in Natal proper before Shaka's day – that there was nothing to fear from anybody in Natal. Anxious as they were to return to their ancestral homes, they poured over the Buffalo and Thukela Rivers in ever-increasing numbers. It is estimated that during the transition period not less than 80 000 Africans entered Natal and subsequently became permanent residents in the Colony. Disunion of the whites prevented any action until it was too late, the various resolutions of the Volksraad in favour of forcing the immigrants back into Zululand, or locating them elsewhere, being thwarted by Major Smith. It is, perhaps, useless to speculate now as to the possibility and advisability of checking this influx. All that concerns us at the moment is that when the new Government entered into office at the end of 1845 it was faced with the problem of ruling not 20 000 but 100 000 Africans; and that it found the European population absolutely decreasing, the majority of the Afrikaner settlers, disgusted with the way in which the British Government had dealt with them, having quitted the Colony by the end of 1848. The new administration thus had to face an entirely new position; Natal had once again become largely an African territory; and the problem now was how to rule and control the vast African population without police, without money and with but a small military garrison.

The hour brought the man. Theophilus Shepstone was the son of the Reverend William Shepstone, one of the first Wesleyan missionaries to labour in the Cape Colony. He grew up at Wesleyville among the Xhosa boys who were attracted to the mission station; he was encouraged by his parents to pick up the language; and while still a boy could understand and speak it perfectly. Xhosa and Zulu are so similar in construction, sound and vocabulary that he had no difficulty at a later date in acquiring Zulu, which he spoke fluently and eloquently. As a youth he was employed at the missionary press in supervising the printing of a Xhosa grammar and parts of the Xhosa Bible. At the age of nineteen, he acted as interpreter for Sir Benjamin D'Urban during the sixth Kaffir War, in which capacity he distinguished himself greatly.[1] When the little expedition of Captain Jervis occupied Durban (1838-9), Theophilus Shepstone – already known to the Africans in the Peddie district as 'Somtseu'[2]– accompanied it as interpreter. This was his first visit to the land of which he was to be the ruler in everything but name for thirty years (1845-75). When he arrived as 'Diplomatic Agent for the Native Tribes' in 1845, he was still under thirty years of age.

The military despotism of Shaka and Dingane had apparently succeeded within a generation in making a dangerous individual out of the Natal African. Even when well-disposed to the European Government – 'Holmen'[3] as he called it – he was not to be relied on. The Natal Native Commission of 1846-7 describes the character of the Bantu: 'Their universal character, as formed by their education, habits and associations is at once superstitious and warlike; their estimate of the value of human life is very low; war and bloodshed are engagements with which their circumstances have rendered them familiar since their childhood and from which they can be restrained only by the strong arm of power; their passions are easily inflamed, while at the same time they have grown up in habits of such servile compliance with the wills of their despotic rulers that they will still show ready obedience to constituted authority.' Shepstone himself was a member of this Commission, and its evidence is reinforced by the fact that the 1852-3 Commission, which was hostile to Shepstone's policy, repeats the description of African character almost word for word, adding however that the Africans were 'crafty and cunning . . . averse to labour and their general habits debased and sensual to the last degree.[4]' Can these horrible monsters be recognised by those who knew and appreciated the Natal Africans of a later date? The change occurred within a generation. One has only to read the two badly-printed and ill-arranged volumes of Evidence of the Natal Native Commission of 1881-2 to discover that thirty years of Shepstone's paternal rule had wrought a transformation. As one heathen after another gets up to bear witness to 'Somtseu's' love of the 'black house', and to soliloquise, in true Bantu fashion over the good old days when 'Somtseu' used to bring his chair out under the spreading tree and talk heart to heart with his people, instead of using one of the new-fangled interpreters who 'eat up the people's words', we feel that there is the vindication and the panegyric which no European commentator can give.

But in 1846 this change was not to be foreseen except by a few patient enthusiasts like Shepstone himself, and the new government was consequently much perplexed as to what it was to do with its vast and apparently dangerous African population. Lieutenant-Governor Martin West – one of South Africa's very forgotten worthies – accordingly appointed on 31st March of that year a Commission to report on the subject and on Native Affairs generally. The Commission consisted of Dr. Stanger, Surveyor-General, Mr. Theophilus Shepstone, Lieutenant C. J. Gibbs, R.E., and Dr. Adams and Rev. D. Lindley, American missionaries. It combined two qualities, not infrequently found in harness together – ability and unpopularity. Of the latter there can be little doubt. Its successor, the Commission of 1852-3, described it, in an explosive and exceedingly Anglo-Saxon paragraph,[5] as consisting 'entirely of officials and foreigners, namely one military man, two Government officials and two foreign missionaries'. The ability of the report is today, by those who have read it, very generally admitted. Earl Grey, in a despatch dated 10th December 1847, describes it as a 'very able document', a very large proportion of the recommendations of which 'he would be prepared to sanction but for the many heavy demands from all quarters made on the Treasury'. 'It is my duty', he goes on, 'at once and distinctly to discountenance the expectation that any plans . . . which would involve large expense can be adopted' – phrases which even in these days have a very familiar ring.[6]

Lieutenant-Governor West, in his instructions to the Commission, dated at Pietermaritzburg, 31st March 1846, had discountenanced the scheme of more or less absolute segregation recommended by the Volksraad of the Republic and supported by Shepstone himself even as late as 1854 but always successfully opposed by authority. In its place, Governor West suggested 'separate locations in the best disposable situations, to be hereafter conveniently superintended by one magistrate (each) and placed under the pastoral care of one or two missionaries each.' The report followed closely on these lines, for Shepstone was too wise to oppose in practice the good, because he could not get what he thought the better. In recommending the location system, it made several additional recommendations, and these must be considered before we approve or condemn the scheme as a whole.

(1) Each location was to be governed by a superintendent or resident agent of the Government who was to be furnished with one or more assistants according to the size of the location.

(2) Order was to be maintained by an African police force officered by Europeans.[7]

(3) In each location a 'model mechanical school' was to be instituted, where (I quote the report) 'the useful arts should be taught and practically illustrated'.

(4) In each location, systematic agricultural instruction was to be given by the superintendent.

As we have already seen, on the miserable pretext of economy, nearly all the constructive suggestions of the report were turned down by the Colonial Office. All that could be done was to lay out the locations and induce the Africans to move into them. This in itself was a formidable task, as there was no military force to back up the Government. Nevertheless by judicious and tactful methods Shepstone – on whom the whole of the burden fell – was able to place the 80 000 refugees in fixed homes in different parts of the country, without the loss of a single life – white or black. It is one of the most brilliant pieces of administrative work recorded in South African history. It may be said that the whole operation was carried out in direct opposition to the instructions of Earl Grey, who was not unnaturally afraid of the result of moving large masses of tribal Africans. He recommended that the actual construction of the locations should wait until the 'Executive Government was armed with military power sufficient to render all resistance to its authority hopeless.' Lieutenant-Governor Martin West rightly pointed out that further delay would be 'equivalent to the abandonment of the whole country to the Africans.' The location system was not, as the 1852-53 Commission suggested, a negrophilist scheme to hand great tracts of Natal over to the Africans but an insurance to save some parts of Natal for Europeans. This insurance, it is true, would have been unnecessary had the Republic and the original population of Natal been suffered to continue in possession, but that possibility had already been precluded by the British Government; Martin West and Theophilus Shepstone had done nothing to create the situation of 1845; but, once it was created, they coped with it with distinguished ability.[8]

Of the hordes of Africans who had to be placed in the locations it is estimated[9] that more than two-thirds were, as a result of the Zulu tyranny, without chiefs and without tribal organisation. As far as the available records go, there appears to have been no definite wish on Shepstone's or any one else's part to resuscitate the tribal system and the Commission of 1846-47 made the appointment of a white superintendent to each location an integral part of its recommendations. But when the Colonial Office expressed its inability to find funds for these posts, what was to be done? Undoubtedly West and Shepstone desired both to control and to civilise. Denied the facilities for civilising, they had in the meantime to control, in the interests of a small and scattered white population and of European prestige generally. The only method of control – and it is an instance of Shepstone's peculiarly administrative genius that he grasped the point and acted so speedily – was to recreate the tribal system artificially. The tribal ties had not disappeared for more than a generation. It was found possible by Shepstone to gather the scattered members of the tribes together, and even in some cases to find a scion of the old 'royal' house. In other cases, purely appointed chiefs had to be given jurisdiction. The policy was a complete success for the time being. Whether Shepstone kept it up when it had become unnecessary, whether in controlling so admirably as he did he gradually forgot the second duty of civilising – these are moot points which we must reserve for discussion later. But in 1847 no able man, in the peculiar circumstances then existing, could possibly have advocated or adopted any other system. It was wrung from Shepstone by the practical exigencies of the position. He cannot justly be either praised or blamed for his policy in this respect. For the administrative skill with which he carried it out he deserves our very warmest praises.

The measures of 1846-47 in Natal have been very vehemently attacked; but they were undoubtedly the best way out of a difficult position, remembering that the British Colonial Office would not countenance any segregation scheme. As for the 'excessive size' of the locations,[10] it must be remembered that they were and are often the most barren, wild and broken parts of an exceedingly rugged and picturesque division of South Africa. 'Only small portions here and there are adapted for cultivation and much of the land is not even fitted for pasturage, but only for the habitation of the eagle and the baboon.'[11] Even today the locations do not form more than about one-ninth of the area of the Province. The Commission, while it undoubtedly gave the African population of 1847 more than enough land for subsistence, did not err on the side of generosity when future generations were borne in mind; and after all nine-tenths of Natal, including most of the best farming land, was still left open for a population of not more than 10 000 Europeans. That the African population has so greatly overflowed the locations and 'squatted' on State Lands and private farms is not a fair article of charge against the West-Shepstone scheme of 1847.

'The Natal Native Policy', said Mr. J. X. Merriman in 1871,[12] 'is summed up in one word – Shepstone.' This is so literally true of the period 1845 to 1875 as to justify an examination of personal character such as would, normally speaking, be out of place in a work of this nature. More than that. After Shepstone's guiding hand was withdrawn, even after his death, and until the present day the whole fabric of institutions and laws affecting the Natal Africans remains a monument to his life-work. The breath of the living personality has gone out of the system: it has become cold and lifeless and stereotyped until there is today, perhaps, more to criticise than to praise in it. But, good or bad, it has been one of the most potent factors in the present situation.

The life of Shepstone is not an unworthy subject for romance. There are few stranger stories in history than that of how a single white man, with no military force, and generally unaided by police, ruled from 100 000 to 200 000 Africans within Natal, and for thirty-six years kept the peace among the still vaster hordes in Zululand, by moral force alone. When we add the unfortunate and questionable but daring episode of 1877 we are bound to say of Sir Theophilus Shepstone's life – to plagiarise – that it was stranger than some men's dreams. Few figures of South African history are more baffling enigmas.

Without the fullest research into all available documents, private as well as public, it seems all but impossible to reach a correct characterisation of the great Natalian; yet the attempt must be made if we are to understand a policy in which personality played so overwhelming a part. If the countenance can only be seen, as through a glass darkly, that represents the writer's state of mind. Yet he believes that the outline, if blurred, is not misleading; and at least it represents the best that a genuinely impartial criticism can produce.

Had we only the Natal part of Shepstone's life to consider the task would be easier. But to reconcile the Shepstone of the 1877 annexation with the Shepstone of early Natal history is a distressing and elusive problem. In the end we seem to see the real Shepstone as neither a spotless knight nor a lying trickster; neither a genius nor an overrated dullard; but a shrewd, patient, laborious, courageous and ambitions administrator, the shadow of whose great name lies across half a century of South African history, and whose career is redeemed from the merely intellectual by his genuine love of and sympathy for the 'black house', which reciprocated it with a passionate and unswerving loyalty to him and his.

Of his insight into the African mind, and of his love for the African people, there can be no doubt whatever. Mr. Charles Brownlee, than whom there could be no more competent judge, tells[13] us that he was thoroughly conversant with the laws, customs and prejudices of the Africans and that his thirty years of constant toil among them and for them had won their entire affection and sympathy. This is the evidence of a contemporary, and of a contemporary who, as Secretary for Native Affairs of the Cape Colony, had no temptation to magnify the abilities of his greatest rival. And yet there is no doubt that while Shepstone controlled, adjudicated, kept the peace, he failed conspicuously to ensure the educational and economic advancement of the people.

The truth is that he was rather a magnificent administrator than a deliberate framer of policy. All the requisites of a good colonial administrator – patience, thoroughness, tact, sympathy, self-reliance, a commanding presence, a full acquaintance with the language and customs of his people and a genuine respect for their traditions – were his in a pre-eminent degree. But there is no doubt that he failed, after his first brilliant measures, to adapt his policy to changing conditions and to give it a direction which would allow of future development.

There is no doubt that he was greatly assisted by circumstances. Few men have had better opportunities of distinction. But few men have used their opportunities better. The view that Shepstone was a very mediocre man who became famous simply because there was no one to compete with him cannot commend itself to those familiar with the written Archives and printed literature contemporaneous with his life.

His good qualities were many. Of his courage there can be no doubt. Charles Barter, a contemporary, relates a striking instance of this in his rhyming chronicle 'Stray Memories of Natal and Zululand':[14]

> Else had I told the thrilling tale
> I heard in Hlabatini's vale

> What time at Lambongwenye Kraal
> With Dunn I held high festival;
> How, when his successor to name
> To Panda's Court the hero came,
> And when, the business fairly o'er,
> Dunn's band had started for the shore,
> A rabble rout by frenzy fired
> Or by the chosen heir inspir'd
> Round Shepstone closed, with fell intent,
> Their murderous eyes upon him bent,
> And assegays in air that gleamed –
> No nearer death impending seem'd
> When sooth it came in after years
> Than then among the Zulu spears.
> Yet calm, with arm extended, he
> Points eastward to the shining sea:
> And 'Yes!' he cries, 'your spears may kill,
> But for each drop of blood they spill
> A host from out yon sea shall come,
> From England sent, my native home,
> And ample vengeance shall they take
> On you and yours, for Somtseu's sake.'
> Clear rang his voice upon the air;
> The lawless rabble crouch and stare;
> Down drop the spears and hark! a cry
> 'Inkosi! Inkosi!'[15] rends the sky.'

Courage again, if not of the most respectable kind, was demanded for the Transvaal expedition of 1877. The Republic was annexed, when all concealing verbiage is removed, by Shepstone himself, eight civil servants and twenty-five police. And Shepstone must have known that he ran the risk of being disavowed. As Dr. E. J. P. Jorissen says:[16] 'Het is duidelijk, Lord Carnarvon zou Shepstone overboord geworpen hebben, als zijn roeklooze daad ware mislukt en misschien eene botsing met de Boeren had uitgelokt . . . Sir Theophilus Shepstone heeft hoog-spel gespeeld, en, gelukkiger dan Dr. Jameson, gewonnen; daarbij den dank van een erkentelijk Gouvernement gekregen. Maar in den grond der zaak waren beide struikroovers.' ['It is clear that Lord Carnarvon would have thrown Shepstone overboard had his reckless deed miscarried and possibly even had it elicited a collision with the Boers . . . Sir Theophilus Shepstone had played for high stakes, and more fortunate than Dr. Jameson, had won; hereby he obtained the thanks and recognition of the Government. But at rockbottom both of them were freebooters.']

The patience of Shepstone was as pronounced as his courage. Let him who doubts this read through the Legislative Council debates of Natal in the 1860's and he will doubt no more. And, rarer still, Shepstone possessed, like General Smuts in later years, a cold magnanimity which refused to take offence at ignorant or malicious criticism. It is safe to say that in ten years of constant parliamentary strife from 1865 to 1875 Shepstone never lost his temper and never said an unkind word. When the British Government disannexed the Transvaal in 1881 and Shepstone fell into disfavour, not a word of public complaint passed his lips. He bore the reverses of fortune with a simple dignity that almost makes one forget that he had deserved them.

Yet with these clear-cut virtues he had the temperament of a trained diplomatist. Sir Bartle Frere describes him, in a despatch dated 3rd February 1879, as 'a singular type of an Africander Talleyrand, shrewd, observant, silent, self-controlled, immobile.' 'Forty years ago,' Sir Bartle continues, 'he might have been great in Continental diplomacy.' It was not without a certain appropriateness that his first official designation in Natal was that of 'Diplomatic Agent to the Native Tribes'. If we are to believe the population of the annexed Transvaal, he possessed some of the less desirable qualities which are customarily associated with the diplomatic calling. In their memorial to Queen Victoria of the 12th April 1879 they said: 'How was Sir Theophilus Shepstone able to annex the country without the burghers offering any armed resistance to it? Your Majesty, it grieves us deeply to have to say it, but we cannot do otherwise than speak the truth: he did it by craft, deceit and threats.' Only very careful research, and perhaps not even that, can tell us how far Shepstone was deceived and how far deceiving, but Metternich himself could hardly have carried through the annexation with more diplomatic finesse.

He was fond of secrecy. Barter, whose testimony as a friend and a contemporary is of the utmost value, tells us:

> When hostile or intruding eye
> Menaced his native policy,
> (Which like the priests of Isis old,
> He chose in shrouded veil to fold
> Unknown alike to friend or foe –
> *Ignotum pro magnifico*) . . .

And Frere, in the despatch already quoted, says:

'He has been driven, more and more, to trust to his naturally excellent memory, and to shut himself up in an irresponsible isolation, as the only man who knew anything about Native Affairs.

'Like many of his countrymen he is inclined to resent inquiry or control, and to treat in a hostile spirit all the information and all the suggestions about his department which do not come from himself. Hence it is not easy to help him, and his reticent habits make him very dangerous in troublous times . . . One never feels sure that one has got his whole and his real opinion and all the information he can give one . . . He has, of course, a vast fund of useful information, if one could get at it; but he is apt to regard it as his own private armoury, and not as belonging to the state. And I always feel, when I think he has gone entirely with me, that he may have said nothing about some fact or opinion which would have entirely altered my view.'

There certainly was throughout his ascendancy in Natal a disposition of secretiveness. Tribal policy was one of the *arcana sacra imperii*, with which it was impious for the average man to meddle. Shepstone did not possess the 'divine oil of delegation'. He trained up, outside his own family, no great administrators: in his own family he had a pathetic confidence, forgetting that two Somtseus in a century is a rare phenomenon in any one family. Both in his policy in Natal and also in the Transvaal he made no attempt to carry public opinion with him, shrouding himself and his schemes in impenetrable and unnecessary mystery. Reserved and self-contained by nature, a generation of contact with a people the least garrulous in the world as far as government is concerned had doubtless confirmed him tenfold in his habit of diplomatic secrecy.

Undoubtedly his temperament was conservative. The policy of *laissez-faire* held many attractions for him. Frere, in a letter to Sir Michael Hicks Beach dated 2nd May 1879,[17] describing the then condition of the Transvaal, says: 'Nothing save lifelong habits of trusting that "something would turn up" can explain to my mind the apparent absence of all effort to devise or substitute a better system . . . When you come to talk to him you find him full of good sense as well as of information, but it never seems to occur to him that he has any duty but to sit still and let things slide . . . He will doubtless give you many intelligent reasons for the whole machinery of administration being in abeyance, but I shall be surprised if he suggests any means of setting it going again.' This particular criticism is not entirely fair, for Shepstone did introduce several definite reforms in African policy during his occupation of the Transvaal; but in many respects it is illuminating and true. There is a sting of justice in the criticism made by Mr. John X. Merriman before the Inter-Colonial Commission of 1903-5:[18] 'You have not elevated the Natives in Natal; you have not raised them; you have not educated them; they are barbarians and you have designedly left them in a state of barbarism.'

That Shepstone was ambitious is a statement for which no evidence can be quoted. So far as a personal impression and a personal opinion can be allowed to find a place in an historical work, I should give my opinion that there was a distinct vein of ambition in him, and that the pride of being the arbiter of the destinies of South Africa weighed as much as anything with him in the episode of 1877.

Shepstone was first and foremost a Natalian. What makes the annexation of the Transvaal and its administration during the years 1877-81 so unreal, so artificial a thing – and that it was such, anyone who, like the writer, has gone carefully through its archives during that period will admit – was that in reality it was an annexation not to the British

Empire but to Natal, by Natal's uncrowned king. Nearly every head of department during the four years was a Natalian. Shepstone's success was felt in Natal as a Natal triumph; the retrocession was far more deeply mourned in Natal than in Great Britain. Such passion as Shepstone had outside his love for the African people was for Natal and for the Empire.

Baffling enigma as he is to the historian, difficult as it is to know what construction to put on so many of his actions, he is, good or bad, beyond all doubt one of the first half-dozen names of South African history.

Such was the man to whom the despotic and all but irresponsible control of the Natal Africans passed during the years 1845-47. The force of his natural ability was such that before long both the British Government and its local representatives became content to leave all administration and all framing of policy in his hands. He had, of course, his preliminary difficulties. Dr. Henry Cloete, the former Special Commissioner, an amiable but vain and pedantic man, had been appointed Recorder of Natal under the new Government; and he was soon engaged in an acrimonious controversy with Shepstone, which lasted all through the year 1848 and which attained such proportions that Mrs. Cloete and Mrs. Shepstone cut one another in the streets of Pietermaritzburg, to the no small discomfort of the tiny official community which was unable, for a time, to hold any social function at which both ladies were present. Cloete maintained that the whole African population of Natal must be treated as subject to Roman-Dutch law – a theory which it was impossible to put into practice and which, had it been possible to apply it, would very likely have provoked disturbances all over the country, even in the cowed state of the refugee population. It would have involved, *inter alia*, the treating of a polygamous marriage as a crime, and the alteration of the tribal law of inheritance by primogeniture to that of equal division among heirs. Shepstone took the view, preferable on both theoretical and practical grounds, that the system of customary law must be taken over *en bloc*, recognised and administered by the courts; and that he, as representing the Lieutenant-Governor, should have some of the jurisdiction previously exercised by the Zulu monarch as paramount chief. As Shepstone proceeded to act on this theory, Cloete felt it his duty to refer to the doings of the Diplomatic Agent in no measured terms in open court. Ultimately Shepstone prevailed in the contest and an ordinance of the 23rd June 1849 abrogated Roman-Dutch law in so far as the African population was concerned and recognised their Customary Law, so far as it was not repugnant to the general principles of humanity observed throughout the civilised world – in other words to the *jus naturale*. This ordinance was the precursor of many similar pieces of legislation in various parts of South Africa. It was largely pioneer work, and Shepstone deserves every credit for it as an original proposal, carried through in the teeth of judicial opposition. Three years later, in 1852, Sir George Cathcart found himself unable to solve the legal difficulty as regards British Kaffraria except by continuing martial law indefinitely in time of peace, and thus enabling each magistrate to do what he liked unhampered by the inappropriate provisions of the Roman-Dutch law, which it apparently never occurred to him to abrogate.

Shepstone was at this time making a very brilliant attempt to reconcile the old African system of government with the existence of a European administration. The recognition of tribal law and the appointment of chiefs as officers for the Government were great steps in this direction. In 1850 a spectacular change was made by the proclamation of the Lieutenant-Governor of Natal as 'Supreme Chief of the Native Population' (replacing the Zulu monarch). This again was at the time an unparalleled enactment, to be imitated in other various parts of South Africa, and subsequently by the Union and the Republic. In later years it came to have unfortunate results.

The framework of the system having been thus laid, a memorandum of instructions was next sent out to all magistrates on the 29th October 1850, from which the following is an extract:

'Whilst humanity, and especially the injunctions of our religion, compel us to recognise in the Natives the capability of being elevated to perfect equality, social and political, with the White man, yet it is as untrue now as it would be unwise to say that the Native is even now in this position, or that he is in his present state capable of enjoying or even understanding the civil and political rights of the White man.

'Her Majesty's Government has most wisely recognised and acted upon these principles by providing a form of government for the Natives in this District, which, while adapted to their present position, is capable of being so modified as to advance their progress towards a higher and better civilisation.

'Magistrates are . . . carefully to bear these principles in mind in all their intercourse with the Natives.'

This memorandum is of great interest, in that it exhibits Shepstone to us as not merely a great ruler, but also as a potential civiliser. It is a matter of great regret that the *laissez-faire* which crept upon him in middle age should have stamped itself on present-day policy quite as much as the brilliant experiments of his youth.

While African law as a whole was recognised, certain of its less desirable features – e.g. punishments for alleged 'witchcraft' – were never adopted into our system, and actively discouraged from the beginning. At the same time some European ideas were skilfully introduced, and the manner of their introduction is a lesson to all rulers of subject races and a strong contrast to the wholesale and unexplained introduction of European criminal law by the Cape Government. Let us take, for example, the grafting into African legal conceptions of the imposition of the death penalty for murder. That a murderer should necessarily suffer death was a conception foreign to the African mind which was still in the *weregild* stage. Shepstone introduced the European ideas on the subject by the argument that a man's life was the property of the Supreme Chief, and that the Lieutenant-Governor was Supreme Chief, and that he would not, in future, be satisfied with cattle compensation for property lost by murder. Thus, by a series of typical African ideas, he gave to the African mind the conception, now well understood, that the appropriate punishment for murder is death, unless the Supreme Chief is pleased to remit it.

I give, in illustration, a full translation from the Zulu of the circular introducing the death penalty. It is dated from Pietermaritzburg the 25th November 1850, and signed by 'T. Shepstone, Diplomatic Agent':

'To all Native Chiefs, Petty Chieftains, Heads of Kraals and Common Native People in the District of Natal.

'Hear ye and listen with both ears. Whereas from your youth up you have been taught to consider a man's life to be the property of the Supreme Chief, and that it is unlawful to destroy such life without his consent; and whereas the Supreme Chief in this District is the Lieutenant-Governor, representing the Queen of England; and whereas several lives have been destroyed without trial, and without his knowledge or consent:

'Know ye, therefore, all Chiefs, Petty Chieftains, Heads of Kraals, and Common People, a man's life has no price: no cattle can pay for it. He who intentionally kills another, whether for Witchcraft or otherwise, shall die himself; and whether he be a Chief, a Petty Chieftain, or Head of a Kraal, who kills another, he shall follow his murdered brother; his children shall be fatherless and his wives widows, and his cattle and all other property shall become forfeited.

'Let this be proclaimed in every kraal and on every hill, so that none may say "I knew it not".'[19]

The process took some little time, but an interesting Government Notice (No. 45 of 31st August 1853) shews that executions did take place in the interval – and public executions, too, to impress the Africans with the new law as graphically as possible. 'The two men of the Inanda,' the Notice reads, 'he of the Umpanza, and the five persons of D'Urban were all hung (sic) by the neck, before the eyes of the people, and in the face of the sun; their guilt had been manifest – their punishment all might see.' The Notice proceeds to remit the death penalty in the case of a Hlubi who had attempted to poison a whole family, stating, however, that in any similar case in future the death penalty would assuredly be imposed.

All that was wanted to seal the policy was the benediction of the Colonial Office, and this was fully and warmly given by Earl Grey in his despatches Nos. 566 and 567 of the 7th and 11th January 1851.

Shepstone was, however, not yet out of the wood. His work, especially the laying out of the locations, had not been popular in Natal, and before he was allowed to settle down to a period of quiet administration it was determined that the Colonists, the practical men who 'knew how to handle Kaffirs', should be given a chance of showing what they could do. On their own claims they should have succeeded far better than a scientific student of the problem, and a Government official at that! It is these magniloquent pretensions which give such a special interest to the Natal Commission of 1852-3. The officials – Messrs. W. Harding, John Bird, Charles Barter and Theophilus Shepstone – were swamped by an overwhelming majority of land-owning colonists, namely: Messrs. J. N. Boshoff, R. R. Ryley, P. A. R. Otto, H. Milner, J. Henderson, G. C. Cato, F. Scheepers, S. Maritz, T. Nel, C. Landman, E. Potgieter, E. Morewood, Dirk Uys, A. Spies, C. Labuschagne, W. Macfarlane, J. Moreland, Dr. Addison and Capt. Struben. Mr. E. Tatham acted as Secretary and Mr. A. F. Fynn as interpreter.

The Commission began by falling tooth and nail on the work of its predecessor. Its vigorous criticism of the personnel of the 1846-7 Commission was followed by an equally vigorous and very illuminating onslaught on the recommendations. 'They failed' – so the report of the 1852-3 body runs – 'chiefly owing to the size of the locations it recommended, which led it to trespass largely on the private rights of proprietors of farms – and *also dried up the source whereby an abundant and continuous supply of Kaffir labour for wages might have been procured.*'[20]

The next object of attack was the resuscitation of the tribal system by Shepstone, which was met with the most vehement protests. The Commission considered, as Shepstone had done, that magistrates should have been appointed for each location; but they did not suggest what other means of keeping order might be adopted under the unfortunate circumstances that neither men nor money were obtainable for the posts. Then, with that eternal tendency of man to idealise the past, they referred, with a frankness which is surprising when we remember that the majority of the members were of English descent, and some recent immigrants, to the Golden Age of the Republic ten years before. 'The Kaffirs,' they said, 'have never felt or acted submissively under British Government either here or in the Cape Colony; and until such habits can be re-established, civilisation will make no progress, and the generally unfortunate effect of British rule on the Coloured races in South Africa will continue unaltered. The leading features in the policy of the Volksraad seem to have been:

'1st. The encouragement of white immigration by every legitimate means, and

'2nd. Keeping the uncivilised Kaffir population in the District (chiefly foreigners) within due bounds as regards numbers, and in strict subordination, in both of which respects that Government deserves our imitation.'

They then proceeded to sketch out a constructive programme. We can quite follow, not without a half-penitent, half-sympathetic fellow-feeling, the kernel of their policy. All that they were concerned with, as land-owners, was, to requote their own words, 'an abundant and continuous supply of Kaffir labour for wages.' With this object in view they recommended agricultural education of an elementary type for the Africans, and economic pressure, by means of hut or other taxation, and by introducing individual tenure of land in the locations with consequent necessity of earning money to purchase a holding, which might constrain the African to come out and work as an agricultural labourer on a European farm. They should be taught to respect the white man (as if respect can ever be 'taught' unless it is deserved, or needs 'teaching' when it is deserved) and realise their own immense inferiority. In order apparently to assist in achieving this desirable end, the Commission recommended[21] that immigration from England should be encouraged of unskilled agricultural labour, of which the ragged schools would be a useful recruiting ground!

Some points of the Report will be read with more appreciative feelings: 'There should be,' it says,[22] 'a Government Industrial School in each village in which the elements of gardening and agriculture, as well as some of the more easy and useful trades, should be taught. This building can also serve as a Chapel.'

'The attendance at school of all young Kaffirs of both sexes in the locations for three years between the ages of seven and twelve years should be compulsory and not left to the caprice of their uncivilised parents.'

'The English and Dutch languages should be taught in these schools.'

Though the report does not face the question of subsequent industrial competition between the Africans so trained and European artisans, of whom there were indeed but few in the Colony at the time, and though there is a very intelligible hint that the Zulu language, one of the finest and most melodious in the world, is to be allowed to die out, the main principle of industrial and agricultural education of a compulsory nature will perhaps recommend itself to many; and it certainly is a very grave omission in the Shepstone policy that systematic agricultural training, in particular, was never undertaken.

Good and bad alike, however, the recommendations of the 1852-3 Commission were quietly and quite definitively shelved. A not unsympathetic magistrate sums up the matter neatly in a report written twenty-five years later. 'The Commission of 1852-3,' he wrote,[23] 'thoroughly exhausted the subject of how the Natives should be governed and taught, and suggested plans for their civilisation and education, but nothing came of the labours of the Commission.'

In many ways this was a good thing; for Shepstone's unhindered administration was considerably wiser than the Commission's suggestions. That its really useful recommendations which Shepstone's Commission had already recommended in 1847 (e.g. industrial schools) were never carried out was to a large extent due to lack of funds. While we blame Shepstone for his *liassez-faire* tendencies we must be generous enough to judge the article he produced remembering that he had to work without tools.

The ten years after the report of the Commission of 1852-3 were devoted mainly to quiet administration. But steps were being taken, in a gradual experimental way, towards the legal securing of the location lands to the tribes inhabiting them. The first scheme which Shepstone had evolved was the granting of separate titles for each tribal location, the land to be alienated by the Crown to separate Boards of Trustees one of whom was to be in each case the chief of the tribe. Such a trust was created by indenture of the 27th May 1858 in respect of the tribe (the Amatuli) occupying the Umnini Location; under the name of the Umnini Trust it still exists. The first trustees were the Secretary for Native Affairs *ex officio*, the chief of the Amatuli tribe *ex officio* and one non-official member. But, on maturer consideration, it was decided not to proceed with this scheme, which would have taken away from Government the power of re-allocating lands between tribes, and instead by letters patent of the 27th April 1864 promulgated in Natal by Government Notice No. 57 of 27th June 1864, the Natal Native Trust was created, the Crown alienating to it all the unalienated location land in Natal in trust for the African population as a whole. The Trust was simply the Executive Council of Natal acting in a particular capacity.[24] Its successor, the South African Native Trust, controls today over 2 000 000 acres of land in Natal.

In the same year that the Natal Native Trust was founded, was introduced the famous system of exemption from Native Law (Law 11 of 1864, amended by Law 28 of 1865). With definite missionary activity largely at work in the Colony many Africans were becoming 'detribalised' and it was deemed necessary to bring law into line with the facts of the case. It was undesirable that a really detribalised African should be under the control of his nominal chief, usually an old-fashioned 'barbarian'. The full legal recognition of this distinction between tribal and detribalised Africans and the providing of a bridge, difficult but capable of being crossed, between the two classes was a very important part of the Natal system. The principle underlying the Exemption laws was a sound one: in practical detail they were full of difficulties, badly drawn up, and provocative of much administrative difficulty.

The applicant for exemption (who could be any male or any unmarried female) had to petition the Governor stating particulars of his family, property, chief, etc., and furnishing proof of his ability to read and write. An unmarried female had, in addition, to produce a European of good standing as guardian. The applicant had then to take the oath of allegiance, and the Governor could either grant or refuse the petition in his discretion.

Exemption in the case of a married man extended to his wife and children under sixteen years of age. No married man who had more than one wife living was to be exempted.

The exempted African was not in the exact political and legal position of a white man, being a *tertium quid*. As regards civil rights and obligations, however, he was entirely under the Roman-Dutch law.

Once exemption was granted, this was strictly applied. An exempted African, for example, taking a second wife during the lifetime of the first, could be tried and punished for bigamy, though, had he not been exempted, such an action would have been no crime.

Natal Africans did not avail themselves largely of the privilege of exemption. It was never thrust upon them and at times the Government actually discouraged it. It is quite possible that Shepstone himself was not in favour of applying the law until a definite movement in the direction of exemption had set in spontaneously among the Africans. It is, at any rate, significant that from 1864 to 1876 not a single application for exemption was received. Between 1876 and 1880, when Sir Theophilus had been replaced by his brother, John Wesley Shepstone, one hundred and forty-nine letters of exemption were granted.[25] It is doubtful, therefore, whether either the merits or defects of the system of exemption can be ascribed to Sir Theophilus Shepstone.[26]

A further step, again more theoretical than practical, was the granting under certain restrictions of the franchise to Africans (Law 11 of 1865).[27] Only exempted Africans could get the franchise, but not every exempted African got it. In a way it was a disfranchisement measure, as the 'Charter of Natal', 1856, had no colour bar.

Giving the kindest explanation possible of the Law, we may say that its underlying principle was that after an African had been exempted from the provisions of Native Law and from tribal restraint a certain time should elapse as a kind of probationary period under the new conditions before the franchise could be granted. The qualifications were stringent. An African had to be a resident of Natal for twelve years, the holder of letters of exemption for seven years and to produce a certificate of recommendation signed by three duly qualified European residents and endorsed by a magistrate or justice of the peace. The grant of the franchise was not automatic but lay in the discretion of the Governor, which was frequently exercised adversely. When the Inter-Colonial Commission of 1903-5 was sitting, it was discovered that, after thirty-nine years only three Africans in the whole of Natal and Zululand had the vote.

The franchise was not hereditary: the son of an exempted and enfranchised African had to apply for special letters of exemption and submit his case to the Governor before he could get the vote. It was a privilege, not a right.

The unkindest explanation of the Natal franchise law – and probably the true one – is that it was a skilful and disingenuous attempt to maintain a political colour bar without saying so. Subsequent legislation enacted three decades later ran on similar lines for the purpose of excluding Indians. Whether the amount of skill expended in these intricacies of *la haute politique* is worth the result is open to question.

At any rate Shepstone cannot be saddled with the franchise policy as a practical one. It was long after he had retired from office that the first African was enfranchised.

The affair of Langalibalele, arising in 1873, need not be examined in detail here.[27] Langalibalele, the chief of the Hlubi tribe living on the foothills of the Drakensberg, failed to respond to repeated orders from his magistrate and finally refused to respond to a command to report personally in Pietermaritzburg. Under the Shepstone system this was gross indiscipline, indeed rebellion against the 'Supreme Chief' (the Lieutenant-Governor). So completely did the rule of Natal with its small garrison and its 18 000 Europeans ruling over 280 000 Africans, depend on moral sanctions and on the prestige of Government, that any failure to respond to an order had to be dealt with promptly if the system was to survive. Moreover the fear of a 'Native rising' entertained by the Europeans of Natal was strong, continued, and at times almost pathological.

In the end, force was employed and both Shepstone and the Lieutenant-Governor, Sir Benjamin Pine, accompanied the punitive expedition. Langalibalele escaped into Basutoland but was ultimately captured. He was tried by a special court which was held in a tent pitched specially for the occasion in the grounds of Government House, Pietermaritzburg. The special court consisted of Sir Benjamin Pine, the 'Supreme Chief' (who had taken part in the punitive expedition and who subsequently outlawed Langalibalele) Shepstone, four magistrates and four principal chiefs of the Colony. Langalibalele was refused counsel with the power to cross-examine witnesses. On the second day of the trial, the four chiefs pronounced him guilty and after this (we are studying South African history, not reading "Alice in Wonderland") evidence was taken.

That great missionary tribune, Bishop Colenso, saw to it that full particulars of these happenings were published in England. (It was a courageous act on his part for he was in very low water ecclesiastically and Shepstone was his principal lay supporter.) The results were startling. Sir Benjamin Pine was recalled and his career abruptly and finally terminated. Shepstone, on the other hand, was knighted (an honour deserved for his three decades of service but falling oddly at this time) and sent out as Special Commissioner to the Transvaal by the Colonial Secretary.

Nevertheless the years 1873-6 marked the end of Shepstone's three decades of benevolent despotism over the Africans of Natal. From 1877 he was embroiled unhappily in the affairs of the Transvaal and of Zululand. He and all his family after him earned the deep hostility of the Zulu royal family and he himself became a kind of 'bogey-man' to the Afrikaners. His years of retirement, however, were kindly and full of goodwill, and he must always be remembered, despite his later mistakes, for his wonderful services in the early days of Natal.

NOTES TO CHAPTER IV

1. Some of the information in this paragraph was derived by the writer from the evidence of Thomas Philipps (an 1820 settler) before the Commons Select Committee of 1836 (Evidence p. 37). But all such references have been superseded by Dr. Ruth Gordon's exhaustive and very valuable book 'Shepstone: The Role of the Family in the History of South Africa, 1820-1900' (Cape Town, A. A. Balkema, 1968).
2. Shepstone explained this name as meaning 'a Nimrod, a mighty hunter'.
3. *Holmen*, or, as transliterated in Doke & Vilakazi's Zulu Dictionary, *uHulumeni*, is a Zulu attempt to pronounce the Afrikaans word Goewerment (see also note on p. 6 of Charles Barter's 'Stray Memories of Natal and Zululand' (Published by Author, Pietermaritzburg, 1897).
4. Report of Natal Native Affairs Commission 1852-3, p. 26.
5. *Ibid*. p. 14.
6. For a further upholding of the work of the 1846-7 Commission as against the criticisms of the 1852-3 Commission, see the views of Rev. C. J. Dohne and Rev. Lewis Grout in 2nd and 3rd Supplements to Natal Government Gazette, 18th January 1853.
7. This may have been to some extent a sop to Earl Grey, who was at the time obsessed with the idea of forming a huge 'Sepoy' army out of the Africans of Natal, an idea which was firmly opposed by Lieutenant-Governor Martin West. (Earl Grey to Sir Henry Pottinger, 4th December 1846; Martin West to Sir Henry Pottinger, 22nd April 1847.)
8. See despatch of Lieutenant-Governor Martin West to the Secretary to Government, Cape Town, dated 7th May 1847.
9. Report of Natal Native Affairs Commission 1852-3, pp. 19-23.
10. The chief criticism of the 1852-3 Commission.
11. Russell, R.: Natal: The land and its story. (Pietermaritzburg, P. Davis & Son, 1904) p. 203.
12. Report of the Select Committee of the Cape Legislative Council on the Basutoland Annexation Bill 1871, p. 27.
13. Report of the Secretary for Native Affairs in the Cape Native Blue Book 1875, p. 123.
14. Pages 11-13.
The whole expedition to crown Cetshwayo was one of the greatest peril. Every member took his life in his hands as is shown by the fact that the Natal Government twice excused itself from sending such an expedition until Shepstone volunteered to go. The expedition consisted of 110 mounted volunteers with two field pieces and 300 friendly Africans from Natal. The Zulu nation numbered some hundreds of thousands. (Russell, R.: Natal: The land and its story. (Pietermaritzburg, P. Davis & Son, 1904) p. 222).
15. 'Prince' or 'Chief' – a salutation of respect.
16. Jorissen: Transvaalsche Herinneringen 1876-1896. 1897. pp. 26-27.
17. Quoted in Martineau: The Transvaal Trouble: How it arose (London, John Murray, 1899) p. 142.
18. Evidence, Vol. II, p. 398.
19. It is interesting to note that this circular was re-issued, *word for word*, by Col. Griffith, Governor's Agent, Basutoland, on 17th December 1872.
20. Report, p. 4. The italics are mine.
21. Report, p. 64.
22. Report, p. 53.
23. Natal Native Blue Book 1878, p. 15. A very unfavourable view of the 1852-3, as against the 1846-7, Commission is given in a despatch of Lieutenant-Governor John Scott to the Duke of Newcastle (Colonial Secretary) dated 26th February 1864.
24. For much of the information in this passage I am indebted to a memorandum of Sir Michael Gallwey, Attorney-General of Natal, dated 12th April 1882 (Papers N.N.T. 32/1896).
25. Papers relating to Native Customs in Natal, 1881.
26. It has even been suggested that the original Exemption Law was drawn up only to throw dust in the eyes of the philanthropic party in England, and that the exemptions of 1876-80 were rushed through in anticipation of a British Parliamentary enquiry.
27. A full account is given in Brookes, E. H. and Webb, C. de B.: A History of Natal (Pietermaritzburg, University of Natal Press 1968) Chapter XII.

CHAPTER V

Natal: The Shepstone Policy II

Brutus, in Shakespeare's 'Julius Caesar', says –
> Oh! that we could but come by Caesar's spirit
> And not dismember Caesar.

His wish was not granted. The conspirators dismembered Caesar and enthroned Caesarism for many centuries. So it was with the policy of Natal after 1875. Shepstone disappears from the scene and only reappears as a retired elder statesman. Shepstonism was more firmly entrenched than ever. Great men like Lyautey, Lugard and Shepstone carry through their policies by the force of their dedicated personalities. Lesser men turn their inspired improvisations into dull systems.

It is perhaps not surprising that Shepstone's brother, John, and his son, Henrique, who succeeded him in turn as Secretary for Native Affairs, should have accepted the family tradition and allowed the Shepstone policy to ossify. But the most surprising convert to Shepstonism was Theophilus Shepstone himself. He had begun his career as an advocate of a civilising policy, he had offered himself to rule the Africans as a great enlightened chief, he only fell back on the 'Shepstone system' when the British Government rejected the latter policy and shrank from providing the funds necessary for the former. So, with outstanding administrative virtuosity, he recreated tribalism and ruled through the chiefs. He came in time to think of this as the ideal system, and to defend it against all change.

The Shepstone system prevailed in Natal up to 1908, and virtually, despite last minute efforts to alter it, until 1910. It became the foundation of later Transvaal policy and it was taken over unchanged by Southern Rhodesia. Its continued existence in an age which seems to have outgrown it is a very dubious blessing.

If this be so, have we perhaps not praised Sir Theophilus Shepstone in the previous chapter beyond his deserts? We may answer in the first place that a history of Natal which denigrated Shepstone would be as sad a performance as a history of Morocco which denied all merit to Lyautey. But there is something more than this. The Natal tribesmen were in danger of being broken up and distributed among European farmers as desired by the Commission of 1852-3. Shepstone would accept nothing of these evil counsels. He stood between the Natal Africans and those who desired to drive them out or to exploit them. He saw that they got land enough to live in and that they were settled there in peace. He refused to let them be used as a mere means to an end. He governed them justly, kindly and with a personal touch. These were great achievements.

From 1875 his actions are less worthy of praise. His share in the annexation of the Transvaal in 1877, motivated partly by ambition, largely by Imperial loyalty, is open to severe criticism. It was also very unwise. He had, to use a vulgarism, 'worked himself out of a job'[1]. Up to 1877 he had stood as the one strong and impartial arbitrator between the Zulu monarchy, the Colony of Natal and the South African Republic. The events of 1877 left him Administrator of the Transvaal with the task of conciliating the Boer population. He could no more pose as their generous protector against Zulu inroads: this had now become his mere official duty. He had to take their part in their long-standing boundary dispute with the Zulu monarchy. The Zulu royal house which had regarded him as a friend found him the friend of their enemies. And while this is not the place to go into the causes of the Zulu war, history must record that Shepstone co-operated with Sir Bartle Frere in bringing it on. It is probable, but not proved, that he was one of the advisers of Sir Garnet Wolseley in the unhappy Zulu 'settlement' of 1879, and he played a very equivocal part in the arrangements surrounding the restoration of Cetshwayo in 1883.[2] The Zulu royal house has never forgiven him.

But we have shot past the administrative watershed of 1875. From then until the introduction of Responsible Government in 1893 we have the spectacle of two lesser Shepstones administering an increasingly ossified Shepstone system. But some changes there were, even during this period. Law 26 of 1875 took away the judicial functions of the Secretary for Native Affairs and set up an independent Native High Court. A case can be made out for the earlier system on the basis that the Secretary for Native Affairs functioned as the deputy of the Supreme Chief (the Governor) who in African law combined executive and judicial activities. Sir Bartle Frere describes the new court (for what his testimony is worth) as 'a most absurd and mischievous High Court',[3] but over its seven decades of existence it did quite useful work. Its civil functions devolved upon 'Native Appeal Courts' and its criminal jurisdiction was taken over by the Supreme Court. No one would wish to go back to the old system where the Secretary for Native Affairs was a Court of Appeal.

It should be noted that this fusion of executive and judicial functions still prevails at a lower level – that of magistrates and Bantu Affairs Commissioners.

Another great change, to which Sir Theophilus Shepstone was opposed,[4] was the introduction of the Natal Code of Native Law.

The original Code was promulgated on 28th February 1878. It differed from the Code of 1891 in being a guide to the unwritten tribal law and not a statutory enactment binding on the courts. In this form it could be of service, for unless magistrates were appointed merely for African cases and specially trained for their work there was great risk of miscarriages of justice, and certainty of conflicting judgments. Unfortunately the difference between the earlier and the later Codes was one of theory rather than of practice, for few magistrates departed from the terms of the 1878 Code, even though it was not legally binding.

The Code of 1891 was a rigid and legally binding one. It remained in force until the date of Union and long after, being only replaced in 1932 and again in 1967, and even the later Codes retained many of the more questionable provisions of that of 1891.

The question of codification is one that is much discussed in jurisprudential circles. It does of course make law plainer – in Bentham's terms 'more cognoscible' – to the people, but in the case of a rapidly changing society exposed to the influences of a stronger civilisation and of far-reaching economic changes, it tends to stereotype obsolescent institutions. One illustration will suffice. In old tribal conditions an orphaned girl came immediately under the guardianship of a male relative, e.g. her paternal uncle. He provided for her and received the *lobolo* for her marriage, and his consent was necessary to the marriage. Today a girl in an urban area desiring to marry must trace in the back blocks of the tribal reserves an uncle who has never provided for her and whom she has never seen, and persuade him to signify consent. Many delayed marriages and much pre-marital sexual intercourse is the result of this originally reasonable but now outmoded provision.

Something must be said at this stage of the third of the four Natal Native Affairs Commissions, that of 1881-2. Its members were the Chief Justice of Natal (Sir Henry Connor), the Bishop of Natal (Dr. J. W. Colenso), Mr. J. W. Ackerman, Speaker of the Legislative Council; Dean Green; Messrs. J. V. Walton, M.L.A., T. Reynolds, M.L.A., R. A. Green, M.L.A., G. M. Rudolph, G. C. Cato, J.P., P. A. R. Otto, J.P., P. R. Botha, J.P., W. H. Campbell, J. E. Fannin, J.P., G. Turner, J.P., and D. L. W. Stainbank. It confined itself entirely to the internal administration of Natal and did not touch on the Zululand question. It is chiefly interesting as providing a remarkable commendation of the main lines of the Shepstone system – doubtless aided by the great and touching confidence of all the tribal witnesses in 'Somtseu' – but on two points it made original recommendations.

The body of the report recommends that Africans not exempted from Native Law, should be allowed to purchase land on individual, freehold tenure. A careful study of the minority reports – of which there were eight, surely a record! – shows that all of them were opposed to this recommendation. As the total membership of the Commission was only fifteen it remains a mystery how the recommendation of the main report could have been carried. It has never been acted on. Mr. G. C. Cato says, in his minority report, with characteristic bluntness and shrewdness: 'I oppose strongly Natives having freehold title to land while under Native law. There is a great deal of fuss made about *ukulobola* and polygamy, which cannot be touched direct, but which can be bombarded all to smash through this wish for land.'

With regard to the franchise, or rather to representation, the African witnesses (whose evidence is one of the most interesting features) are unanimous in desiring a representative or representatives as advisory members of the Legislative Council. They are quite willing to have a European as a representative, and entirely agreeable to his being nominated by the Government. This is the gist of the evidence of Chiefs Teteluku and Faku and also of Nambula and Makukula, Christian Africans. But they do want someone definitely to speak their views and to expound the Legislature's views to them. In other words they want another 'Somtseu'; but 'Somtseus' do not grow on every bush. There is no difference really between the measures contemplated in this request and Shepstone's earlier system, and it is interesting to note[5] that Shepstone himself supported their request.

'One touch of Nature makes the whole world kin', and before leaving the 1881-2 report, I must digress to quote one very amusing piece of evidence:[6]

'*Chief Umnini and followers.*

Q. "Is there much drinking of *ishimiyana*?"[7]

A. "That is the food we eat."

Q. "Is it food or poison?"

A. "It is neither: it is the devil. Stealing, fighting and adultery all arise out of *ishimiyana*. I complain of it greatly. The consumption of it has always gone on since the mills started. I cannot check it."

Q. "Would you advise that treacle should not be sold?"

A. (In alarm) "I must qualify what I have said about *ishimiyama*. I do not wish it to be understood that this is a very great grievance.

I use it myself when I have any work to be done." '

The saddest features of the whole period 1875-93 are (1) the perpetuation of the policy of *laissez-faire* in African matters, (2) the loss of touch with the African people and the replacement of paternal government by officialdom. As Mr. Stainbank said in the Legislative Council of 1889:[8] 'I have no doubt the Government will repeat their stock assertion: "See how loyal and obedient and peaceful the Natives have been during that forty years – see how easily we have collected taxes, *as if the end and aim of good Government is merely to keep people from rebellion and get as much money as it can out of them. That is not the end of good Government.*" '

Undoubtedly too not only the magistrates but also the Secretary for Native Affairs had become much less accessible to the people than in the good old days when 'Somtseu' used to bring his chair under the great tree and speak heart to heart with them. It is pitiful to think of the son and successor of the great 'Somtseu' admitting, and defending the admission, that he rarely or never visited the locations. Whoever reads the Legislative Council debates of the years immediately before the introduction of Responsible Government will not wonder that there was a desire for change. There was much talk of a certain wagon which the Secretary for Native Affairs insisted on having built to carry him about before he could visit the Africans in the locations. Members made merry over this vehicle, which indeed seems to have had at least one of the qualities of Van der Decken's ship – that it never got there. Unfortunately their constructive ability was less than their gift for destructive criticism.

Before passing on to the Responsible Government era it may be as well to quote one or two extracts from Legislative Council debates in illustration of these statements:

Mr. Yonge: 'It will be remembered that on a former occasion this House expressed a wish that the Secretary for Native Affairs should visit these Native Locations. When, in furtherance of that view, the question was put to the hon. gentleman, the questioner was told he could not really carry out this desire by the Council because a peculiarly cumbersome, unworkable, untrustworthy and frightful-looking wagon was not provided. That is the sort of answer with which he puts you off projects of that description. He puts you off by saying that the transport to carry him about this beautiful portion of the country is not ready. That does give many of us a feeling that the hon. gentleman is not so capable of looking after and representing in this House the Natives as we should wish him.' (Debates, p. 334, Vol. XIV, 1889.)

Sir J. Robinson: 'I maintain that the Administration of Native Affairs such as now exists does not help the Government of this country apart from the Native population of the Colony. We have had it from the hon. gentleman's own lips that he never or rarely visits the Natives in their locations. We have it on record that the Magistrates of this Colony do not confer regularly with the Chiefs with whom they are brought into contact. We know also that the Magistrates of the Colony do not confer periodically, as they ought to do, with the hon. member.[9] The Native Department is like a body with a wooden head, and in making that remark I do not desire to be personally offensive to the hon. member. I say the Department is a body with a wooden head.' (Debates, page 354, Vol. XIV, 1890).

Mr. Binns: 'And here I have a more serious charge still to bring against the hon. member. He is entirely out of touch with the Native population of this Colony. There was a time in those good old days under the trees here when that could not be said of the Native Department of Natal, because, however primitive it might have been, there was a close touch between the Secretary for Native Affairs at the time and the Native Chiefs of this Colony. That cannot be said at the present time.' (Debates, page 402, Vol. XIV, 1890.)

At the same time, it is only fair to add the following complaint of one of the early Responsible Government Secretaries for Native Affairs (Debates, page 49, Vol. XXVIII, 1899): 'I do not know whether my hon. predecessor found the office that he held to be one that was a bed of roses. I can tell him distinctly that I have found it anything but that, but rather a bed of thorns. The public can have but little appreciation of the labour that falls upon the Native office. And whatever is attempted in the Native Department seems to receive severe criticism all round on account of every individual believing in his own soul that he is able to solve the Native question.'

In 1893 the British Parliament conferred responsible government on Natal. It may well be argued that this, as in the later case of Southern Rhodesia, was premature. The ultimate control of the African tribes in Natal (and, after 1897, in Zululand) now fell to the white farmers, merchants and lawyers who made up the Natal Parliament.

Shepstone had controlled, but had failed to civilise. The political leaders of the Responsible Government era lost control while still failing to civilise. Their sometimes rash and often selfish interventions were unequally yoked with the strong conservatism of the permanent officials of the Native Affairs Department. The policy of that Department, as stated in a memorandum of Mr. S. O. Samuelson, Under-Secretary, dated September 1907, was 'to maintain and strengthen the tribal system in the interests of the Colony.' That is to say the principles which Shepstone had adopted in the peculiar early circumstances of the Colony – with neither money, magistrates nor police available in sufficient quantity – were to be perpetuated under entirely different conditions. A spirit of rigid conservatism and *laissez-faire* had settled on the Department, and the fact that so many of the changes made by political heads after that date were ill-considered doubtless did much to confirm the permanent heads in their attitude. Yet only a few years before the laying down of the maintenance of tribalism as the essence of Natal policy, the beginnings of tribal disintegration were apparent to an observant eye in the fact that Government had to issue instructions to prevent the permanent movement of individual tribesmen away from their hereditary homes and the control of their hereditary chiefs.[10]

At the same time, while the permanent Department was undoubtedly too conservative to recognise the signs of the times, it did draft several remarkable and interesting Bills which would have ameliorated certain aspects of African life had they been passed. But these Bills never became Acts. In justification, to some extent, of this legislative sterility, it must be pointed out that the South African War of 1899-1902 held up all domestic legislation to a marked extent. Immediately thereafter the Inter-Colonial Commission was formed to report on every aspect of the African question. Its report did not appear until 1905. In 1906 the Natal Native Rebellion had broken out.

What were the causes of that rebellion? Partly, no doubt, unwise legislation. We have remarked on the legislative sterility with regard to measures for the amelioration of the Africans. But time was found to pass *inter alia* Act 40 of 1894 regulating the relations between European Masters and African Servants, Act 15 of 1899, dealing with stock theft by Africans, Act 28 of 1902 providing for 'togt' or day labour in boroughs and Act 48 of 1903 raising the squatters' tax. Anything that affected the interests of the European farming community was sure to receive attention. These rapid changes did not all make for the good of the Africans. The frequent breaks in continuity of policy irritated and perplexed them, used as they had been for half a century to the rule of 'Somtseu' or some scion of his house under unvarying principles. Finally a very ill-considered poll tax, levied in addition to the existing hut tax, precipitated matters.

Secondly, it must be said that the Government was not sufficiently in touch with African opinion. When Mr. S. O. Samuelson succeeded to the permanent Under-Secretaryship in 1893 it might have been thought that this would have been remedied, for few Natalians knew the African better and few were more accessible. But at the very moment that he succeeded to office, that office, under the conditions of Responsible Government, was shorn of much of its power by the creation of a political secretary with a seat in the Cabinet. The usual results of the divorce of knowledge from responsibility – a not infrequent state of affairs under the cabinet system – were apparent in this case also. The political Secretary who, comparatively speaking, knew nothing, controlled policy. The permanent Under-Secretary who, comparatively speaking, knew everything, was reduced virtually to the position of a chief clerk. To this change Samuelson conformed too readily, and in any case he, though an able man, was a strong conservative.

But the cause of the Natal rebellion goes deeper than this. It was essentially the result of omissions rather than of hurtful acts. In the writer's opinion it was due ultimately to the fact that the Africans had been left alone in their locations for half a century, free from all economic pressure and from all danger of inter-tribal warfare, without any attempt having been made to provide safe channels into which their energies might be directed. Untrained in agriculture or local government, without the compelling influences of competition, what more natural than that the discontent so fundamental in human nature should have combined with their hereditary proclivities to make them protest actively? The poll tax doubtless kindled the spark, but the train had been laid by many years of *laissez-faire*.

One thing must, of course, not be overlooked. Even with all these contributory causes the rebellion did not spread. The majority of the Africans were quiet: many were actively loyal to the Government. The worst of the trouble was in or adjacent to the recently-annexed

Zululand. But the African evidence before the Commission of 1906-7[11] shows how widespread was the discontent that had burst into flame in so few cases. The ineptness, and indeed bankruptcy, of Natal policy, had brought about the 'rebellion'. When it happened it was met with panic and handled with unjustifiable severity, and the record of the Natal troops in the field was not good.

The fourth of the great Natal Commissions assembled late in the year 1906 and presented its report on the 25th July 1907. The Commission consisted of Justice H. C. Campbell, I.S.O., President of the Native High Court (Chairman), the Hon. Sir T. K. Murray, K.C.M.G., J.P., the Hon. Sir J. Liege Hulett, K.B., M.L.A., J.P., the Hon. C. J. Birkenstock, M.L.C., Col. H. E. Rawson, R.E., C.B., Rev. Jas. Scott and Mr. Maurice S. Evans, C.M.G., M.L.A., J.P.[12] Messrs. J. Stuart and A. Canham acted as Secretaries.

The report is a curiously unequal document. Its list of detailed recommendations for administrative reform is so useful, sensible and interesting that it seems best to quote it in full; and it therefore appears as the first appendix to this chapter. Its proposals for a new general framework of government were, however, of but dubious value.

The Commission considered that there was a 'striking syncretism'[13] between the Shepstone system and parliamentary control. Parliament was an oligarchy as far as the Africans were concerned.[14] The frequent changing of the political headship of the Native Affairs Department was misunderstood.[15] The ordinary Minister, with his uncertain tenure of office, when faced by the many aspects of the African problem was content to tide over difficulties and maintain the *status quo*.[16]

It was therefore proposed that Native Administration should have a self-contained constitution[17] and that Parliament should grant a charter to the Administration,[18] empowering it to govern the Africans without the necessity of a frequent intervention of either the Legislature itself or the responsible Minister, who was only to concern himself with the final approval of policy.[19]

The chief features of the proposed new scheme were:[20]

(1) The Governor to retain the title of Supreme Chief and to remain, as a figurehead, at the head of all African administration.

(2) The office of Minister for Native Affairs to be abolished and the Prime Minister to be the political head of the Native Affairs Department (the existing Cape system).

(3) As a permanent head, the Under-Secretary for Native Affairs (henceforth to be termed Secretary) assisted by the Board.

(4) This Board or Native Council, to consist partly of the four Native Commissioners referred to in para. (5) and of four non-official members, all nominated. The Secretary for Native Affairs to be Secretary of the Board. The Board to have legislative powers, subject

to the veto of Parliament (on the lines of Law 44 of 1887, repealed in 1891).

(5) As executive officers of the Department, four Native Commissioners, one of whom was to be Chief Native Commissioner, were to be appointed. They were to undertake purely administrative duties, judicial duties being still left to the magistrates.

About the first of these points there was no criticism.

The second was vigorously opposed by the Hon. W. H. (later Sir William) Beaumont who happened to be Administrator of Natal at the time the report was submitted. His opposition was successful and the Native Administration Act of 1909 which introduced most of the changes recommended by the Commission left the Ministry of Native Affairs a separate portfolio.

The remaining points were enacted by the Native Administration Act of 1909 in spite of strong opposition. The chief points of opposition were (1) the general division of authority, (2) the untenable position assigned to the Secretary for Native Affairs, (3) the separation of administration from judicature in local areas.

(1) On this point it is best to quote from the actual minute of Sir William Beaumont:

'There does not appear from the scheme to be any permanent and distinct personality who can be regarded by the Natives as the Chief Administrative Officer. The Natives quite well understand that the powers and functions of such an officer are limited and controlled by "the Government" but "the Government" is to them impersonal and they require some Chief over all, to whom they can make a final appeal in all administrative matters . . . Under the Scheme there is no one who can co-ordinate the policy and the actions of the several District Commissioners and the Native Council, unless it be the Prime Minister, and that is not practicable. There must be a continuity and uniformity of policy based on definite principles throughout the land, and to ensure this there must be a clearly defined chain of authority from the lowest to the highest.'

Such a chain of authority is described very effectively and the best that can be said for the Shepstone administrative system is said, in a report by the ultra-conservative Mr. S. O. Samuelson, appearing in the Government Gazette of January 22nd, 1908, an extract from which is printed as appendix II to this chapter.

(2) The position allocated to the Secretary for Native Affairs was such that Mr. S. O. Samuelson refused to accept it and resigned in 1909, being succeeded by Mr. A. J. Shepstone, C.M.G. Sir William Beaumont, in the minute already quoted, had expressed his conviction that the Secretary for Native Affairs should be chairman, not secretary, of the Council for Native Affairs. This, which was a distinct improvement, was adopted in the Act of 1909, but even so, what with the Minister,

the Council and the Chief Native Commissioner, the unfortunate Secretary was more or less crowded out. The fact is that mere administrative re-arrangements, even if they had been less open to question, could not transform the situation without radical economic and social reforms. Stagnation in different channels was still stagnation.

(3) As regards the District Commissioners, nearly everyone of expert authority outside the Commission was opposed to the fatal division of authority involved in their appointment. Judge Chadwick of the Native High Court vigorously opposed the change as being derogatory to magisterial authority which needed strengthening instead of weakening[21] and Mr. Samuelson insisted that the proper separation was not between administration and judicary but between officers for Europeans and officers for Africans. His view was that, as far as possible, separate magistrates should be appointed for African affairs.[22] In the Senate debate of 14th February 1912 on the Bill which repealed most of the provisions of the Native Administration Act of 1909, the Minister for Native Affairs said: 'The specific functions of the Commissioners will not be carried out by any one in future. These special functions have been found not to work out. The officials have no scope.'

Less than three years sufficed for the discrediting of the re-arrangements of 1909. By Act 1 of 1912 the Council for Native Affairs and the District Commissionerships were abolished. The Chief Native Commissioner was left alone, high and dry, without any judicial authority, without any direct control over the magistrates, and without any subordinate officers of high status immediately under him. The Commission of 1906-7 had made its recommendations in vain.

APPENDIXES TO CHAPTER V

APPENDIX I

DETAILED ADMINISTRATIVE REFORMS RECOMMENDED BY THE NATAL NATIVE AFFAIRS COMMISSION OF 1906-7
(see para. 122 of the Report)

(1) The advisability of creating more magistracies with special regard to distance and population.

(2) More attention and consideration at all offices. All business (court work excepted) should be disposed of as it arises at magistrates' offices.

(3) The use and abuse of the salute of 'Bayete'*and the issue of instructions forbidding its general application beyond the provisions of the Code.

(4) Where deprivation of rights or position may be intended as a result of administrative action, the desirability of not deciding thereon except after open inquiry or trial.

---

*The royal salute.

(5) The reference to the Native Department of all Borough By-Laws before confirmation.

(6) Directions to magistrates to be guided by the spirit of Section 76 of the Code in maintaining discipline at kraals.

(7) Pending legislation, magistrates, as public officers, to be urged when attesting promissory notes for money lent to Natives, to enquire into the amount, circumstances of loan, and rate of interest, as a means of affording them some protection.

(8) Arranging for magistrates' officers receiving, remitting and paying out wages (subject to a small commission, say, 3d. per £) as a simple and safe means of earnings of sons reaching kraal heads in distant places, thus helping to increase the supply of labour.

(9) Adequate means for acquainting Natives with contemplated and completed legislation.

(10) The publication in the Zulu language of Laws and Regulations specially applicable to the Natives.

(11) Police out-stations – the advisability of withdrawing them from locations, Native districts and Mission Reserves.

(12) Police methods – unnecessary arrests and hand-cuffing of kraal heads should be avoided. Notifying attendances to and through Chiefs, where practicable, should be resorted to.

(13) The employment of educated Natives as Interpreters and Policemen, and at the principal Railway Stations.

(14) Official notification to tenants of intended and completed sale of Crown Lands.

(15) Inquiry into the ability of kraal Natives and others complying with the Crown Lands buildings clause, its feasibility and comparison with the advantages of cultivation as a more practical condition.

(16) Consideration of joint action with neighbouring Colonies in connection with Inward and Outward Passes, and immediate revision of the existing rules and forms to remove doubts.

(17) Reserve for the education and welfare of the Natives.[23] The desirability of increasing the sum of £10 000, as by natural increase and the incorporation of Zululand and the Northern Districts, the Native population has increased by 100 per cent since 1893.

(18) The application of the rents collected from Natives on Mission Reserves.

(19) The position and claim of the Native Mission at Impapala, Zululand, to special consideration and compensation. (See evidence of Sir Charles Saunders, Mr. C. R. Glynn, the Rev. J. D. Taylor, the Rev. H. D. Goodenough and Plant Makanya; also the report of the Zululand Delimitation Commission, 1902-4.)

(20) The reconsideration of the action of the Native Trust in dismantling buildings used for worship, where at a distance from the station of the Superintendent Missionary.

(21) Repeal of the Act requiring registration of births and deaths, having regard to Native feeling thereon, the incompleteness of records, the exclusion of Zululand from its operation, and the cost of such registration.

APPENDIX II
Mr. SAMUELSON'S DESCRIPTION OF THE SHEPSTONE ADMINISTRATIVE SYSTEM

(Extracted from Report by Mr. S. O. Samuelson, Under Secretary for Native Affairs, No. S.N.A. 2958/07, published under Government Notice No. 39 of 20th January 1908)

The patriarchal or tribal system was reduced to a concrete legal form by the Code of 1891, and has been brought under statutory control by that law and subsequent legislation. It was taken over from the Natives and is peculiarly suitable and adapted to their social conditions and circumstances. It is essentially a representative form of government. If the kraal-heads and councillors, the district chiefs and councillors, the paramount chief and councillors, each in effect elected, have not embodied a form of representative government, what did they embody? The tribal organisation has been used as a vehicle of administration, and has provided machinery of government in this Colony for more than half a century. By this system all the efficient machinery of the Native form of government was brought into play, adapted and made available by the Government of this Colony. The Secretary for Native Affairs in this system answers to the Principal Induna or Prime Minister, and the magistrates to the indunas or rulers of districts, to whom are transmitted all the orders of the Supreme Chief through the principal induna and by whom all these orders are transmitted to the Native chiefs and minor Native authorities residing within their respective jurisdiction.

The detail of the authorities in the system is as follows, commencing from the lowest in regular gradation upwards, each being responsible in the first instance to the authority next above him:

1. The head of a family.
2. The head of a kraal or kraals, a collection of families.
3. The headman or induna of a territorial division or district.
4. The principal headman or induna.
5. The chief of the tribe.
6. The magistrate of the division in his capacity as Native Officer.
7. The Secretary for Native Affairs.
8. The Supreme Chief, being the Governor of the Colony for the time being.

The Native population fully understand the several links which connect them with the same head as that which is acknowledged by their white fellow-subjects.

Into the system which has served us so well in the past it is now proposed to introduce a dry-rot fungus in the shape of a raw and unfamiliar set of officials.

NOTES TO CHAPTER V

1 See a detailed study in Brookes, E. H. and Webb, C. de B.: A History of Natal (Pietermaritzburg, University of Natal Press, 1965) Chapter XIII.
2 *Ibid.* Chapter XV.
3 Martineau: The Transvaal Trouble: How it arose (London, John Murray, 1899) p. 78.
4 Cape Native Laws and Customs Commission, 1883, minutes of evidence. Questions 151, 289, 326, 435, 436, 437.
   David Welsh's excellent study of Shepstone (The Roots of Segregation (Cape Town, Oxford University Press, 1971)) makes it clear that Shepstone, despite his disposition to shore up traditionalism, disliked codification because it rigidified the situation (see his Chapter II).
5 Evidence, p. 289.
6 Report, Vol. II, p. 193.
7 i.e. Fermented treacle from sugarcane.
8 Debates, p. 382.
9 i.e. The Secretary for Native Affairs, who was an *ex officio* member of the Legislative Council.
10 See Secretary for Native Affairs Circular No. 2, dated 6th January 1898, and Government Notice 49 of 1902 dated 18th January 1902.
11 Approximately 500 African witnesses appeared before the Commission.
12 The author of 'Black and White in South-East Africa' and 'Black and White in the Southern States of America', books which had a considerable influence on contemporary opinion.
13 Report, para. 34.
14 Report, para. 33.
15 Report, para. 39.
16 Report, para. 23.
17 Report, para. 35.
18 Report, para. 40.
19 Report, para. 21.
20 Extracted from paras. 41 to 52 of the Report.
21 Minute dated 28th August 1907 in Papers S.N.A. 14/08.
22 Minute undated in papers S.N.A. 3394/07 (Samuelson papers).
23 A sum of £10 000 per annum was specially secured for this purpose in the Constitution Law of 1893, introducing Responsible Government.

CHAPTER VI

The Evolution of the Transkeian Policy

In an earlier part of this book it has been shown how the provisions of the Fiftieth Ordinance (1828) applied not only to Hottentots but to such Africans as lived within the borders of the Colony. As one annexation after another extended the Colony's boundaries and increased the number of its African inhabitants, the rulers of the Cape shrank from the logical application of this policy which would ultimately have led to an African majority in the electorate. By measures such as the Glen Grey Act (1894) the franchise was withheld from the majority of the Africans in the annexed areas, and a system of partial self-government replaced it, which may fairly be claimed to be the precursor of the autonomy of the Transkeian 'homeland' at the present day. Yet up to 1910 formal equality and the principle of a non-racial franchise held good even in the Transkeian Territories, and these ideals were warmly defended by the majority of the Cape delegates to the National Convention of 1908-9.

The Cape really spoke with two voices. The policy of integration, of which the non-racial franchise was a living symbol, prevailed in the Colony proper. The policy of separate development, despite the existence of some voters on the non-racial franchise, prevailed in the Transkei. What came to be called 'the Ciskei' (roughly the old British Kaffraria) occupied an intermediate position. This was the situation at the time of Union. Of course the abolition of the African franchise, the development of Transkeian autonomy and the greater assimilation of the Ciskei to the Transkei have led to great changes since.

There have in every generation been, and there are today, South Africans true to the principles of 1828. The supporters of integration and of a non-racial franchise have not all been missionaries, overseas visitors or 'cranks', but have included men deeply rooted in South Africa, such, for example, as Sir James Rose-Innes, W. P. Schreiner and F. S. Malan. But it would be idle to claim that their views have affected modern South Africa to the same extent as the views of those who have supported separate development and the Transkeian system.

In a way separate development was thrust upon the Cape by the policy which led to the annexation of Basutoland (Lesotho) to it in 1871. The Cape rule of Lesotho (1871-84) is marked by some inept and some disgraceful features, but it undoubtedly gave Cape Ministers and officials lessons in ruling a large, compact African area which could not well be administered as the districts in the Colony had been administered up to that date. It should be noted moreover that the grant of responsible government to the Cape took place in 1872 only one year after the annexation of Lesotho.

The Cape Legislature had been decidedly averse to incurring the responsibility of Basutoland, as it was then called, when the subject first came up for discussion; but when a possibility of Natal being entrusted with its rule became apparent a Select Committee of the pre-responsible government Legislative Council (of which Mr. John X. Merriman was a leading member) reported strongly in favour of annexation, and a Bill providing therefor passed its third reading on the 10th August 1871.

The permanent interest of the annexation of 1871 is the precedent it subsequently furnished for the government of the Transkei. Contrary to the principles of the British Kaffrarian annexation, Lesotho was not incorporated with the Colony but treated as an autonomous territory. Colonial law did not apply within it. The legislative authority was the Governor (later the Governor-in-Council) subject to the veto of Parliament. Acts of the Cape Parliament were not to apply to Lesotho unless expressly declared so to apply by the terms of the Act itself or by a subsequent proclamation of the Governor.

The administration was entrusted to magistrates, of whom there were four, one of these being also chief magistrate and Governor's agent. Supreme judicial as well as administrative powers vested in him, with an appeal to the Governor only in certain serious cases. Thus the whole framework of the subsequent Transkeian political and administrative system was already adopted for Lesotho in 1871. Those who were responsible for it included John X. Merriman, Charles Brownlee and Col. C. D. Griffith, the first Governor's agent. It failed in Lesotho partly owing to magisterial errors on the spot, mainly owing to the ignorance and perversity of politicians in the Cape Parliament, to changes of government and to the rise of the 'Native problem' as a party cry. Taught by their mistakes, the Cape Government after 1884 avoided these pitfalls in their administration of the Transkei.

What was of questionable wisdom was the rapid extension to the magistrates of authority which had hitherto belonged entirely to the chiefs. The general principle of replacing the chief by the magistrate may have been better than the principle of educating chiefs until they are fit for their position, but such a change requires time. In these matters statesmen must build to a definite plan, not merely drift; but at the same time they must not be in too much of a hurry. The Cape Government failed to take this excellent rule into account, forgetting that they were dealing not with the tractable Mfengu or the conquered Xhosas, but with the unbeaten and obstinately conservative Basotho.

From the beginning the magistrates were given jurisdiction over all criminal cases (except those punishable with death, reserved for the chief magistrate) and all civil cases. The chiefs were allowed to adjudicate on petty criminal cases and on all civil cases, but any judgment could be reviewed on appeal by the magistrate. As a matter of fact, the overwhelming majority of cases went to the chiefs and public opinion was so strongly in their favour that it was unusual to appeal. Even if an appeal was lodged, the appellant ran the danger of being 'eaten up'[1] by the chief, and the magistrates had not always enough force at their disposal to redress the wrong.[2]

A series of new rules came into force at the end of 1871. 'Eating up' became a crime – a rule difficult to enforce. It was forbidden to compel a woman to marry against her will, and all marriages had to be registered with the magistrate and a small registration fee paid. The *bohadi* (*ukulobola*) cattle had also to be registered, otherwise the magistrate's court would not entertain litigation regarding them. A widow was granted rights of guardianship over her children.

The fact that these reforms were liberal and enlightened must not prevent us from realising that they were subversive of the whole legal and social structure of Bantu society, which was still in the agnatic stage, and that they were introduced hastily without any genuine effort to conciliate public opinion regarding them, and so soon after the annexation as to arouse the deepest suspicion of the Basotho relative to their new position. They were thus in some measure inexpedient and impolitic, though without any doubt some of them ought to have been accepted as ideals to be gradually introduced by the Government as public opinion permitted. An even more questionable step was the nominal suppression of *letsima* (*isibhalo*), i.e. forced labour for the chiefs, an old Bantu custom far less reprehensible perhaps than our civilised custom of conscripting thousands of young men to be shot in national quarrels in which they have no interest. As might have been expected, the 'suppression' of *letsima* merely caused open defiance of the Government, for the common Mosotho was even more attached to his chief than averse to forced labour.

After these rules had been promulgated a commission was appointed which drew up a handbook of Basotho customs, used from 1873 as a guide to magistrates. The work of the commission was hurried and imperfect, its conclusions were sometimes incorrect and sometimes hampered by the regulations already in force and above adverted to, but it is of interest as being the forerunner of the historic Native Laws and Customs Commission of 1883.

For some time the position of the Government, though precarious, did not appear to be dangerous. A distinct tendency was apparent towards bringing cases to the magistrate instead of the chief,[3] but experienced observers realised that this could not have been done but for the tacit consent of the chiefs who found themselves freed from the routine work involved and that in the event of a real conflict between the chiefs and the Government, the mass of the people would follow their chiefs almost to a man.[4]

From the beginning a hut tax of 10/- per annum was imposed, and collected with little difficulty owing to the fact that chiefs were allowed to retain a large commission on the tax collection. No further salary was paid to the chiefs, but this commission proved adequate for their remuneration and assisted in reconciling them to European magisterial jurisdiction. We see, thus, in Lesotho the characteristic Transkeian feature of financial independence, with detailed variations skilfully adapted to local conditions. Unfortunately this hut tax was raised later to £1 per annum probably at too early a date.

Nevertheless it seems as if the Cape Government would still have had a chance of success had it not been for the crowning folly of the Disarmament Act of 1878. The motives and effects of this Act have been eloquently described by Dr. Theal,[5] and it only remains to draw attention to some of the surrounding influences at work and to some details peculiar to Lesotho.

One cannot help being struck at the undignified and unworthy partisanship which surrounded the whole disarmament question. Reading through the voluminous official correspondence of the period, the writer could not but carry away the impression that both the Cape Parliamentary parties were 'playing to the gallery' rather than working in single-hearted love of their country. Such an attitude in practical politics is so common today that we tend to regard it as excusable, yet surely it is inexcusable in the field of African policy. Whoever reads the speeches of Mr. J. Gordon Sprigg and Mr. J. W. Sauer at succeeding *pitsos* must blush to feel that these were the representatives of white South Africa before a dignified and unconquered people.

The tactlessness of Sprigg at the Pitso of 1879 when the Basotho were first definitely asked to surrender their arms is as amazing as it was doubtless disastrous.[6]

The time selected for pronouncing on disarmament was singularly unhappy. It was in the year of Isandhlwana, too soon after Ulundi for the news of that victory to have sunk into the African mind, and must have created the impression – perhaps true – that the white men were afraid!

As is well known, the appeal to the Basotho to surrender their arms voluntarily failed. The majority who had defied the Government turned on the obedient minority, maltreated and plundered them. The white man's government had become an object of contempt: the Sprigg ministry had made war inevitable, and it might be thought that the right course of action to pursue under the unfortunate circumstances was to vindicate law and authority as vigorously as possible.

Instead of this Sprigg, with J. M. Orpen, first made an ineffectual attempt to parley with the Basotho. An inadequate number of troops were sent, the difficulties which these men experienced added to the Basothos' self-confidence. When the war was in full train (early in 1881) an event took place for which the Sprigg ministry, which had blunders enough to its discredit, was not responsible. This was the desertion of a large proportion of the burgher forces in the face of the enemy. Not all the special pleading of Theal[7] can justify this act of disgraceful cowardice and bad citizenship.

The Legislature at home proceeded to rival the forces in the field. The Sprigg ministry was turned out of office and replaced by a ministry under Mr. (later Sir) T. C. Scanlen with J. W. Sauer as Minister of Native Affairs. The avowed object of this ministry was the disannexation of Lesotho. With its assumption of office on the 9th May 1881 the war was at an end. The Basotho had defeated the Cape Colony. The next three years up to the date of the disannexation were a period of humiliation and shame. Colonel Griffith, who had done so much for the Basotho, found his health conveniently bad and retired in August 1881, to be succeeded by J. M. Orpen. On the 6th April 1882 the proclamation applying the Disarmanent Act to Lesotho was repealed.

South African history is never dull, whatever its faults may be. Into the blackness of this period of shame and anarchy came the meteoric presence of Charles George Gordon. The 'official' (if the term 'official' may be used) correspondence between him and the Government in the six weeks while he was in Lesotho gave the writer a couple of hours' hearty amusement in the dusty precincts of the Archives little used to such irreverence, and it is much to be regretted that Mr. Lytton Strachey had not this material before him when writing his controversial monograph on Gordon.[8] Gordon's plan of reconstruction, not necessarily bad but characteristically drafted *before* he had visited the Basotho,[9] was the withdrawal of the military forces and the existing magisterial administration and the appointment by the Colonial Government of a Resident and two sub-residents as advisors to the paramount and lesser chiefs.

The Government compromised. At a great Pitso held from the 16th March to the 2nd April 1883, the new Scheme was propounded and discussed with the chiefs. The Governor's agent or 'other officer' – the term magistrate was not used – was to try all cases in which Europeans were concerned and to sit with the chiefs to try all purely African cases, except those of treason or sedition, to be reserved for the Governor's agent alone. An African Council of Advice was to assist the Governor's agent in administration. Mr. Orpen had meanwhile been replaced by Captain Matthew Blyth, an officer who deserved a less unpleasant position. On the 24th April Captain Blyth called a meeting of the Basotho nation to discuss the scheme propounded at the Great Pitso. Not a chief of importance was present. The cup of humiliation was almost full.

The final surrender was, however, yet to come. The Cape ministry had sent John X. Merriman to England to lay its needs before the Colonial Office. On the 29th May 1883 he placed before the Earl of Derby, on behalf of his colleagues, a proposal that the Cape – in other words the nucleus of self-governing South Africa – should abandon almost all its responsibilities with regard to African affairs to the Government of the United Kingdom. 'The best solution,' the memorandum reads (par. 36) 'from a Colonial, and also from an Imperial, point of view would be found in the assumption by Her Majesty's Government of the control of all the Native Dependencies of the Colony including Basutoland, Fingoland, Tembuland, East Griqualand and St. John's. These together would form a tolerably homogeneous and self-supporting territory with a seaboard, independent of the Colony proper, who would be by such an arrangement placed in a position to contribute liberally towards the support of such a scheme, while Natal, who derives a considerable amount from the customs dues of East Griqualand might also be fairly called upon for a contribution. These amounts, with those raised by taxation, would supply a revenue amply sufficient for administration on the most efficient scale, while to South Africa and to the cause of law and order generally such a step would be of incalculable advantage.'

This far-reaching suggestion was received coldly and only Lesotho, where the prestige of the Cape Government had been so destroyed as to make continued Cape rule impossible, was detached from the Cape Colony. The Disannexation Act passed the Cape Parliament in September 1883. On the 18th March 1884 it received the royal assent, and Captain Blyth handed over his duties to Colonel Marshall Clarke, the Resident Commissioner of the British Government.

A change of government in the Cape reversed the disannexation policy. Port St. John's was annexed in 1884. Despite protests to England by the Africans concerned, Thembuland and Gcalekaland were annexed in 1885, and the Xesibe territory in 1886. Eight years later Pondoland was also annexed.[10]

The new regime in Lesotho preserved order perfectly among the people. It did little directly to civilise. There were many grievances but peace was preserved and white prestige was largely restored. The work of Sir Marshall Clarke, under the most difficult circumstances, proved markedly successful. At Sir H. B. Loch's visit to Lesotho in 1890 every chief, except Letsie, incapacitated by age, attended the Pitso[11] – a contrast indeed to the last Pitso under Colonial auspices in 1883. Thereafter respect for authority was maintained. Economically the territory stagnated, if it did not actually go backward. Civilising activity was almost confined to the missions. New life only came flowing in after the period covered by this book, and was perhaps only marked in the 1960's.

While the Cape politicians were bungling the Lesotho question the Cape statesmen – in other words the permanent Civil Service – were successfully coping with the problem of the Transkeian Territories, part of which had been annexed in 1877 as a result of the Ninth (and last) Frontier War.

The man to whom above all others credit is due for the inception of the Transkeian system is Charles Brownlee, permanent Secretary for Native Affairs. His report for the year 1875 is a magnificent document. Its high note of moral obligation and idealism combined with sturdy common sense and expert personal knowledge of the African, struck the right keynote for African policy in South Africa. We know beyond all doubt that the lines of Transkeian African policy did not grow up accidentally but were deliberately and designedly laid down from the beginning by Brownlee himself.[12] In spite of the attacks on his system by such people as J. M. Orpen,[13] who accused him of unduly hastening detribalisation, we have the outstanding fact that the Transkeian African under the system laid down by Brownlee became the most advanced in South Africa. With exemplary public spirit, after his laying down the lines of policy, Brownlee quitted his Secretaryship and, as the first chief magistrate of Griqualand East, gave his colleagues a lesson as to the putting of theory into practice, which was invaluable in assisting to build up the high tradition of Transkeian administration.

The Transkeian African policy was well described as being from the beginning a 'unique progressive policy adapting itself to the various stages of advancing civilization'.[14] Its framers realised that to treat all the Africans (including the progressive Mfengu removed to the Transkei in 1865) as being on one dead level of barbarism would be the height of folly. 'It is most wise and proper,' wrote Captain Matthew Blyth, the first and perhaps the best chief magistrate of the Transkei, in 1881,[15] 'to hedge these people on either side with strict laws and regulations, but the road forward should never be blocked and there should be no bar placed to their advancement.' From 1881 Mr. Sauer, the Minister of Native Affairs in the Scanlen ministry, instituted the practice of constant public consultation with the Africans – a practice which took regular and institutional form in the Council system first brought into being in 1894-5. The whole lines of the Glen Grey system were clearly sketched out by Captain Blyth in a memorandum dated the 13th January 1882.[16] Thus from the beginning the Transkeian administrators pursued a definite course and Transkeian policy presents itself to the student as a coherent, intelligible, progressive and conscious evolution. The Ministers at far-off Cape Town had the good sense to leave men who knew something about their subject a free hand in policy. Great credit is due to Mr. Sauer for the precedent which he set in this direction. Everyone knows that the Transkeian experiment succeeded, as far as Europeans are concerned, owing purely and simply to the permanent staff of the Native Affairs Department and particularly to the resident magistrates. It may be convenient for panegyrists and other garblers of history to credit Cecil John Rhodes with the Glen Grey policy and to suggest to us that it sprang full-grown from his brain as Pallas Athene from the head of Zeus. Sober and accurate history must step in with regret and destroy this legend in the interests of the just fame of the great administrators who really deserve such praise as may be given – in particular Charles Brownlee, Matthew Blyth, H. G. (later Sir Henry) Elliott and W. E. (later Sir Walter) Stanford.

The main points of the Transkeian policy have already been mentioned in discussing the Government's early policy in Lesotho. The magisterial system – magistrates definitely replacing chiefs, of course gradually – was from the first adopted. There were three chief magistrates – of the Transkei, of Tembuland and of Griqualand East – later amalgamated. Parliament was persuaded at the date of the annexation to grant a charter to the administration. The Governor-in-Council (in practice the permanent Native Affairs Department) became the normal legislative authority. Parliament retained a right of veto over his proclamations, and a theoretical right to legislate for the Territories; but Acts of Parliament were not to apply unless expressly extended by the Acts themselves or subsequent proclamations. From the first, care was taken to co-operate with the people and a council system discussed favourably, though the time was not considered ripe for its adoption.

The essence of the Grey policy – to civilise and not merely to preserve peace and the *status quo* – was a feature of Transkeian life from the first. The material progress of the people was fostered and ensured. The Government at Cape Town, taught by the bitter lesson of Lesotho, refrained from oppressive legislation.

Tribal law was administered from the first. But in some parts of the territories it had a legal standing and in others not. It was, therefore, considered advisable to appoint a commission to go into the whole question of 'Native Laws and Customs' and to report. Thus we get the famous Cape Native Laws and Customs Commission of 1883 – probably the most useful commission that has ever reported on African administration in South Africa.

The commission consisted of Sir Jacob Dirk Barry, Judge President of the Eastern Districts Court (chairman), Mr. Charles Brownlee, Chief Magistrate of Griqualand East, Mr. (later Sir) W. E. Stanford, Chief Magistrate of Tembuland, Dr. James Stewart, Principal of Lovedale, Dr. (later Sir) W. Bisset Berry and Messrs. W. B. Chalmers, Thos. Upington, Jonathan Ayliff, Emile S. Rolland and Richard Solomon. Mr. John Noble acted as secretary. Very unfortunately, Mr. Brownlee was unable to attend the sittings of the commission, though he forwarded his views in writing, and Mr. Chalmers had to retire early in the life of the commission. These vacancies were not filled.

The commission was of great value, first by reason of the material it collected. All its witnesses were experts[17]– a strong contrast to the Inter-Colonial Commission of 1903-5 – and beside their evidence the commission collected and printed or reprinted much useful matter. Among other things there was the first draft of the Transkeian Penal Code, draft Bills relating to African marriages and succession, a monograph by Sir T. Shepstone on the African tribes of Natal, an epitome of Maclean's Compendium of Native Law, Hammond Tooke's genealogy of the African chiefs, and the first Natal Native Code. It remains today the best single volume to put into the hands of a student anxious to learn something of African administration.

Secondly, the commission merits attention by reason of the manner in which it dealt with tribal law. The result of its labours is the characteristic Transkeian method of fully recognising and administering tribal civil law without codifying it. Tribal criminal law (which, strictly speaking, is really a branch of tribal civil law) was abandoned, and a code – the Transkeian Penal Code – drawn up which expounded the existing criminal law of the Colony, with a few absolutely essential modifications, very lucidly and simply. It was obviously drawn up for Africans only, but in order to save parliamentary susceptibilities, it was enacted[18] for the Territories as a whole, including the small European population – i.e. on a territorial instead of a personal basis.

Beyond these two points – the collection of information and the putting of legal matters on a satisfactory basis – it cannot be said that the report of the commission was brilliantly successful. It recommended,[19] for example, a chief executive officer for the Territories distinct from the chief magistrate – a division of authority the antithesis of the subsequent successful administrative system of the Transkei.

It also recommended the erection of a Native Council. This body in the form of a council of chiefs had been strongly and distinctly advocated before the commission by Sir Theophilus Shepstone.[20] The commission's own proposal, however, contemplated an informally elected body.[21] Africans exercising the ordinary parliamentary franchise were to be debarred from voting for the Native Council though they would still be eligible for election thereto.[22] Neither Shepstone's nor the commission's scheme was actually put into practice; and when a council system was actually introduced a decade later, it took a definitely original form.

The ten years after the issue of the report of the Native Laws and Customs Commission were years of steady material progress and advance in civilisation. With these desirable features, however, it is sad to compare the constant references in the annual Departmental Blue Books from 1884 onwards to the spread of drunkenness and venereal diseases. In spite of all the activities of magistrates and missionaries it was impossible to prevent the tares of civilisation from growing up with the wheat. An interesting feature is the beginning of systematic historical and ethnological research relative to the tribes inhabiting the Territories and a special interest attaches to the valuable reports of this nature appearing in the Blue Books of 1886 and 1887 over the signature of 'Geo. M. Theal, First Clerk, Native Affairs Department'.

In 1889 passed away Captain Matthew Blyth, one of the finest administrators of Africans that South Africa has known. 'To commemorate his memory the people of the six Districts over which he ruled so well have voluntarily raised a large sum of money to be expended in erecting a monument over his grave.'[23] Blythswood Industrial Institution also commemorates his name; but his best monument is the prosperity and advancement of his people.

The parliamentary franchise was extended to such Africans (not many) in the Transkei as were able to qualify for it with the vital condition that communal property was not to be accepted as a property qualification by Act 30 of 1887. But Act 8 of 1892 instituted a restriction on the franchise which prevented this measure from materially affecting the Transkeian system. Col. C. D. Griffith, C.M.G., formerly Governor's agent for Lesotho, was the first member for the Tembuland constituency.

Annexations proceeded apace, the last being that of Pondoland in 1894. The simplification of administration which began with the amalgamation of the Transkeian and Tembuland chief magistracies in 1891 – a change which was well received by the people[24]– progressed until there was but one chief magistrate for all the territories east of the Kei. Control, peace and order were secured, and it became possible to devote more direct governmental attention to civilising and educative measures – measures which had been gradually prepared for ever since the first annexation.

Of these measures by far the most important was the Glen Grey Act (No. 25 of 1894). Its details are more fully discussed later, but it seems advisable to give a brief resume of its general effect here.

Briefly, then, the Glen Grey system combined an improved form of land tenure with a measure of partial self-government intended to have an educative effect and to lead up to better things. Quit-rent tenure had, of course, been known since the days of Sir Harry Smith, but the Glen Grey tenure was far in advance of any previous scheme in its details. It was argued that the quit-rent furnished a useful revenue and the necessity for its payment an incentive to work, while the clauses providing for forfeiture of title on conviction for treason or stock theft or on proof of non-beneficial occupation provided most admirable safeguards against the abuse of the new privileges. At the same time adherence to the principles of 'one man, one lot' and of following the existing lines of occupation, though a hindrance to progressive agriculture, were designed to ensure that nothing of permanent value in primitive African society would be lost under the new state of affairs.

The councils were intended to provide a limited right of local self-government, to train the people in administration, to give them a sense of responsibility in raising and expending money for their own benefit and to teach them to remedy their grievances instead of deploring them.

Introduced into the district of Glen Grey in the Ciskei first of all, the system was almost immediately extended to the Transkeian districts of Butterworth, Idutywa, Nqamakwe and Tsomo by Proclamation No. 352 of 1894. The general council came into being in 1895 and rapidly became one of the most important African bodies in South Africa. A general extension and reconstruction of the councils took place in 1903. The council part of the Glen Grey system was ultimately extended to each of the eighteen districts of the Transkeian Territories. The Native Affairs Commission describes it as undoubtedly successful and a most valuable means of ascertaining representative African opinion.[25] The best proof of its success is that Act 23 of 1920, making a similar council system permissive for the whole Union, passed the House of Assembly without a division.

The reforms of today may become obsolete and even harmful tomorrow. In many (though not all) ways the Transkeian system led to the policy of 'Bantu authorities' in the 'homelands' which is so controversial at the present day. While the Transkeian Council system did much to foster self-respect among the people concerned and to give them political experience it is not necessarily an adequate alternative to real participation in national government.

Of course the change was greeted at first with vigorous opposition, as reforms often are. The people themselves, with characteristic conservatism, were suspicious of the new arrangements and magistrates were for a time apprehensive of trouble.[26] But in a year or two all was calm. The highest encomiums were passed on the newly appointed councils.[27] The labour tax, the only really unpopular feature of the Act, was quietly allowed to drop.[28] The end of the century saw the Territories in a state of great tranquillity and prosperity[29] and there was a unanimous consensus of magisterial opinion in favour of the Act as it had proved itself at the end of 1899.[30] One district – Kentani – came under the Act voluntarily in that year.[31] Before the Commission of 1903-5 the chief clerk of the Native Affairs Department, Mr. E. E. Dower, repeatedly expressed his opinion that the Act had proved most beneficial in working.[32] The only real criticism came from other officials, Messrs. Job Scott and W. Power Leary, who expressed the fear that the General Council, by combining the Africans, had been a strategical error of policy.[33] If the proper attitude towards the African population be one of intense fear, there is point in this criticism; otherwise, not.

Pondoland, though progressing favourably, was as yet far behind the rest of the Territories in general advancement and it was thought impracticable to extend the Transkeian council system (much less the quit-rent tenure) thereto. In 1911, however, just after Union, a modified scheme was introduced. The delegates were nominees of the chiefs, not elected.

That there has been criticism on the subject of the Transkeian council system on the part of Africans is true, but only on the grounds that it did not go far enough.

We have now traced briefly the history of the evolution of what was undoubtedly the most successful African administration in South Africa before Union. We have seen how the Smith-Calderwood policy contributed the ideas of individual tenure on quit-rent and the encouragement of agricultural and industrial progress; how the Grey policy set up the positive encouragement of civilisation as the end and the magisterial system as the means of an ideal African administration; how the Brownlee policy of legislation by proclamation, the recognition of tribal law, and the commanding position of the chief magistrate, first applied in Lesotho in 1870-2, won its way into the Transkei and how, from the Lesotho disaster, the Government learned the lessons that reforms must proceed by gradual stages, that oppressive legislation must not be enacted, that policy must be lifted above party considerations, and that the Cabinet and the Legislature must give as free a hand as possible to the permanent administration. We have seen how, armed with this knowledge and with a good will, the Government did actually carry out from 1879 what has been correctly termed 'an unique progressive policy', a policy which won the loyalty and confidence of the African people.

It would be idle to pretend that the Transkei has been free from all ills, or that its government has been absolutely perfect. Yet during a period within which the European peoples of South Africa were twice engaged in fratricidal strife it experienced profound peace. Its people advanced not merely in material wealth but in civilisation, in the sense of responsibility and in the power of managing their own affairs. A century of missionary endeavour has assisted even the heathen in their progress in the scale of evolution. If there, why not elsewhere? Why can we not find applicable to all our other African areas those majestic words of the hundred and forty fourth psalm:

... 'That our sons may grow up as the young plants: and that our daughters may be as the polished corners of the temple.

That our garners may be full and plenteous with all manner of store: that our sheep may bring forth thousands and ten thousands in our streets.

That our oxen may be strong to labour, that there be no decay: no leading into captivity, and no complaining in our streets.'

Admittedly in recent years the growth of population and the pressure on the land has turned the Transkei into something of a rural slum. But we are here considering the years 1877 to 1910.

More than to anything else this cycle of progress and this happy result must be attributed to the permanent administrators of the Native Affairs Department and to them tribute must be paid. They were 'paternalists' in a discredited system of 'colonialism' but paternalism is surely preferable to negligence, uncaring indolence or cruelty. It is to South Africans, but not to South African legislators and politicians that the credit is due. That must give us room for pride and room also for self-examination and humility. Perhaps Hamlet's definition of a politician is not out of date yet – 'one that would circumvent God'. Our permanent administrators did not, perhaps, have these gifts of subtle cunning, of polished and practised ambiguity, of dexterous tactical skill and of profitable anticipation of public opinion. They have been merely just, upright, clean, honourable South African gentlemen – not always perhaps very clever, certainly not possessed of the Baconian 'wisdom for a man's self', labouring without much hope of recognition and reward, but exhibiting a single-hearted loyalty to the good of their people which is the essence of a practical Christianity. To them South Africa, white and black, owes a debt which it can hardly hope to repay.

NOTES TO CHAPTER VI

1. i.e. Of losing all his movable property, usually livestock.
2. Report of W. A. Surmon, Magistrate, Kornet Spruit, Lesotho, dated 31st December 1883; Cape Native Blue Book 1884, p. 85.
3. *Vide* Cape Native Blue Book 1887, pp. 3 and 8.
4. Despatch of J. H. Bowker, Governor's Agent, to Secretary for Native Affairs, Cape Town, dated from Mohale's Hoek, 18th April 1878 (copies of correspondence, telegrams, etc., in re Morosi's Rebellion, Basutoland, 1879, pp. 30-31).
5. Theal, G. M. History of South Africa 1873-1884, Vol. II, (London, George Allen & Unwin Ltd.) pp. 55-6.
6. Report of Pitso of 16th and 17th October 1879 (White Book).
7. Theal, G. M. History of South Africa 1873-1884, Vol. II, (London, George Allen & Unwin Ltd.) pp. 67, 68 and 80.
8. In Strachey, L.: 'Eminent Victorians'. (London, Chatto & Windus, 1931). The pidgin English in which Gordon addressed Masupha and which is solemnly reported in full is very funny when one realises that it had to be interpreted into Sesotho.
9. See Report of Interview between the Premier and the Secretary for Native Affairs and certain Basuto Chiefs, Councillors and Headmen, 16th March – 2nd April 1883, pp. 108 and 109.
10. I am deeply indebted to Dr. Christopher Saunders of the University of Cape Town for allowing me to draw on his, as yet, unpublished thesis for this information.
11. U.K. Blue Book, Basutoland Papers, c. 5896 (1890), p. 1.
12. Report of Secretary for Native Affairs 1878-9, especially pp. 11-12.
13. In 1880, after Brownlee's resignation of the Secretaryship.
14. Report of Wm. Goodwood, Resident Magistrate, Tsomo, dated 31st December 1881 (Cape Native Blue Book 1882, p. 19).
15. Cape Native Blue Book 1881, p. 39. See also Cape Native Blue Book 1883 (including memorandum of 13th June, 1882).
16. Cape Native Blue Book 1882, p. 6.
17. Among the most interesting portions of the volume must be classed the evidence of Sir Theophilus Shepstone (which seems to me to have carried more weight than that of any other witness), of Mr. J. M. Orpen and of Cetshwayo.
18. By Act 24 of 1886.
19. Report, para. 119, p. 44.
20. *Ibid*. para. 121, p. 45.
21. *Ibid*. para. 122, pp. 45-6.
22. *Ibid*. para. 125, pp. 46-7.
23. Cape Native Blue Book 1890, p. 27.
24. Cape Native Blue Book 1892, p. 37.
25. Report, 1921, p. 30.
26. Cape Native Blue Book 1896, pp. 88-9, 91 and 95.
27. Cape Native Blue Book 1897, pp. 23, 83, 85 and 90.
28. *Vide* Report of Select Committee of the Cape House of Assembly on the Glen Grey Act, 1898, p. 2.
29. Cape Native Blue Book 1899 *passim*.
30. Cape Native Blue Book 1900, pp. 72-74.
31. Cape Native Blue Book 1899, pp. 72 and 81.
32. e.g. Questions 178, 637, 652 (Evidence, Vol. II, pp. 19 and 64).
33. S.A. Native Affairs Commission 1903-5 Evidence. Questions 14500 (Vol. II, pp. 1060-1) and 16442-16449 (Vol. II, pp. 1195-6).

CHAPTER VII

The Transkeian Council System (continued)

Before passing on to the study of the Transvaal and Orange Free State it would be as well to go a little more fully into the history of the Transkeian council system discussed in outline in the previous chapter.

The first move towards it was made in 1882 when Captain Matthew Blyth recommended that 'a sort of municipal council be formed in each district.' The Native Laws and Customs Commission of 1883 recommended a general council for the Territories – a suggestion of Sir Theophilus Shepstone.[1] Some years elapsed before action was taken on these recommendations, but ultimately it was decided to make a beginning with the district of Glen Grey in the Ciskeian Territories as an experiment, and Act 25 of 1894 was passed to this end. This Act provided for the election of location boards by registered plot-holders, and for the creation of a district council of twelve members, six elected by the location boards and six appointed by the Governor, presided over by the local magistrate. The council had the power to levy a rate of not less than five shillings on every owner of an allotment and every adult male resident in the district, and to expend the funds so raised on education, dipping, roads, etc.

The location boards proved a failure. Less than nine years after the Act came into operation the magistrate of Glen Grey found it necessary to report unfavourably on them.[2] The Cape Native Affairs Commission of 1910 recommended their abolition.[3] Their defects are generally admitted today.

On the other hand the district council proved from the beginning markedly successful. After its first year of work, Mr. C. J. Sweeney, magistrate of Glen Grey, reported as follows:[4]

'The Council, formed as it has been of leading advanced Natives in the District, has secured the confidence of the people, its members have taken a keen interest in the welfare of the district, and have evinced a considerable grasp of work which at the beginning of the year was new to all of them.

'The Council rates have been well paid up, the Natives realising that, under the changed condition of affairs, this tax is expended for their benefit by their own representatives.

'The Council meetings have been well attended, and the business brought forward intelligently discussed.'

In 1897 he reports:[5]

'The District Council continues, I am pleased to say, to work well, and I think that body has reason to feel satisfied with the work performed during the past year.'

In 1903 a Select Committee of the Cape House of Assembly appointed to enquire into the working and administration of the Glen Grey Act reported, *inter alia*, as follows:

'Speaking generally . . . your Committee are convinced that the operations of the Act have been, as they were intended to be, most beneficial to the Natives concerned. Individual tenure and local self-government have done much, and will in the future do more to lead the aboriginal Natives in the path of improvement.'[6]

The Cape Native Affairs Commission of 1910, hostile to some forms of African local government, commended the working of the Glen Grey District Council highly.[7]

The Union Secretary for Native Affairs reported in 1919: 'A keen and intelligent interest is taken by the Councillors, not only in affairs of the district, but in matters of wider concern.

'As providing means for the expression of public opinion amongst the Natives the institution is of great service in the administration of Native Affairs in the district.'[8]

In 1895 the operation of the Glen Grey Act was extended to the Transkeian Territories, when district councils and a general council were established. The weight of evidence available tends to show that these bodies proved very successful indeed. At the time of Union there was in each of the eighteen districts in the Transkei a district council, consisting of six councillors, holding office for three years with the magistrate as chairman *ex officio*. The Governor-General nominated two councillors, while the remaining members were elected by the landowners in 'surveyed' areas by a process of indirect election, and by the headmen of 'unsurveyed' areas, subject in all cases to the Governor-General's approval. The 'unsurveyed' areas could follow the system prescribed for 'surveyed' areas if so desired.

'District Councils meet quarterly or when specially summoned by the Magistrate. Minutes of meetings are kept and forwarded to the Chief Magistrate, who brings before the Transkeian Territories General Council matters required to be dealt with.

'District Councils practically act as advisers or agents of the Transkeian Territories General Council, which consists of the Chief Magistrate as Chairman, the Magistrates of the Districts, and three Native Councillors from each District, two of whom are nominated by the District for the Governor-General's approval and one by the Governor-General.

'The General Council meets once a year for business.

'The funds of the General Council are obtained by a rate levied by the Governor-General on every Native occupier of a hut or piece of land, and on every Native male domiciled within the jurisdiction of the Council. Its estimates of expenditure must be approved by the Governor-General.

'Besides dealing with matters of local government, such as roads, dams, fences, dipping, health, education (scholastic or industrial), etc., the Council is the forum for the discussion of every conceivable aspect of Native interest.

'The resolutions adopted by the Council which require Government action or legislation are discussed at a meeting of Magistrates, carefully and sympathetically considered by the Government, and form a most valuable means of ascertaining representative Native opinion in the Territories.'[9]

How has the system worked in the Transkei?

During the first year after its proclamation there was very little evidence as to the actual working of the councils, but what little there was is good. Mr. W. C. Scully, the well-known poet and novelist, then magistrate at Nqamakwe, wrote:[10]

'I have been particularly struck with the resourcefulness, the carefulness, the sense of responsibility and the generally excellent tone displayed by the local members. Important road works have been authorised, and will soon be commenced. Dipping tanks, to be paid for out of the Council funds, are to be constructed under the supervision of the local Scab inspector. Liberal grants have been made in aid of different schools.'

Mr. V. M. Watermeyer, Magistrate of Tsomo, reported:[11]

'The Councillors ... evince great pride in knowing that they have the principal voice in the management of local affairs. One or two of them are rather too conservative, but some show a remarkable acuteness in carrying on the business of the Council on liberal European ideas. Almost all the Natives who were loudest in their protestations against the introduction of the new laws have now completely changed front, and acknowledge the wisdom and expediency of the measure.'

In 1897 satisfactory reports were received from Idutywa, Butterworth, Nqamakwe and Tsomo: there were no unsatisfactory reports. The remarks of Mr. W. T. Brownlee, Resident Magistrate, Butterworth, deserve quotation in full:[12]

'Election to membership in the Council is regarded as a great honour. The various members are as a rule most exemplary in their attendances at Council meetings, where all matters brought forward are carefully and intelligently discussed, and the proceedings are carefully watched by the Natives generally. Much good work is being done. Wattle plantations have been started in each of the four districts, and wattle planting is progressing apace. Extensive road works have been undertaken, and the control of all schemes has been taken over by the Council. A bridge is to be built over the Butterworth River. The extermination of burr-weed has been taken in hand.'

Before the Commission of 1903-5 voluminous evidence, the overwhelming majority of which was favourable, was given on the conciliar system. No witness of standing was against the district councils. Two gentlemen, ex-magistrates, whose names carry weight, Messrs. W. Power Leary[13] and J. H. Scott,[14] were against the general council – not because it had not worked well, but because by combining the Africans it was politically a mistake. But 'divide et impera' is surely at rock bottom the method of a coward. The council system was not among the Commission's terms of reference, but there is little doubt that the majority of members of the Commission were sympathetic towards it.

In 1908 a deputation was sent[15] by the Natal Government to inquire into the working of the council system and the system of individual land tenure in the Transkeian Territories. The deputation, consisting of the Rev. F. B. Bridgman and Messrs. Martin L. Luthuli and P. J. Gumede, timed its visit to coincide with the meeting of the General Council, attended all its sessions and was thoroughly convinced of its success. Although this chapter is over-burdened with quotations already, it would seem absolutely necessary to give here an extract from the report of the deputation:

'The Transkeian Territories General Council convened at 10 o'clock on the morning of April 27th, and adjourned on May 9th. The Council was usually in session each day from 9.30 a.m. to 1 p.m., and from 2.15 p.m. until 4.15 p.m. The General Council met this year for the first time in its own building, having a fine spacious hall, besides committee rooms and offices, recently bought and fitted at a cost of £2 500. The Council hall is arranged in assembly style, with platform for the President, and with two rows of elevated desks and seats placed horse-shoe shape for the Councillors, and in the centre of the house a long table at which sit the magistrates. There were also seats provided at either end of the hall for visitors, European and Native. At the session of the Council there were present the magistrates and forty-four Native councillors, representing fifteen magisterial districts and a total population of 476 000.

'In opening, the Council was led in prayer by the Chief Magistrate, who followed with an address reviewing the year's work, and touching upon important matters to come before the present session. The Agenda comprised about sixty topics and notices of motion. To illustrate the variety and scope of the matters discussed, the following subjects may be mentioned:

'Dipping of sheep and scab regulations; improvement of breed of horses; cotton growing; unlawful killing of animals and burning of huts; attendances of children at beer drinks; Inter-State Native College; Native hospitals; increase of grants to school teachers; agricultural and industrial schools, etc.

'Nothing will give so clear a comprehension of the work carried on under the auspices of the General Council as a review of its finances. The annual report for 1907 shows an income of £49 962. Of this amount more than £46 000 represents revenue from the general rate. The principal items of expenditure were as follows:

(1) General Election, £14 000.
(2) Agricultural and Industrial Institutions and tree plantations, £8 000.
(3) Public Works, salaries of surveyors and engineers, roads, of which there are 3 000 miles under Council management, dipping tanks, and dams for irrigation schemes, £17 000.

'More particularly as regards education the following points may be noted:

'(1) The General Council gives grants to Government-aided Schools on the following basis: Towards the salaries of head teachers, the Council gives 15s., and for assistant teachers 10s., for every £1 Government aid. Grants are also given to *unaided* schools for a period not exceeding two years. The Council also aids in the purchase of school furniture on the £1 for £1 basis. The number of pupils in Council aided schools is over 37 000.

'(2) These schools while receiving Government and Council grants are primarily mission schools and are under missionary management. The large number of schools and churches was very noticeable during our travels in the Transkeian Territories.

'(3) Towards the Inter-State Native College the General Council has granted £10 000.

'(4) Agricultural Institutions. The Deputation paid a visit to the Agricultural Institution, located at Tsolo. Our impression of this effort to instruct Natives in cultivation and stock-raising was most favourable. The School, not quite four years old, has a splendidly situated farm of more than 3 000 acres, and a good equipment of stables, sheds for cattle and sheep, a dairy, farming machinery, besides quarters for the superintendent and apprentices. At present there are twenty apprentices engaged in a three years' course of instruction, which includes cultivation of various crops (there being 150 acres under irrigation), dairying and stock-raising. Limited attention is also given to carpentry and blacksmithing.

'The Institution has a fine lot of livestock and is doing much to improve the breeds of Native horses, cattle and sheep. The stallions, 19 in number, include both Colonial and imported throughbred stock. One of these stallions is valued at £500, while several cost from £150 to £300 each. In the breeding season the stallions are distributed, to the several council districts, no charge being made to the ratepayers. The past season 629 mares were covered, a proof that the Natives are taking interest in the improvement of their horses. In cattle the Institution has some prize stock. Two-year-old Shorthorn bulls are sold to ratepayers for £6 each, while in the open market they would bring £20. Rams worth £6 are supplied to ratepayers at £1. The Superintendent told us that results showed that sheep bred from these rams were shearing wool to the value of 5s. or 6s., instead of 1s. 6d. to 2s. to the fleece.

'The General Council this year voted an appropriation of £3 500 for the establishment of another agricultural institution, to be located in the Butterworth District, this to be on similar lines to that just described at Tsolo. No one feature of the varied operations under the General Council so impressed the Deputation as this very serious and practical effort to teach the Natives improved methods of agriculture and stock-raising.

'(5) Industrial Trade Schools. There are two situated in the Umzimkulu District and at Butterworth, the latter having been established eight years. These Institutions, it is generally conceded, have not been thus far a great success, the primary cause for this partial failure as pointed out by a Special Council Committee are two: (*a*) The attempt to run the Institutions upon a paying basis financially, and (*b*) the lack of discipline over the apprentices together with the want of attention to character-building. After thorough investigation, measures are now being adopted for reorganisation and a better report of these Institutions may be expected in the near future. At the Butterworth Institution there are at present fifteen apprentices who are being taught carpentry, wagon-making, stone-cutting and masonry.

'The General Council is responsible for many activities besides those mentioned above. These that have been touched upon are merely illustrative.

'As to the conduct and personnel of the General Council, we received several impressions which should also be noticed.

'1. The Management of Council Finances

'During the session a letter was read from the Auditor-General speaking in highest terms of the sound and business-like administration of the Council funds. The accurate, painstaking accounting of the Council's Treasurer[16] was also warmly commended.

'In conversation with us the Chief Magistrate emphatically declared that the administration of finances must remain in charge of Europeans; experience having shown that in dealing with considerable sums, and particularly as regards trust funds, Natives have not yet obtained sufficient breadth of view or adequate sense of accountability to qualify them for this work. This was partially illustrated during the Council's session. Despite warning that the Treasury could not meet the demand, the Councillors passed several votes requiring a large increase of expenditure. Later, when it came to the consideration of the budget, the Chairman appointed a committee of Natives to draft the estimates. After two days' struggle this Committee reported that it was unequal to the task, and requested that the work be undertaken by the Magistrates.

'2. The Spirit pervading Officials and People

'On the part of officials from highest to lowest there was evident an attitude of friendliness towards the Natives. The Chief Magistrate and Resident Magistrates, not only at the Councils, but also those whom we saw in the discharge of duty in the home districts, showed a genuine interest in the welfare and advancement of these people, and seemed ever ready to render practical help in securing the material and moral betterment of those under them.

'On the part of the people there was manifest a feeling of confidence and trust in both their own Magistrates and the Government generally. Neither was the element of gratitude lacking as indicated by two incidents in the Council, when, first, Magistrate W. T. Brownlee was presented with a seal ring by the people of his late charge at Butterworth, and second, when the Council very heartily voted the retiring head clerk a gift of £250. It may also be observed as an evidence of the contentment of the Native population that the average police force in a magisterial division of from 25 000 to 40 000 population is one European and from six to eight Native constables; but it should be stated that in addition to this small force the headmen, twenty-five to thirty-five in a district, are subject to police duty if occasion requires.

'3. The personnel of the Native Councillors

'Viewed as a body, there was nothing remarkable about the education or ability of the Councillors. There were a few well-educated and able men, but, as far as could be ascertained, fully half the representatives could not read or write. Judging from their confusion, some seemed to be having their first experience in the procedure of voting.

'4. The Relation of the "red Kaffir" to the General Council

'As may be inferred from the last paragraph, the majority of the councillors being "red Kaffir" representatives, so, of course, the vast majority of the ratepayers belong to this raw type. In most of the Council districts, there is but a sprinkling of adult Natives who may be classed as civilised. It was most difficult to realize that it was the *raw* Native who was supplying the bulk of the £50 000 with which the Council finances its operations, and that, therefore, it was the "blanket kaffir" who holds the larger share in the proprietorship of the "Bhunga"[17] roads, wattle plantations, dipping tanks, agricultural institutions, with its prize livestock, etc. These considerations are all the more surprising when we recall the fact that the Proclamation providing for the council system is, as with the land tenure, only *permissive:* and that the council system, with the 10s. rate, only becomes operative in a given district when the Natives of that district express a desire for the extension of the Proclamation to that area.

'The Deputation was forced to seek an explanation of this strange phenomenon of self-imposed taxation by a people for the most part still in barbarism. But the only answer was the patent fact that the Government was determined to do all in its power for the material, intellectual, and moral betterment of the Natives in the Transkeian Territories, and the people, being persuaded that this was the purpose of the Government, have given their co-operation. From observation and inquiry we were convinced that the extent and success of both the land tenure and council system were directly due to the persuasive measures and tactful pressure exercised by officials from the Chief Magistrate down. While the provisions of the proclamations have been proved excellent, they would have been a dead letter, but for the philanthropic spirit which has animated this administration.

'In conclusion, while the opinion of the Deputation as to the operation of the Glen Grey idea has been already foreshadowed, yet the delegates feel it incumbent to record their unanimous and enthusiastic endorsement of both the land tenure and council systems, as administered in the Transkeian Territories. Doubtless there are defects of detail, but the Deputation has but one opinion as to the broader principles involved.'

In 1919 the Union Secretary for Native Affairs reported;[18]

'Council operations embrace the maintenance of about 3 210 miles of roads, and the construction of new ones at a charge of about £25 000 a year; the construction and repair of dipping tanks, of which it has 295 for large stock and approaching 650 for small stock; the provision and upkeep of wattle plantations, the dipping of large stock, grants in aid of scholastic education, hospitals, lastly its own institutions for the teaching of trades and agriculture, and for the improvement of stock-breeding among the Natives and experimenting in and encouraging the cotton-growing industry. On these institutions, of which there are four – one industrial and three agricultural – it has spent some £96 595 to 20th June 1918, which includes purchase of farms, fencing, buildings, irrigation, stud stock and general maintenance. The present value of the stock is estimated at £7 500, including about 20 stallions of good breeding, which are distributed among Council districts during the season on free service to ratepayers.'

The Native Affairs Commission, in its first Annual Report (1921), refers to 'the undoubted success of the Transkeian system'.[19]

There seems to be very little room for doubt, then, that the district councils and the general councils proved remarkably successful so far as their powers and activities go up to the time of Union and beyond.

In 1911 the council system was extended to the districts of Libode, Ngqeleni and Port St. John's, collectively known as Western Pondoland. There were three district councils and a general council known as the Pondoland General Council, constituted on lines analogous to those of the Transkeian Territories General Council, the principal difference being that the members who in the Transkei were elected, were in Western Pondoland nominated by the chief. The Pondoland council system was therefore, as the Native Affairs Commission has pointed out,[20] a useful variant of the Transkeian system specially adapted to more tribal Africans. The activities of the Pondoland Council were on a more restricted scale than those of the Transkeian Territories General Council, with which it was subsequently amalgamated. Still, in the seven years 1911-18 it collected £70 110 and disbursed £70 026, of which £8 314 was devoted to scholastic education, £34 034 to agriculture and industries, and £21 777 to public works, and had also constructed 42 dipping-tanks for large and 80 for small stock.[21]

Some ten years after Union, African leaders began to express certain grievances about the council system. They especially resented the fact that the meeting of magistrates which regularly followed the General Council sessions unduly revised the budgetary and other proposals of the Council.[22] For a time this point was met by inviting a small deputation elected by the Council members to attend the annual magistrates' meeting. A further complaint was the filling of all the higher posts by whites. Both these complaints have been met, and more than met, by Dr. Verwoerd's Transkeian policy. Compared with the council system the new policy of Transkeian autonomy has meant a big move forward in true autonomy. But, of course, major change that it is, it has dealt only with local self-government and does not give the Transkeian Africans any real share in forming national as well as local policies. For what it is, however, it is good, and any impartial student of Transkeian affairs must admit that the council system was an excellent and educative preparation for it.

NOTES TO CHAPTER VII

1. Report, para. 121.
2. Memorandum dated 6th May, 1903.
3. Report, pp. 28-9.
4. Memorandum, dated 20th January 1896.
5. Cape Native Blue Book 1897, p. 23.
6. See article 'Native Councils as an aid to Administration' by Sir Godfrey Lagden in the compilation 'The S.A. Natives' (London, John Murray, 1905) p. 111.
7. Report, p. 29.
8. Report of the Department of Native Affairs, 1913-18, p. 21.
9. This and the following paragraphs from Report of Native Affairs Commission, 1921, p. 20.
10. Cape Native Blue Book 1896, pp. 93-4.
11. *Ibid.* p. 95.
12. Cape Native Blue Book 1897, p. 85.
13. Questions 16442-16449, Vol. II, pp. 1195-6.
14. Question 14500, Vol. II, pp. 1060-1.
15. See report published under Government Notice No. 420 of 17th July 1908.
16. A Scotsman.
17. The local term for the General Council.
18. Report of the Department of Native Affairs 1913-18, p. 20.
19. Report, p. 30.
20. Report, pp. 30-2.
21. Report of Native Affairs Commission 1921, p. 32.
22. See, e.g. D. D. T. Jabavu: 'The Black Problem', (Lovedale, Lovedale Press, 1921) p. 28.

CHAPTER VIII

Transvaal and Orange Free State Policies

The Voortrekkers who left Natal were ultimately successful in establishing two Republics – the Orange Free State which early exhibited the characteristics of a settled and stable state, and the South African Republic (Transvaal) which had a more chequered and tempestuous career. Of the policies of the Orange Free State towards the Africans within its borders there is little to be said. Up to 1868 the difficulties of the Orange Free State were bound up with frontiers and particularly with frontier wars with the Basotho. The British annexation of Lesotho ended this phase of Free State history, and three years later the British annexation of the diamond fields, however unjustified, relieved the Free State of yet another problem of government.

From 1871 up to the time of Union, the Orange Free State (from 1901 to 1910 the Orange River Colony) was responsible for only two tribal areas – Witzieshoek in the north-east and Thaba Nchu near the Lesotho border. Both of these were on the whole well governed and contented. The rest of the African population was scattered over hundreds of white farms as labourers, kept indeed in strict subordination but in general reasonably well treated.[1]

The Transvaal, on the other hand, was faced with a large African population and many important tribal areas. Its record was by no means as good as that of the Orange Free State. This is to be explained, first by the character of the Transvaal settlers, and second by the absence until 1877 of effective central government.

The Transvalers were the guardians of the last frontier. They were the frontiersmen *par excellence*, with both the merits and defects of frontiersmen in an exaggerated form. These were the men who would not submit to British rule in Natal, who left the Orange Free State when the British annexed it.

The Transvaal's independence was not recognised until 1852. Thereafter the country was for many years divided into quarrelsome little republics (e.g. Lydenburg, Zoutpansberg) and into parties, especially the parties headed respectively by Pretorius and Potgieter, the latter being the more intransigent. In the tenuous Archives of the Republic of Lydenburg at least one attempt can be traced to preserve African tribal rights,[2] but this and all other legislation in the early days of the northern Republics depended for its effectiveness on an almost non-existent police force and a very weak public service.

Farms were granted, often irrespective of tribal boundaries. An African might go to sleep in his tribal area and wake up a squatter on a white man's farm. These and other incidents provoked natural resentment among the tribes, and certainly in the early years of the South African Republic there was no possibility of its ruling large masses of tribal Africans. It was much if it could prevent them from attacking the white population and safeguard the territories of the State. Thus the question of the government of Africans presented itself mainly as an external one needing, unfortunately, military resources, and so the Department most appropriately placed to deal with the Africans was that of the Commandant-General.[3]

Occasionally settled policies were promulgated. For example, Law 9 of 1870 imposed a tax of 2/6d. per hut on Africans in service living on their masters' farms, 5/- per hut on Africans in service not living on their masters' farms, and 10/- per hut on other Africans.[4] Good or bad this policy was not carried out.[5] Ten years later a careful examination of revenue receipts showed that the Africans had during that period contributed little or nothing to the general revenue.[6]

Several laws endeavoured to limit and regulate the supply of African labour – precursors of the Plakkers Wet (Squatters Law) of the restored Republic.

No statutory recognition was given to tribal law. Legally Roman-Dutch law plus Statutes and Volksraad resolutions applied, but on vital matters such as marriage or inheritance these were grotesquely inapplicable.

Where the feeble resources of the State permitted, sporadic attempts were made to right injustices. In one or two instances the Government of the Republic bought farms for occupation by Africans,[7] but as the Republic would not recognise African ownership of land the ownership of these farms remained vested in the State.

With the election of the Rev. Thomas Francois Burgers as President of the Republic (1872) hopes might have been entertained of a more systematic policy. But, intelligent and patriotic as Burgers was, he had to rule a country so short of funds that the Postmaster-General had to take his salary in stamps and the Surveyor-General in land, and the neighbouring States had to finance the Transvaal mail contractor. An unsuccessful attack on Chief Sekukuni, chief of the Bapedi, lost Burgers his last chance of retaining office, and Shepstone's annexation of the Transvaal followed.

With Shepstone's coming and the first British rule of the Transvaal (1877-81) a more coherent policy as regards African affairs might have been expected, for Shepstone had the necessary experience and more funds than the Republic had ever possessed. But a devastating procrastination had set in. Shepstone had lost the initiative he had had in earlier days, and his son, Henrique, seems to have succumbed to the same disease. One of the first acts of the British administration was, however, to set up a special Department of Native Affairs – an entirely admirable departure and one to the credit of the new administration. It was retained after the retrocession.

It took Henrique Shepstone two and a half years to bring out a memorandum setting forth the general condition of tribal affairs in the Transvaal, based on information derived from the various Landdrosts as a result of a questionnaire sent out a few months earlier, the replies to which[8] are very interesting reading today.

We now come to the policies propounded – too late – by Henrique Shepstone. Before doing so, we must go back to recount the renewed war with Sekukuni. Sekukuni was indeed subdued but at a greater loss of life (on both sides) and of money than had been incurred in the Republic's war. British soldiers were shot down in large numbers by rifles which Sekukuni's subjects had bought at the Kimberley Diamond Fields, then under the administration of that very Owen Lanyon who succeeded Sir Theophilus Shepstone as Administrator of the Transvaal, and bought against the heated protests of the Republics and also of Natal.[9]

Henrique Shepstone in his policy memorandum deals with the question of tribal law. His remarks shed such light on the Shepstone policy generally that it is perhaps better to quote than to paraphrase them:

'The government of the Natives cannot be carried on under the common law of the country. They are not yet sufficiently advanced in civilization to understand or be ruled by it. It is essential that they should for some time to come be governed under and by their own laws and customs, and for this purpose it will be necessary to pass a law authorising such government, and that the Governor or Administrator should be appointed Supreme Chief with the power of appointing administrators of Native Law to govern the Natives in accordance with their laws and customs, subject to appeal to him as Supreme Chief. This was contemplated by Sir T. Shepstone as will be seen by a reference to the High Court Proclamation which withholds from that Court all jurisdiction in cases between Native and Native except such heinous offences as murder, etc., and proceeds to state that a proclamation will be issued regulating Native management.'

After a typically long delay an Ordinance was at last passed (No. 11 of 1881) on the 14th July 1881, four months after the Preliminaries of Peace had been signed and only three weeks before the autonomous Transvaal State came into being, creating the Administrator Supreme Chief and all the landdrosts administrators of Native Law; and recognising Native Law (uncodified) in all the courts of the Transvaal. On the 8th August the Triumvirate took over the government on behalf of the Transvaal State. This ordinance of the moribund 'Legislative Assembly of the Province of the Transvaal' was treated as having no valid force and effect. But many of its provisions were embodied in Law 4 of 1885 of the restored South African Republic.

It is interesting, as a further confirmation of what has been said in an earlier Chapter regarding Shepstone's antipathy to the Native High

Court to note that this ordinance of 1881 did not set up a Native High Court in the Transvaal but left a right of appeal to, and review by, the Executive Government – a provision confirmed by Law 4 of 1885 and remaining in force until withdrawn by Act 29 of 1907 of the Transvaal Colony, leaving the Supreme Court the only court of appeal.

A new hut tax ordinance imposing a tax at the rate of 10/- per annum was enacted in 1880. The Administrator of the Province expressed the view, in introducing the ordinance, that 'it would be the duty of the Government to institute measures to improve the condition (of the Natives) and bring them more closely under the humanizing influence of civilised law and customs. The promotion of education and the encouragement of useful and industrial pursuits will greatly tend to effect this object.'[10] Nothing was done in these directions before or after the retrocession; but a beginning was made successfully with the actual collection of the hut tax.

With regard to the location question there was an inexcusable delay in applying the provisions of Burgers' Law 3 of 1876. Towards the end of 1879 the urgency of the agrarian problem was pressed on the Administrator by the Secretary for Native Affairs, but to no purpose. Not a location had been properly surveyed and laid out when the war of independence began. The British Government accordingly considered it necessary to incorporate provisions in the Pretoria Convention of 1881 for the setting up of a permanent location commission. This location commission was to have two duties. The first was to demarcate locations. The second was to receive transfers of land bought privately by Africans in trust for such Africans. As has already been stated, the laws of the Republic did not permit ownership of land by an African in his own name. But in 1880 Henrique Shepstone introduced the system of permitting such transfers to the Secretary for Native Affairs in trust, thereby practically admitting such ownership while retaining, theoretically, the prohibition against it. The powers of the location commission in this connection passed, by Executive Council resolution of the 4th January 1886, to the Superintendent of Natives, and thence, under Crown Colony government, to the Commissioner for Native Affairs and in 1907 to the Minister for Native Affairs. Though in 1905 the case of *Tsewu* vs. *Registrar of Deeds* established the principle that an African could own his land directly (subject later to the provisions of the Natives' Land Act of 1913), the bulk of African-owned land other than Government locations in the Transvaal was, strictly speaking, owned by the Minister in trust.

The duties of the commission were clearly laid down in an address delivered by the Royal Commission in the presence of the Triumvirate at a great Pitso at Pretoria and printed for circulation among the landdrosts and communication by them to the tribesmen of their districts shortly after the retrocession:[11]

'Aan de Opperhoofden, Hoofden, en Inboorlingen van de Transvaal . . .

'Het zal U toegestaan zijn land te koopen of op de eene of andere wijze te verkrijgen, maar het transport zal in uwen naam geregistreerd worden op naam van drie heeren, die zullen uitmaken eene Inboorlingen-Locatie-Commissie. De Commissie zal inboorlingen-locaties uitmeten, welke de groote inboorlingen-stammen in vrede mogen bezetten. Bij het opmeten van zulke locaties zullen bestaande regten stipt gehandhaafd worden; en het Transvaalsche Gouvernement aan de eene en de inboorlingen-stammen aan de andere zijde zullen de alzoo bepaalde grenzen steeds moeten eerbiedigen. Op dezelfde wijze zullen de verschillende stammen elkanders locaties moeten eerbiedigen, en waar zulks niet gedaan is, zal de beledigde stam zijn klagte voor het Gouvernement van het land brengen.'

The commission as originally constituted, consisted of His Honour S. J. P. Kruger, Vice President of the Transvaal State (chairman), His Honour George Hudson, British Resident, and Mr. H. J. Schoeman, Native Commissioner[12] for Pretoria and Heidelberg. Its first meeting was held on the 9th May 1882. On the whole during its not very lengthy existence it proved a useful body, and many existing locations were delimited by it. But a number of tribes to whom land had been promised at one time or another never had their locations beaconed off.[13] No Transvaal government up to the time of Union, whether of Burgers, Shepstone, Kruger or Milner, ever honestly faced the African land question. Here the Transvaal failed badly. Under the provisions of General Hertzog's Native Trust and Land Act, 1936, considerable areas of land, however, were bought, but there was never enough.

The Pretoria Convention of 1881 had contained, among other vexatious provisions, an Article[14] retaining a right of veto for the Suzerain over legislation differentially affecting Africans. After prolonged efforts this, with most other restrictions on the sovereignty of the State, was removed by the London Convention of 1884. It is remarkable that legislation on African affairs lay dormant between the two conventions; and this is almost certainly to be explained by the desire of the Transvaal State not to give the British Government the opportunity of exercising a vexatious and disputed right. The restored South African Republic (1884) was, however, active from the very first in constructive legislation affecting Africans, and of such legislation the earliest and best example is Law 4 of 1885.

The primary object of this celebrated Law was to provide a more satisfactory administration of justice for the Africans while at the same time bringing them more under Government control as opposed to the unchecked rule of the chiefs. The preamble recognises that the time is not ripe for bringing the African population under the general laws of the Republic; and in accordance with this principle section 2 enacts that the laws, habits and customs hitherto observed among the Africans shall continue to remain in force in the Republic except in so far as they are inconsistent with the general principles of humanity recognised throughout the civilised world, while section 5 provides that all civil disputes between Africans shall be dealt with in accordance with 'Native Law' for the time being in force.

It must be added that from the beginning the Government took the view that *lobolo* formed a practice inconsistent with the general principles of civilisation, and the courts refused therefore to undertake *lobolo* cases – a practice confirmed by Law 3 of 1897. This was not only a display of ignorance of the real nature of *lobolo*, but also assisted to defeat one of the main ends of the legislation – the weaning of the Africans from the tribal courts to those of the Government. The non-recognition of *lobolo* for long remained a defect in the Transvaal system.

At the head of the whole system set up by Law 4 of 1885 stood the President, who was recognised Paramount Chief over all Africans in the Republic, exercising as such all powers and authorities customarily vested in a paramount chief by tribal law. He was authorised to depose chiefs for treasonable conduct, to remove them from the places in which they had resided, to place them under supervision, or in safe custody, and to replace them by suitable persons. These powers were to be exercised in conjunction with the Executive Council, but were not to be subject to revision in any court of the Republic (section 13). The President had the right to review any decisions of courts affecting Africans and might also fine a tribe (sections 7 and 10). These judicial powers of the Executive were withdrawn by Act 29 of 1907.

Below the President stood the Superintendent of Natives, the chief executive officer of the administration, who was also (section 4) the court of appeal from the decisions of inferior courts. This power also disappeared by virtue of Act 29 of 1907.

A special system of administration was provided for, embodying the germ of the principle that Africans must be dealt with only through specially qualified African affairs officers. Commissioners were appointed over Africans in districts where the Volksraad, owing to the density of the population, considered such a step necessary, the landdrost serving in other areas. Provision was also made for the appointment of sub-commissioners. The duties of these officers were redefined and the system brought into its later form by Ordinances 3 and 44 of 1902.

Chiefs 'appointed by the Government' were to exercise primary jurisdiction in civil cases, concurrently with the Government courts. No Chiefs were 'appointed' till long after Union, but, as a special proviso to Law 4 of 1885 continued the powers of existing chiefs pending appointment, the real objects of the Law were achieved in this connection.

Altogether then, the policy of the Republican government in this connection ran on improved and rational lines. Moreover it must be said that the actual carrying out of the policy was, on the whole, kindly and not unduly oppressive. A somewhat stringent pass law was however felt as a grievance by advanced Africans. Provision for their exemption was rightly made by an ordinance of 1902.

Where the policy of the South African Republic might really be open to question was on the economic side. Coupled with provisions against 'squatting' and 'kaffir farming'[15] ran the rule that Africans could not acquire land in their own name – a rule justifiable, surely, if at all, only if the location system had been fully worked out, which was not the case. Adequate land was never provided for the tribes and no effort was made to assist tribal agricultural development in tribal areas. At the same time, after the opening up of the Reef, the Superintendent of Natives officially exhorted Africans to go and work on the mines and so earn their hut tax money. That may have been a wise policy at the moment, but by diverting Africans unnaturally from agriculture to industry and closing doors of remunerative activity to the surplus 'poor white' agricultural population, it involved a heavy mortgaging of the future for the present. The Crown Colony government accelerated this unwholesome development and it has been one of the less satisfactory features of Transvaal policy generally.

No barriers were placed in the way of Africans who wished to exercise trades or carry on business among their own people.[16] Such barriers as existed were against Africans carrying on businesses for a white clientele.

Such was the state of affairs when the South African War of 1899-1902 broke out. That war, as is well known, resulted in the entire suppression of the Republic and its emergence as a Crown Colony under the rule of Lord Milner.

It is well known that the Milner policy was to procure an early federation of the South African States, while the Transvaal and Orange River Colony were still under Crown Colony government. It was his hope that some common 'Native policy' might be worked out by the various South African governments prior to that federation,[17] and in particular that the Transvaal, whose policy as we have seen, was of a somewhat mixed and inconsistent character, should receive some guidance from experts in the other colonies. Accordingly on the 29th September 1903 there met together at Cape Town one of the most brilliant gatherings of Native administrators ever brought together in South Africa. A defect of the commission – and a vital one – was the inadequate representation of the Afrikaans-speaking population, and of course at that date, no one thought that Africans should report on their own future. Sir Godfrey Lagden was chairman. The Cape Colony was represented by Col. (later Sir Walter) Stanford and Mr. F. R. Thompson; Natal by Mr. S. O. Samuelson, Under Secretary for Native Affairs, and the Hon. Marshall Campbell, M.L.C., the Orange River Colony by Captain Quayle Dickson and Mr. Johan Bestandig de la Harpe; the Transvaal by Messrs. J. C. Krogh and J. A. Hamilton; Rhodesia by Sir Thomas Scanlen; and Basutoland by Mr. H. C. (later Sir Herbert) Sloley. Mr. H. M. Taberer acted as secretary and Mr. G. A. Godley (subsequently Union Under-Secretary for Native Affairs) as chief clerk. After hearing a vast number of witnesses – some qualified and many otherwise – during the years 1903 and 1904, the commission produced its report bearing date the 30th January 1905.

As the report of this commission is referred to constantly in the succeeding chapters, it is unnecessary to do more at this stage than refer to some of its most salient points.

The three sections of the report which were of most importance to the Transvaal were those relating to land tenure, labour and representation.

The commission was not in favour of any compulsory introduction of individual tenure, but recommended the encouragement of any African movement in that direction on the general lines of the Glen Grey Act.[18]

With regard to the distribution of land between Europeans and Africans, the commission made a series of recommendations,[19] which formed the ground work and basis of the Natives Land Act of 1913. It recommended that the evil of unrestrained squatting should be checked and that Africans should not be permitted to live on farms, except as labourers, unless Government sanction had been given on proof that such residence was necessary and desirable. The commission proceeds to say (paras. 192 and 193):

'If this process [the purchase of land by Africans] goes on, while at the same time restrictions exclude Europeans from purchasing within Native areas, it is inevitable that at no very distant date the amount of land in Native occupation will be undesirably extended. Native wages and earnings are greater than they used to be, their wants are few, and their necessary expenses small. They will buy land at prices above its otherwise market value, as their habits and standard of living enable them to exist on land that it is impossible for Europeans to farm on a small scale. There will be many administrative and social difficulties created by the multiplication of a number of Native units scattered throughout a white population and owning the land equally with them. Such a situation cannot fail to accentuate feelings of race prejudice and animosity, with unhappy results. It will be far more difficult to preserve the absolutely necessary political and social distinctions if the growth of a mixed rural population of landowners is not discouraged.

'The Commission has arrived almost unanimously[20] at the conclusion that it is necessary to safeguard what is conceived to be the interests of the Europeans of this country, but that in doing so the door should not be entirely closed to deserving and progressive individuals among the Natives acquiring land, and has resolved as follows:

'That certain restrictions upon the purchase of land by Natives are necessary, and recommends:

'(1) That purchase by Natives should in future be limited to certain areas to be defined by legislative enactment.

'(2) That purchase of land which may lead to tribal, communal or collective possession or occupation by Natives, should not be permitted.'²¹

The Natives' Land Act was obviously a result of these recommendations. This, however, was a Union Act. As far as the Transvaal was concerned, the land recommendations of the commission produced no result; partly because the question was immediately overshadowed by the more spectacular Chinese labour and Responsible Government questions, partly doubtless because the new responsible ministry of the Transvaal wished to avoid for a time any legislation which might, by arousing the wrath of the ruling Liberal Party in Great Britain, bring into play the formal veto of the Crown.

On the subject of labour, the report of the commission is inadequate and disappointing. The members, from the pages of the report, would appear to have been unaware of the existence of a poor white problem and its economic bearing on the question of African labour. Further, there is a significant *petitio principii* on the subject of the proper sphere of African labour, the main recommendation of the report having regard chiefly to mining and large industrial concerns without the consideration of the question whether the employment of Africans in these spheres is really for their good or that of South Africa as a whole. It may indeed have been so, but the question was not really examined. We must, however, remember that tens of thousands of lives had just been lost in the Anglo-Boer War on questions largely concerned with mines, and naturally they loomed large in the public eye at the time.

The concrete recommendations of the commission with regard to labour are contained in paragraph 383 of the report (the sub-paragraphs have been numbered here for convenience of reference). It may be said that the only one which had any effect in the Transvaal was the fifth, but since Union the seventh recommendation has been partially met by Act 15 of 1911 (Native Labour Regulation Act) and the regulations thereunder, while the third found a place in the legislation relative to urban areas.

Paragraph 383 reads as follows:

'The following are the recommendations made with a view to stimulate industry among the Natives.

'(1) The checking of the practice of squatting by refusal to license all but necessary or desirable private locations, and the imposition of a tax on such locations as may be authorised, based on the number of able-bodied Natives domiciled thereon.

'(2) The imposition of a rent on Natives living on Crown Lands, as distinct from recognised reserves or locations, such rent to be based upon the value of such land and to be regularly and punctually collected.

'(3) The enforcement of laws against vagrancy in municipal areas and Native labour locations, whereby idle persons should be expelled.

'(4) The encouragement of a higher standard among Natives by support given to education with a view to increase their efficiency and wants.

'(5) The encouragement of industrial and manual training in schools.

'(6) The protection of the Native worker in his health, his comfort, his safety, and his interests, by provision for his accommodation and transport when travelling by rail or road to and from his work.

'(7) The enactment of regulations which will so far as possible secure that at the larger labour centres his food, his housing, his sanitation, and his medical treatment, should be satisfactory. In this respect the Commission recognises that very much has already been done at Cape Town, Kimberley, Johannesburg and other centres.

'(8) The abolition of all taxes or charges upon passes when travelling.'

The recommendations of the commission with reference to the franchise are striking. Briefly they involved the creation of an indeterminate number (one or more) of special African constituencies in each Colony, returning members to one or both Houses of Parliament. Africans were to be restrained from voting at the ordinary elections. The qualification of the African representatives (i.e. whether they should be Africans or Europeans) was left to be determined by each separate Colony.

This proposal was still-born. In the National Convention it failed to act as an eirenicon among warring parties, and the only recourse was to preserve the *status quo* (see sections 35 and 152, South Africa Act). Nothing is more convincing of the unrepresentative character of the 1903-5 Commission than this fact – that the representative National Convention only five years later failed to approve its most important political recommendation. In the Transvaal, under the terms of the Vereeniging Treaty, nothing could be done until the introduction of responsible government. It was understood that the authorities under the new regime would take action on the lines indicated. The first responsible ministry, however, was not enthusiastic for the commission's scheme, and it had hardly got into office before the closer union question absorbed all others.

It will thus be clear that the report of the 1903-5 Commission produced but few results in South African African policy. Why was this?

Really because – to go to the heart of things – it produced no true South African policy. It became very evident, as the commission deliberated in committee on the report, that the Natal delegates were unwilling to sacrifice the essentials of their system, which indeed received insufficient attention and respect from their colleagues. Time after time they were left in a minority of two in the voting. On many points their dissent is recorded in the body of the report.

This unfortunate fact left the Republics *vis-a-vis* the Cape with its policy of identity, expressed in the franchise. The contrast was too striking to make a compromise practicable. As we have seen, a paper compromise was arrived at, but it went too far in the direction of differentiation to satisfy public opinion in the Cape, and too far in the direction of identification to satisfy public opinion in the Transvaal.

It became clear at an early date that the Cape government did not propose to abolish its existing franchise scheme, nor to restrict the rights of Africans in respect of the purchase of land. What inducement was there for the Transvaal government, representing from 1907 mainly the older population smarting under the sense of injuries received and not ready to undertake experiments against traditional policy, to create a special African franchise, or participate in any of the other changes recommended by the commission? The Cape had not budged. Could the Transvaal be expected to move?

The commission, then, failed because it did not evolve a real, practicable South African policy. It failed also because it was not fully representative of South African public opinion, because it did not go to the heart of things from the economic side, because it ignored in its report the existence of a 'poor white' question and lastly because none of its members (from the Colonies which ultimately made up the Union, at any rate) had had practical experience of more than one system. Had a wide interchange of officers been undertaken in 1903, instead of the appointment of a commission, more good would have resulted than was actually the case.

It would be ungenerous to deny the real usefulness of the commission. Its evidence is of great interest (though marred by the admission of many incompetent and unqualified witnesses). The annexures to its report are of very much greater value than the report itself, and furnish the student with a mine of information. Yet the whole work of the Commission falls just short of greatness.

On the Transvaal it left no impression whatever – a crucial test, since it was the Transvaal only whose policy was plastic enough to be moulded. Up to the date of Union, Transvaal African policy remains a curious combination of the old ideas of the Republics, some valuable conceptions borrowed from Natal, but insufficiently worked out, and a little not very skilful tinkering with the problem by the Milner administration.

NOTE ON THE 'TRANSVAAL SLAVERY' QUESTION

Allegations were made in the early days of the Transvaal that slavery was practised on a large scale in that Republic. The best refutation of this charge is that the Shepstone regime of 1877 found no slave system to be destroyed and no slaves to free.

On the other hand there existed in the early days of the Republic an unpleasant form of veiled slavery – the 'apprenticeship' of African children, captured in warfare, sold to farmers or otherwise acquired. These children were almost invariably described as 'orphans', presumably as an excuse for their being taken over. They remained apprenticed for a period of years only, but very often stayed with their masters, having lost all touch with their tribes and having no home to go to. This nefarious system appears to have been prevalent mainly in the remote areas of the northern and eastern Transvaal, and I have not traced any reference to it even there after 1881. Of its existence on a considerable scale in the earlier years of the Republic, none can doubt who have studied Chapter IX and Appendixes II and III of Dr. J. A. I. Agar-Hamilton's 'Native Policy of the Voortrekkers' and the authorities quoted therein.

NOTES TO CHAPTER VIII

1 The invaluable research work of Dr. H. J. van Aswegen has made the author question whether he ought not to say more about the policy of the Orange Free State, but he has come back to the feeling that the policy of the Orange Free State in two small African areas has not had very noteworthy effects on South African policy as a whole.
2 Volksraadsbesluit No. 44 of 30th March 1860 (Archives D 4/2).
3 In whose files are to be found such papers as there are dealing with the 'Native Policy' of the Republic prior to 1877.
4 *Vide inter alia* Leyds: First Annexation of the Transvaal (London, Unwin, 1906) p. 136.
5 For its application in later years *vide* section 3, Law 24 of 1895, and Staatsprokureur's minutes 370/96 and 739/96 of 1896.
6 Speech of the Administrator (Sir Owen Lanyon) in opening the first Legislative Assembly of the 'Province of the Transvaal', 10th March 1880.
7 Memorandum of the Secretary for Native Affairs of the Province of the Transvaal dated 25th November 1879 (Transvaal Archives G 1200/1).
8 Preserved in the Archives G 1200/1.
9 See the authorities (mainly British) quoted in Leyds: First Annexation of the Transvaal (London, Unwin, 1906) pp. 158-9.

The following official minute was found by the writer in the Archives, dated Kimberley Diamond Fields, 4th August 1874 – two years after Sir Henry Barkly had deliberately refused to stop the gun trade. It had apparently been intercepted by the Republican Government.

'To the Chief Sekukune

'From the lieut-Governor of Griqualand West.

'The lieutenant-Governor avails himself of the return of Mamaree from the Diamond Fields to his own country and to his Chief Sekukune to write to the Chief and to send his greeting.

'Mamaree will be able to tell Sekukune how his people who came here to work have been treated, and he will, the Lieutenant-Governor feels assured, speak favourably on that subject and say that the people are well treated.

'The Lieutenant-Governor will, so far as he can, cause this good treatment to be continued towards all who come here to earn money and to work in the Mines.

'The Lieutenant-Governor will be glad to hear from Sekukune in return.'

In the Annexing Proclamation of 12th April 1877, Sir Theophilus Shepstone gives as one reason for the annexation: 'That the Secoecoene war ... has ... proved suddenly fatal to the resources and reputation of the Republic'. Shepstone is not to blame; he had always been against the sale of guns. But what of the Government which authorised the traffic in arms and then used its inevitable results as a pretext for annexation?
10 Administrator's Speech in opening the first Legislative Assembly of the Province of the Transvaal, 10th March 1880.
11 Undated but apparently printed towards the end of 1881. Archives T 1/125. The English translation reads as follows:

'To all Paramount Chiefs, Chiefs and Natives of the Transvaal.

'You will be permitted to buy land or acquire it in any manner, but the transfer will be registered on your behalf in the name of three gentlemen who will comprise a Native Location Commission. The Commission will delimit Native Locations which the great Native tribes will be able to occupy in peace. In the delimitation of these locations, existing rights will be strictly preserved; and the Transvaal Government on the one hand, and the Native tribes on the other, shall respect on all occasions the boundaries so determined. In the same way the various tribes shall respect each others' locations; and where this is not done, the injured tribe shall be able to lay its complaints before the Government of the country.'

12 The early existence of Native Commissionerships in anticipation of Law 4 of 1885 may be noticed.
13 Evidence of W. Wyndham, Secretary for Native Affairs, Transvaal Colony, before the S.A. Native Affairs Commission of 1903-5, questions 39, 245-49, 755 (Vol. II, pp. 427-8).
14 Article III.
15 Not more than five families were allowed to reside on any farm occupied by a European and not more than two on a farm not occupied by a European (Law of 1887, Staats-Prokureur's Interpretation of 1894).
16 See e.g. Staats-Prokureur's ruling 396/96, 'Geen bepaling in die Wet bekend is waardoor het verboden zou zijn van een Kaffer een Winkel-lisentie te geven in zijne Locatie. Te Pretoria worden dergelyke lisenties reeds verleend.'
    [*Translation:* We know of no provision in the law whereby it is forbidden for a Native to obtain a shop licence in his area. Such licences have already been issued in Pretoria.]
17 Report of S.A. Native Affairs Commission 1903-5, paragraph 2.
18 *Ibid.*, paras. 147 and 154-164.
19 *Ibid.*, paragraphs 181 and 184-197.
20 The dissentients were Colonel Stanford (Cape), Mr. Samuelson (Natal) and Mr. Marshall Campbell (Natal).
21 The commission further recommended (para. 197) that whatever principles governed the purchase of land should apply also to the leasing of land by Africans. The same three gentlemen dissented.

CHAPTER IX

African Customary Law

We leave now the task of tracing governmental policies towards the Africans within the different colonial or republican boundaries and pass to an analysis by subject-matter of South Africa as a whole

We begin with the study of what governments and even universities used to refer to as 'Native Law'. The term 'Native' has been so much bound up with colonialism that Africans resent it. Nor are they satisfied with the Zulu word 'Bantu' which the South African Government has used to replace it. 'African' can be misleading as it would cover areas with legal systems differing considerably from those prevailing in the Republic of South Africa. On the whole it has seemed, however, advisable to adopt the phrase 'African customary law' and to define it.

African customary law, as the term is used in this book, denotes the indigenous system of customary law existing among the various tribes within the Republic of South Africa. It must be carefully differentiated from laws affecting Africans, such as pass laws or laws relating to Christian marriage among them. The test is that African customary law, properly so termed, was in existence among them prior to any European influence or control.

African customary law is customary law, exactly like Roman-Dutch Law or English Common Law, and obviously it is unwritten. Can we distinguish it from mere custom? It is a profitless question, perhaps, for the frontier line between the two cannot be definitely ascertained and beaconed off; and we might very well adopt the usual and question-begging phrase 'Native law and custom'. But there is a danger, if we do this, of creating the false impression that African law is not law in the sense that the unwritten common law of any country is law. African law is every whit as valuable, as fixed, and as rational a system (so far as the law of persons is concerned) as Roman-Dutch Law. In primitive times – and that means less than a century ago, for our purposes – it was duly administered by courts of chiefs and counsellors, who possessed power to put their decisions into practice, all over South Africa. It exists *proprio vigore*: our legislation has not created but merely recognised it. Our courts ought, on all principles of sound jurisprudence, to have recognised it without recourse to authorising legislation. But alas! the hand of Bentham and Austin was heavy in all parts of the British Empire during that part of the nineteenth century in which the problem of the recognition of African customary law first presented itself for solution.

A more insular, a less philosophical and a less historical theory of law it would be impossible to produce.

If we do not draw a hard and fast line between African law and African custom, this must not be understood as impugning the validity and authority of the African legal systems. But many authorities have in the past satisfied themselves that such a distinction could be drawn, and, while the writer is not prepared to dogmatise on the subject, he personally would approve of such a differentiaton. In an African marriage, for example, all kinds of ceremonies were customarily observed. Certain visits were made between the kraals concerned. Certain dances and feasting took place. It was most unusual to omit any of these ceremonies, but had they been omitted there is no doubt that the chief would, in adjudicating upon succession, nevertheless hold such marriage valid, provided only that the *ukulobola* cattle had been passed. The *ukulobola* cattle affected status: the dances did not. In other words *ukulobola* was African law: the dances were merely African custom. Consciously or unconsciously this differentiation has been made by all the courts in South Africa which recognise African customary law at all.

But is it not misleading to speak of 'African customary law' as if there were only one system of law among the whole of the South African tribes? There are, it is true, many differences of detail from tribe to tribe, but the broad principles of law involved are the same. The various tribal systems are very much closer than the systems of common law of those countries which build on the Code of Justinian. They are different legal dialects of the same language. For instance, *ukulobola* among the Amagwamba often took the form of hoes manufactured from iron,[1] in Lesotho of cattle, sheep and goats together,[2] among the Amatonga of Portuguese money;[3] in times of scarcity of baskets of corn[4] and even stones as tokens.[5] But the institution of *ukulobola* itself and its effect on status and inheritance is exactly the same in every case.

Parts of African customary law are today not recognised by white courts anywhere in the Republic – on the ground that they are 'repugnant to the general principles of humanity obtaining throughout the civilised world'[6]. In other words the *jus naturale* prevails even over a definite existing system of jurisprudence. This is in accordance with the highest legal traditions. In these circumstances accusations of witchcraft, which formed a very large part of the litigation of a chief's court in primitive days, are not entertained even in those parts of the Republic where the recognition of African customary law is most complete. Similarly the compounding of murder or other criminal offences by a cattle fine has disappeared, though it is open to grave doubt whether European administrations were justified in regarding the compounding of theft by restitution and fine as being against the *jus naturale*. Our philosophic jurists, in whom we have been singularly rich for a small country, have rarely devoted their talent to African customary law hitherto, and therefore it is natural to discover errors which are juristically inexcusable.

Again parts of this customary law have not been recognised everywhere. *Lobolo* for instance is recognised in Natal and the Transkeian Territories, but was not, before Union, so recognised to any extent in the Cape Province proper, the Transvaal or the Orange Free State. Communal responsibility was recognised in Natal, the Transkeian Territories and the Transvaal, but not in the Orange Free State or the Cape. Hence it must be clear that absolute African customary law and African customary law as recognised by our Courts are two different things, and that the term 'Native law' has had different meaning in different Provinces and at different times. For this reason it is necessary to devote special consideration to the question of recognition of African customary law.

'Native Law does not deserve the very grave condemnation with which it is so universally visited by those who are wholly unacquainted with it or who only possess a very limited knowledge of it. It is a law suggested by circumstances, it is essentially just, and has been found effectual for the protection of individuals, and necessary for the good government of men living in a tribal condition . . . To those who are intimately acquainted with the Natives there is much indeed to admire both in them individually and in the laws which govern them. Many may think that, because they are barbarous and wholly uneducated in our sense of the word, any laws emanating from them must be worthless, but such is not the case.'[7]

The background of all African customary law is the tribal system. 'The individual is absorbed in the commonwealth, the man is lost in the citizen.'[8] The chief is the embodiment of the tribe, the head and centre of the whole fabric. The system is perfectly understood by the Africans, carrying with it mutual responsibility and suretyship and requiring implicit obedience to authority. It embodies an unbroken chain of responsibility – the responsibility of the headman for his people, of the head of a kraal or family for its members, and of every individual of a tribe to the chief.

'The followers of the chief, while in attendance upon him at his kraal are generally designated *amapakati*, understood by Europeans to mean counsellors . . . The chief generally occupies each day with his Amapakati, the topics of the times engage their attention – trials of criminal or civil cases occupy a portion of their time; these trials may correctly be said to be conducted in open court, for, as there are no professional lawyers, every Umpakati may freely enter into the case under investigation, and from the ridicule which would result from the interference of an Umpakati incompetent to argue in the case, it seldom happens that any display of incompetency occurs; thus the chief's residence may be appropriately termed the school where law is taught, and its rules transmitted from one generation to another.'[9]

African criminal law can hardly be said to have formed a distinct system from civil law. But all European administrations in South Africa have drawn the distinction and, even where recognising civil law, have virtually ignored the rules of African customary law regarding crime.

The punishments in such law were death and cattle fines. Imprisonment was unknown. Death was the penalty commonly inflicted for murder of a chief or parent or for desertion from the tribe, and of course for 'witchcraft'. The main crimes punishable by fine were murder, adultery, rape, arson, theft, maiming or injuring cattle, causing cattle to abort, false witness, speaking disrespectfully of authorities, and using love philtres. The last four were considered deserving of specially heavy fines. Murder, apart from incidents of warfare, was not common.

In many of these cases, particularly theft, the procedure was what we should call a civil, rather than a criminal one. The cattle, or the bulk of them, went to the injured individual, but in the case of murder all usually went to the chief.

Of all this mass of public or quasi-public law, all that remains recognised by European courts today is the status of chiefs, headmen, kraal heads, etc., and the doctrine of communal responsibility – illustrated in the so-called 'spoor law' – a law based on intimate knowledge of African judicial conceptions – which provides that if the 'spoor' of stolen cattle be traced to a certain kraal, and it proves impossible to detect the actual thieves, the whole kraal is responsible.

This chain of mutual responsibility is very fully and admirably worked out in the Natal Code of 1891.

The whole system is strikingly illustrative of Maine's and Vinogradoff's contention that status is the determining factor in all systems of archaic law.

Coming now to that part of African customary law – frequently termed African Civil Law – which has received more adequate recognition from the various governments of South Africa, we find ourselves in a region of intense interest to the legal investigator. 'The main elements of Native Law hinge on a few leading principles. The subjection of the female sex to the male and of children to their father or the head of their family – primogeniture among males as the general rule for succession, the incapacity, generally speaking, of women to own property, polygamy with its accompanying lines of demarcation according to "houses" in parts of the polygamist's property – adoption or guardianship or other conventional or hypothetical fatherhood.'[10]

It will be gathered that African customary law is in the main a law of persons. And as a law of persons it is admirably worked out with exquisite skill, comparing very favourably with early Roman or Germanic law. Its rules of intestate succession are such as to make professional exponents of Schependomsrecht and Aasdomsrecht grow pale. Parenthetically it may be pointed out that testate succession is unknown – a striking proof of Maine's contention that intestate succession was first in the history of legal development.[11] As regards relationship the African is still in the agnatic stage: a mother may, and frequently does, come under the guardianship of her own son. The most interesting features of the African law of persons to laymen are the institutions of polygamy and of *ukulobola* – the passing of cattle prior to marriage – and these it is proposed to deal with at length.

The law of property is much less worked out. Individual property in land is unknown in African customary law. All the land at the moment occupied by a tribe is held to vest in the chief, not in his personal capacity but (to import our ideas into an earlier system) in trust for the tribe. A chief could not, e.g. alienate tribal land with any binding effect except by a tribal act, involving full and public discussion with his *amapakati*. The tribe is the utmost entity normally conceived of by African customary law. A paramount chief had, in practice, no power to adjudicate between tribes as to the ownership of land. A quarrel between tribes would be analagous not to a lawsuit but to a war – a matter of 'international law' shall we say? The individual tribesman possessed nothing but the right to occupy at the chief's good pleasure.

The movable property of the Africans under tribal conditions consisted mostly of livestock. The only normal ways of acquiring this property, under such conditions, were by inheritance, gift or *ukulobola* payment. Sale was absolutely unknown and barter very uncommon.

Naturally, as the simplest and most rudimentary forms of contract were practically foreign to the African mind, there was no law of contract at all, except in so far as *ukulobola* can be regarded as a contract. This provides us with two interesting points of departure. The entire absence of a law of contract suggests to us that, as a legal system, African customary law is more archaic than the oldest extant Roman law; and a detailed study of it is therefore a matter of intense interest to the scientific investigator of jurisprudence. Secondly – to flog a dead horse – the absence of contract among a people like the Africans, possessing the rudiments of civilisation, a distinct and effective government and an admirable system of personal law is a very convincing disproof of the suggestion that government is based on contract and a clear indication that the State has evolved from the family, and is to be explained ultimately by sex, the divine sacrament of Society.

How far is African customary law really law? Today a slip-shod student might be tempted to anwer 'so far as recognised by the courts'. But this is to evade a very interesting legal question. African customary law is in full operation in districts where the European courts do not recognise it. Most African marriages in the Transvaal involve the passing of *lobolo* cattle, yet the institution of *ukulobola* was not recognised by the Transvaal courts before Union. If we adopt the sound and philosophic view of Savigny and deduce all law as springing from the *Volksgeist*, the spirit of the people, undoubtedly African customary law is worthy of the name. Perhaps the whole question may be met by applying to tribal law Lawrence's famous remark on international law:[12] 'The controversy . . . is a mere logomachy. If we hold that all laws are commands of superiors, international law is improperly so called. If we hold that whatever precepts regulate conduct are laws, international law is properly so called.' If we are to take sides, it is sufficient perhaps to say that one immeasurably greater and wiser than John Austin has told us 'Diuturni mores consensu retentium comprobati legem imitantur.'[13]

The value of the study of African customary law is thus twofold. It is of assistance to the student of comparative jurisprudence, and it is also a useful avenue by which to approach the problem of concrete policies affecting Africans in South Africa.

To the student of comparative jurisprudence it presents, to summarise what has already been said, an example of custom evolving into law, and of definite law based on custom. It provides him with a worked-out legal system more archaic than those which he is accustomed to study. From its elaborate rules regarding the status of individuals, he is able to reconstruct society as it existed centuries before the preparation of the Twelve Tables. The study of the problem of codification as applied by Europeans to African customary law[14] suggests many themes of value and utility as to the merits of written and unwritten law, and as to the principles which should guide the philosophic legislator who attempts to reduce a system of common law to writing. To the student who approaches jurisprudence and politics from the institutional side, African customary law presents an acid test which may be applied with advantage to many of the theories enunciated from comfortable study chairs by abstract speculators. The Hobbist theory of the origin of government, the Austinian theory of law, the Marxian doctrine that government is a nefarious institution to protect private property – all these disappear before the simple test of the African customary law. Aristotle is the only political theorist who emerges from the test absolutely unscathed!

It may be added that one vast field of legal science – the *Jus Naturale* – receives valuable illustration from the manner in which African customary law has been recognised in South Africa. Every legislative enactment recognising such law has been accompanied by the phrase 'so far as compatible with the general principles of humanity obtaining throughout the civilised world', or words to that effect. By examining those parts of primitive African law which have been rejected by our courts and our codifiers, we can get some indication – not much, perhaps, because our best legal theorists have not devoted their full attention to the subject – of modern views of the content of the *Jus Naturale*.

Speculations and enquiries such as these are of interest to jurists and political scientists the world over. But the study of African customary law is also of immense value to the South African, legally-minded or not, who is interested in the practical, concrete problems of African life. To arrive at the soul of the African people is, after all, our ultimate aim. Into that citadel there are many entrances, and the gateway of African customary law is as useful as any other.

In African customary law the institution of polygamy and the accompanying *ukulobola* contract are perhaps the two things most foreign to white legal conceptions.

'*Lobolo* and polygamy,' said Chief Teteluku in his evidence before the Natal Commission of 1881-2, 'are the two great questions which divide us from the white man.' As such they deserve our serious attention, and the more so as an examination of *lobolo* in particular illustrates very clearly the scientific nature of African customary law and the folly of interfering with it without adequate knowledge and due cause.

Whilst it requires no argument to demonstrate the advanced nature of a monogamic as compared with a polygamic system, yet it is as well to remind ourselves that for man to pass through the polygamic stage is natural if not inevitable. In a system which politically is patriarchal and legally agnatic, polygamy is in perfect keeping.

Polygamy is today on the decline among the Africans.[14] This is due partly to missionary influence and the example of Europeans, but probably even more to economic causes. Among the chief of these is the agricultural revolution which replaced the hoe by the plough. In the days of the hoe, agricultural labour was commonly performed by the women, consequently the more wives a man had the greater was his labour supply. Moreover, his implements cost him next to nothing and he was therefore in a position to meet the *lobolo* obligations which each succeeding marriage involved. Today – at least in all but the most backward parts of the Republic – the plough is commonly used. The man drives it himself: he needs less labour but more money, for ploughs are expensive. The result is a perceptible diminution of polygamy and an increased willingness to work – both desirable results. The introduction of the plough is one of the best services which Europeans have yet rendered to Africans in South Africa.

Yet though polygamy is waning and though the majority of Africans in the Republic are monogamists, polygamy still claims a sufficient proportion of the people to make its investigation not merely an academic matter. Its implications are far-reaching. It is one of the chief hindrances to Christian missionary enterprise – largely, be it said, owing to the methods of some Christian missions in the matter. That no convert should be allowed to marry additional wives after baptism is a rule to which no exception can be taken. But that a convert who is a polygamist should be required to put away all but one of his wives already married in good faith according to African customary law before baptism seems to many laymen, as it seemed to Bishop Colenso, as unjustifiably harsh as it has been manifestly impolitic. 'A Native has three to six wives; the missionary comes along and converts him, and he has now to be married to one of his wives according to Christian rites before he can become a member of the Church. Usually he chooses the youngest wife. In any case, whichever he marries, the remainder are put away or sent away: and if they have grown-up children they resent the stigma cast upon their mother, and there is trouble over the property, followed frequently by litigation, which often ruins the whole family.'[15] This is the case where a polygamist adopts Christianity. Too often he finds the sacrifice above his powers, and the mission knows him no more.

The general attitude of governments in South Africa has been to discourage polygamy by indirect means, while not directly interfering with it. There is, for example, the provision in the Transkeian marriage regulations of 1879 that the first marriage – but no other while the first wife survived – might be registered at the magistrate's office, in which case that marriage was accorded a slightly different legal status, divorce, e.g. being governed by Colonial and not by African customary law. This device has proved a hopeless failure, only an infinitesimal proportion of Africans registering – apparently among other things because the inducement was insufficient.

A much more drastic step was suggested by the Native Laws and Customs Commission of 1883, which recommended that after a fixed date, not less than five years after the promulgation of any regulations issued in consequence of the commission's report, recognition should be accorded to the first marriage only, and that after that date any *ikazi (lobolo)* or other claim relating to any wife other than the first should not be entertained by the courts.[16] The old fault is again apparent in this enactment – utilising the machinery of courts and codes to change social institutions, which in point of fact will not change. The recommendation was, however, not carried into effect.

It had been anticipated in Natal by the majority report of the 1881-2 commission.[17] Dean Green in his minority report[18] offers a not uninteresting suggestion, viz.: that 'the law should require the insertion of a clause in every title deed where land is transferred to a polygamist setting forth that he may by testament bequeath such land as he will, but that if he die intestate the law shall treat him as a monogamist.'

In 1903 the National Council of Basutoland decided that the eldest son of the *first* wife is the general heir of a chief or commoner alike.[19] (It is perhaps needless to say that the eldest son of the great wife usually succeeds among African tribes. The great wife, whose *lobolo* is paid by the tribe, is usually married late in life, sometimes being the twentieth, thirtieth or even fortieth wife. Hence the prevalence of minorities and regencies in African polity.)

It was hoped that this step would discourage polygamy. It was adopted by the Africans themselves, after being duly explained to their principal men in Council, but undoubtedly such a step by such a method would be the furthest one could go generally at present.

The 1903-5 Commission summed up the position as follows[20]: 'The Commission is satisfied that considerable disadvantages in their advance towards Christianity result to the Natives from Polygamy which, however, is an old-standing and prevalent social institution amongst these people. The Commission does not regard it as among those customs which have to be put down with a strong hand, but looks forward to its gradual extinction by such means as greater spread of Christianity and of civilisation, by the labour of women being more than it is supplanted by that of men, and by the ordinary law being voluntarily adopted; and owing to the absence of any great surplus of women in the African population without which general polygamy is impossible for any length of time.'

We now come to the question of *lobolo* – What is this institution?

'*Ukulobola* (*ikazi, bohadi*) may be taken to be a contract between the father and the intending husband of his daughter, by which the father promises his consent to the marriage of his daughter, and to protect her, in case of necessity, either during or after such marriage, and by which in return he obtains from the husband valuable consideration, partly for such consent, and partly as a guarantee by the husband of his good conduct towards his daughter as wife. Such a contract does not imply the compulsory marriage of the woman. The "ikazi" may, upon every principle of sound law, be recoverable under such a contract.'[21]

'It is not a contract of purchase and sale. The terms "buying and selling" are scarcely fair terms to apply in describing the transactions referred to. The property given in the case of marriage amongst these people forms a provision for the widow and family in case of the husband's death which arrangement is held sacred and universally respected by all Fingos and Caffres. Now in this view of the case there is much to be considered, and by hastily and harshly breaking it up, quite as much evil as good may be effected.'[22]

The more or less official definition cited above has not found universal acceptance of recent years. Some students of social anthropology have preferred to consider *lobolo* as *compensation* to the bride's social group rather than to her parents. This explanation may possibly have been the origin of the present *lobolo* custom, but the fact that the cattle are invariably handed over to the bride's male guardian and never, e.g. to the chief, prevents us from accepting it as an adequate explanation of the state of affairs today.

More fruitful is the conception of *lobolo* as the purchase not of the woman, nor yet of the *manus* over her, but of her childbearing powers, a conception which explains much that would otherwise be obscure in the detailed working out of the custom.[23] Some authorities consider that the *bogadi* of the Basotho is to be explained differently from the *lobolo* of the Zulus, the former being correctly characterised as compensation to the father, the latter as purchase of the woman's child-bearing powers. If this is correct, it would to some extent, though not wholly, explain the difference in the attitude of the French missionaries in Lesotho from that of all the reputable Natal authorities.

Personally the writer feels that this differentiation goes too far. He would claim that *lobolo* (*ikazi, bogadi*) has everywhere a two-fold character, viz. (1) compensation to the father, perhaps developed from a more primitive compensation to the tribe or sib; (2) purchase of the woman's child-bearing powers. In some parts the first, in others the second, of these factors is stressed, but both are present everywhere to a greater or lesser extent.

What is at any rate absolutely clear is that *lobolo* (*ikazi, bogadi*) is not a purchase of the woman in the sense in which that term would be used by the average European.

As clear indications that *lobolo* is not a contract of purchase and sale, we may notice the following points as forming part of the substantive customary law on the subject among every tribe in South Africa, exceptions thereto being distinctly felt as breaches of tribal morality. (i) The woman does not become her husband's slave. (ii) He may not kill, injure or maltreat her. (iii) If she leaves him, owing to his misconduct, he does not have a claim against the parents for the *lobolo* cattle, thus losing bride and cattle together. (iv) He may not sell her to another man.

These points are well brought out in a memorandum prepared in 1880 by Mr. T. Shepstone, Junr., C.M.G., which reads as follows:[24]

'Regarding the suggestion "to do away with woman-selling legislation" I consider that it is a misapprenhension to say that the selling of women among the Natives either exists or has been legislated for in Natal. It is true that on the occasion of a marriage some consideration more or less valuable – such as cattle where cattle are to be had – passes from the man's family to that of the woman; but this is not a sale of the woman; the husband cannot sell her or in any way dispose of her to another; she does not become his chattel in any sense of the word, nor he her owner in the sense of owning property, and the consideration given to her father at her marriage becomes practically a security for her proper treatment, and a provision for her support should her marriage become dissolved on account of ill treatment; because in that event, the girl returns to her father's family and the consideration is not returned to the husband or his family.

'No doubt it is desirable that feelings of a higher order should answer the purpose accomplished by this material guarantee, but such a result can be effected only after the lapse of time has brought about a great advance in the social conditions of the Natives.

'*Ukulobola* is the Native[25] word exclusively used to describe the handing over of the consideration; and is different from, and does not carry the same meaning as the word "tenga" which is used as exclusively to indicate sale or barter.'

To the view thus presented, objections will doubtless be raised by missionaries, some of whom have apparently ineradicable prepossessions against *lobolo*, and by others. Take for example the written evidence of the Revs. R. M. Dyke, L. Mabille and H. Marzolff of Basutoland before the 1903-5 Commission:[26]

'A cattle marriage is a genuine sale . . . Women are transferable as well as heritable . . . Some cases have occurred in which one man has sold his wife to another; and we know of one case in which a man was unable to pay a fine and the Paramount Chief directed that his wife should be sold to pay the balance, which was done.' Or this of Peter Mti, an African of East London:[27]

' "Lobola" is in vogue even among school Natives. "Lobola" is a good custom in itself, but it is liable to great abuses. Originally it was intended to be a sort of settlement on the wife which was paid over to her father or lawful guardian in trust for herself or her children. But the way in which it is now manipulated by Natives in British Kaffraria leads the most conservative among Natives to remark that "lobola" has degenerated into a matter of purchase and sale . . . It is often the case in this district for a Native to sell his daughter to this man this year and to the next man next year. These matters have come under my personal observation, and I wish to emphasise them.'

This view is supported by a good deal of evidence. Even as far back as the Natal 1881-2 Commission, Dean Green in his minority report was constrained to write:[28]

'Few things were more sad, in hearing natives' evidence before the Commission than to observe the barefacedness, so to speak, with which they referred to their daughters and sisters as being means of their procuring wealth through the *lobola* on their marriage.' In urban areas in particular this conception of *lobola* is being increasingly adopted, particularly on the Witwatersrand, and a case was brought to the writer's notice where a man '*lobola*'d' a woman for a new pair of trousers! This debased conception of *ukulobola* is certainly increasing in urban areas, partly because money there counts so much more than cattle and it is doubtful whether it should be recognised there.

Is there any way of reconciling these views? . . . *lobolo* as a contract of great value in a primitive society: *lobolo* as a matter of sordid purchase and sale of women . . . *lobolo* as an innocent and even laudable practice: *lobolo* as contrary to the *Jus Naturale*.

It is suggested that the reconciliation is this: in African customary law proper the transaction was never one of purchase and sale; but European influence has tended to suggest this view to Africans of recent years, partly by the errors of the Codes and partly by the influence of the ideas of European commerce.

Mr. A. F. Fynn, resident magistrate of Pietermaritzburg, one of the finest authorities on early tribal custom of his day, gave evidence before the 1852-3 commission as under:[29]

'The bride is not designated as a wife until she has borne a child or has a house under charge, until which she is called *Umlobokazi*, implying that the cattle given for her have not as yet been delivered to her parents.

'In the evidence which I now give before the Commission I wish to be understood as showing those Kafir customs as they prevailed prior to Europeans coming among them; if cases ever occurred in the tribes of a stipulated amount of cattle being given by a bridegroom for his bride, it was not a common occurrence. The general mode is that on the ceremony being concluded, the male friends of the bride make their demand for cattle, but not for any particular number; the bridegroom having previously arranged as to the number he will give on that occasion, presents them with apologies for the smallness of the number, or as the case may be, and is desired to come on some future occasion. The number of cattle given depends more on the wealth of the bridegroom than on any other circumstance.

'Trade, as implying buying and selling, is understood by Kafirs under the term "tenga", which originally meant "exchange". This word is applicable to every description of trading, but the word was never used among themselves in connection with marriages. Such an application of the word would be ridiculed by all who heard it.

'I admit that it is now sometimes used by the Natives who have been in the service of Europeans, and I am bound to conclude that this introduction of the word has been forced upon such Natives by those Europeans who have arrived at the conclusion that women were bought for a stipulated price, and suppose the word "tenga" an appropriate one.'

Practically every authority on *lobolo*, great or small, whether for or against *lobolo* today is agreed that in primitive African customary law the *lobolo* contract was as above described – a contract not involving purchase or sale. The change obviously must have taken place under European influence, and that influence must have been partly, as suggested by Mr. Fynn, personal. It is impossible to acquit some missionaries of grave error in this matter. They seem to have made up their minds to condemn *lobolo* anyhow. Notice the way in which Messrs. Dykes, Mabille and Marzolff put the change among the Basotho similar to that above described by Mr. Fynn among the Natal Africans.

'A cattle marriage is a genuine sale. This is a position which was indignantly denied by the old Basutos. White men, they said, knew nothing about it. "The girl was not sold," they said, "she did not cease to be her father's child, and the money or cattle was given as a thank-offering and a compensation to her parents for the trouble and expense of bringing her up, and for the loss of her services." The fact was, they were shocked to hear a spade called a spade. That position was untenable, and the more candid heathen will now admit (especially among themselves) that the transaction is a sale.'[30]

The history of the influence of codification upon *lobolo* is a series of lessons how not to codify. Instead of reproducing the existing law, the Codes put down what the estimable gentlemen responsible for them considered the law ought to have been. The Natal Code of 1878, for instance, withdrew from the husband the right to recover the *lobolo* cattle in case of the wife's misconduct. 'The Natal Code in this way created, according to the report of the Natal Commission of 1887, an evil which the Native law avoided and this shows that their customs are all parts of a well-considered system.'[31] This error has since been rectified. Not so the error of stipulating maximum amounts of cattle and insisting on the payment in full of *lobolo* prior to marriage. This is an exceedingly serious departure from Native Law, perpetuated in the Code in 1891. The only reason for it was the desire to save the (European) courts the trouble of *lobolo* litigation. Comment on that is needless.

Mr C A Wheelwright, one of the best authorities on later African administration in Natal, said in his evidence before the 1903-5 Commission:[32]

'The system worked admirably until it became codified and a limit was placed on the amount of the *lobolo*.

'*The idea of barter is to be traced to this period, as it did not exist before.* Unscrupulous natives at once made use of our law courts to claim the highest rates authorised by the Code and the whole principle of lobola lost its virtue.'

The draft 'Bill to amend the Code of Native Law, and to extend the same to the Province of Zululand', contained a very questionable proviso[33] that *lobolo* must be paid in cattle unless it is not practicable to procure cattle for such a purpose. But very fortunately this last error never became law.

An attempt has now been made to demonstrate the true principles of *lobolo* in African customary law, and the reasons for any changes that may have occurred in African feeling regarding the institution. But it is advisable, before proceeding to examine the attitude of the various South African administrations towards *lobolo*, to point out what to sociologists would be a platitude – that *lobolo* is not a mere local idiosyncrasy of the Africans, but as widely spread as polygamy itself, and discoverable in the course of natural evolution among nearly all peoples whose laws and policy were similar to the natural laws and policy of the Africans.

An able paper on this aspect of the subject was prepared by the Reverend A. Kropf of the Dohne Mission Station, Cape Colony, and published in the 'Kaffir Express' of August 4th, 1873. Thence it was taken over by the Native Laws and Customs Commission of 1883 and printed among the Appendices to its report.[34]

It has profoundly influenced African administrators since that date; and bearing this in mind it has been thought advisable in view of the historical importance of the document to quote extracts from the original report, in spite of its occasional stressing of the obvious.

'From the earliest age of history "*ukulobola*" was practised among all oriental nations, and in their migrations towards the west they brought it even to Europe, where it died away after the new wine of the Spirit of God had thoroughly fermented in the disciples of Christ.

'Those that contend that *ukulobola* is a mere buying and selling, I wish to refer to the Bible, where the Hebrew verb *Mohar* never means buying or selling in the ordinary sense now commonly accepted among us. Its primary sense is that sense of exchanging which also proved [sic] by the softened form *Mar* and the hardened *Makur*. The nearest signification of this word is given by Gesenius: *uxorem pretio parentibus soluto. It is the equivalent which the bridegroom gives to the bride's father for the services which she can no more render to him, but must render to her husband.*

'That *ukulobola* is not buying and selling can also be proved by the husband having no liberty to sell his wife again, which he can do with bought chattels.

'The use of this word in the Old Testament is restricted to this transaction only, and cannot be used in any other connection, just as it is in Kaffir, when it is alone used for marriageable women.

'We find the word for the first time in Genesis XXXIV, 12, where the English Bible reads: 'Ask me never so much *dowry* and gift.' It is here connected with the word *Mathan*. The first, *Mohar*, is given to the father and the second, *Mathan*, to the bride. Also Genesis XXIV, 53, where the servant of Abraham gives to Rebecca jewels of silver and jewels of gold and raiment; but to the brother (mark the brother stands first) and the mother precious things.

'That the custom of *Ukulobola* became at that time consolidated, we infer also from Genesis XXIV, 27.

'The daughter was of valuable service to the father in the house or in the field by minding sheep, etc. *By giving her to be married he lost those services and therefore a part of his property or wealth*, which had to be redeemed by the bridegroom, either by money, precious things or cattle, or by serving the father-in-law in the fields like Jacob, or as a warrior like David, I Samuel XVIII, 25. In this sense the customs prevail to this day among the Arabs, the Mohammedans in India, the Kurds, Turkomans, Circassians and Kabyls, the latter giving eight pots of fat and thirty hamels for a girl. The Wiguls in the district of Perm in the Ural Mountains gave five roubles for a lean, and to twenty-five for a fat, girl. The Tahiers in Western Africa ask *Ukulobola*, but the parents often refuse it for the purpose of claiming the children But if the girl has the courage to ask for and to accept the *ukulobola*, then the issue does not belong to the parents.

'If any doubt should still exist about the meaning of the word *Mohar*, this doubt will be removed by a careful study of Exodus XXII, 16 and 17. The whole paragraph from XXI, 18 to XXII, 17 speaks of the indemnification to be given for the loss, damage or violation committed to any one's property, and, most remarkably, the last subject coming under this head is the daughter, whose violation is to be redeemed according to the signification of *ukulobola*, which we have given above. In this passage occurred both the noun and the verb. The violator had to pay the *ukulobola* even if the father refused to give the daughter to him Here we see that the *ukulobola* was already fixed, and Deuteronomy XXII, 29 mentions only the highest *ukulobola* in such a case, when this human property had been injured

'From the foregoing we infer:

'1. That in ancient times the brother, just as it is among the Kaffirs, had a nearer right of control and protection over his sister than the father. Genesis XXIV, 53 and XXXIV, 15.

'2. The *Mohar* or *ukulobola* is never mentioned as given to the bride, which the English word "dowry" will infer, but to the father. In Deuteronomy it is said: "He shall give to the damsel's *father* fifty shekels of silver."

'For our purpose it shall be of minor importance to mention that Homer in his Iliad, Hymn XI, 241, says of Iphiclamus: "The unfortunate, far away from his wife, never having enjoyed her charms, for whom he had given first a hundred bullocks, and further promised for her a thousand goats and the same number of sheep." Or in the Odyssey where Hephaistos says: "Till the *father* shall give me back all the presents which I have given *him* for the girl, the dog-eyed." '

'Though the German woman, as Tacitus says, was held in the highest respect by the man, she was nevertheless not independent, like him who, weapons in hand, fought for his right and liberty. The unmarried women were in the power of their male relatives, called *Schwertenagen*, who had to defend them, and who enjoyed and received as an equivalent for their defence and protection the indemnification which those had to pay who offended the woman. This right, analagous to the Roman *Manus*, was exercised by the father or brother as guardian, and was called *Mandwald*, i.e. advocation, attorney or guardianship. As the girl, by being married, was transferred from the guardianship of the father, brother or other male relative to the guardianship of the husband, the marriage could only be concluded by the formal public transfer of the bride from her guardian to her future husband: and as at the same time the guardianship was looked upon as a complex of property rights on account of those moneys that fell to the guardian for defending and protecting the woman, the transfer therefore was done as a purchase – mark, not of the woman but of the *guardianship* which was considered to be a property right. This transfer of the wife to the future husband was executed in the open market-place, and marriage was legalised by paying down a fixed sum.

'The *ukulobola* obtained also among the Pruczi and the Slavonians who inhabited the eastern parts of Europe.'

To these erudite instances may perhaps be added the better known one of the old method of marriage by *coemptio* in Roman law. 'Coemptione vero in manum convenient per mancipationem, id est per quandam imaginariam venditionem; nam adhibitis non minus quam euinque testibus civibus Romanis puberibus, item libripende, emittis mulierem cuius in manum convenit.[35]

What has been the attitude of our lawmakers and administrators relative to *lobolo*? We have already discussed what the attitude of the Church ought to be. What, we ask now, should be the attitude of the state?

Lobolo is not illegal, in the sense of being punishable by law anywhere in the Republic.

Lobolo is not essential to the validity of a marriage under recognised African customary law anywhere in the Republic. The Natal Code treats it as usual, not indispensable.

Lobolo is fully recognised (i.e. cognisable) in the specifically 'Native' courts set up throughout the Republic.

The two defects – one rectified and one continuing – of the Natal Code regarding *lobolo* have already been adverted to. Otherwise the Code reproduces the genuine African customary law fairly well. In the Transkei, where magistrates are expected to work on the actual tribal custom, obviously *lobolo* is closer to primitive African customary law, though even the Transkeian practice is not unexceptionable.

Even in the two areas where *lobolo* is recognised, suggestions have been made that that recognition should be withdrawn – in the case of Natal by the Commission of 1881-2. 'We do propose,' say the Natal Commissioners,[36] 'that, after a certain time, our courts shall take no cognisance of suits originating directly or indirectly in a claim for *lobolo*, either as a cause of action or as a ground for execution in carrying out a chief's judgment in a matter connected with *lobolo*, *nor should the chief have any coercive jurisdiction*. We propose that a law or rule to the above effect be promulgated . . . It would have to be fully explained to the people that the only alteration made, was that they must settle *lobolo* claims among themselves, and it should also be made known that any breach of the peace resulting from their being so left to settle the matter among themselves would be liable to severe punishment.'

This is a most fatuous proposal when one realises that on the same page of the report the commissioners say: 'It is generally admitted that almost all litigation among Natives is connected directly or indirectly with *lobolo*'!

The chief arguments for the recognition of *lobolo* by our courts are four in number.

In the first place, it enhances the value of a woman, both to her father and to her husband, and thus protects her against ill-usage. This argument holds good in the overwhelming majority of cases, even where there is a tendency on the part of the Africans concerned to regard *lobolo* as a commercial transaction, for there is probably not one case in ten thousand where the woman is transferred by her husband to another man.

One aspect of this protection is well put forward by Mr. H. C. Campbell, magistrate, Inanda, and later Judge of the Native High Court:[37]

'It may startle many to be told that this custom of *ukulobola* is practically the only power which operates as a restraint upon the Native woman. Whether married or single, she is the representative of a certain value, and because of having a value easy of depreciation, she is carefully and jealously guarded. Objectionable as is the practice of giving woman a legal value in many of its phases, it cannot be denied that without the compensating checks of religion and education, difficult to be applied, implanted and retained, its abolition would be productive of wide-spread disorder.'

In the second place *lobolo* is a valuable safeguard to the woman's self-respect. She feels that her husband has had to work and give valuable recompense for her. It is a remarkable and very well-known fact that the African women are, if possible, even more attached to the *lobolo* custom than the men. 'A respectable Caffre or Fingo woman considers herself, and is considered, as forming an improper connection if married without the giving of cattle by the husband, as much as a respectable white woman would do to live with a man to whom she is not married. Such matters require to be carefully dealt with.'[38]

This leads one to the third argument for the recognition of *lobolo*, which is perhaps itself sufficient to prove the point – the strong support accorded to it by African public opinion. It is estimated that even in the Transkeian Territories and even among Christians, ninety-five per cent of the marriages that take place are accompanied by a *lobolo* contract.[39]

Lastly, the *lobolo* cattle supply the wherewithal to provide for a woman who has left her husband owing to ill-usage – a very important practical point.

Against *lobolo* it has been argued not merely that it involves a species of slavery, but also – and this is a very important argument – that it has the economic effect of concentrating the productive energy of Africans on cattle, instead of agricultural pursuits proper. In turn, this necessitates more land than a real agricultural community would need, and the land problem is a source of grave disquiet and unrest.

In reply to this really serious objection it may perhaps be argued that 'man does not live by bread alone', and that a custom of social and ethical value must not be discarded on mere economic grounds. It could be further argued that the actual form the *lobolo* must take is not material.

The conclusion of the 1903-5 Commission on the subject of *lobolo* is as follows:[40]

'The Commission is of opinion that the Native system of passing cattle, known variously as *lobolo*, *ikazi* and *bohadi*, in connection with marriage by Native custom and usage, should not be interfered with by prohibitory legislation, but be left to die out gradually as the outcome of an advance in civilisation. Evidence taken points to a tendency in that direction.

'That provision be made for the hearing and determining of claims arising under Native custom for restitution of *lobolo* or such portion thereof as may be deemed equitable where a husband is deserted, without sufficient cause, by his wife.'

As far as the Government is officially concerned, the above recommendation may appear to meet the case. The general recognition of *lobolo* in all courts administering African civil law throughout the Republic is right. It must be said, however, that what our courts should administer is the existing customary law *so far as not contrary to the Jus Naturale*, which, as we know, forbids slavery,[41] or any similar transference of persons. The application of this principle would come to the same thing as recognising the primitive customary law of *lobolo*, as uninfluenced by European misconceptions. The recognition thus accorded should probably apply even in the case of Christian marriages and of all marriages of exempted Africans where there is definite evidence of the contract having been entered into.

NOTES TO CHAPTER IX

1. Evidence of Sir T. Shepstone before the Cape Native Laws and Customs Commission 1883, questions 596 and 597.
2. Evidence of L. Barnett, Assistant Commissioner, Quthing, Lesotho, before S.A. Native Laws and Customs Commission 1903-5, Vol. V, p. 379.
3. Special report of C. C. Foxon, British Resident, Maputaland, 31st August 1896.
4. Evidence of Sir T. Shepstone before Cape Native Laws and Customs Commission 1883, question 469.
5. Evidence of E. Blyth, Asst. Commissioner, Berea, Lesotho, before S.A. Native Laws and Customs Commission 1903-5, Vol. V, p. 380.
6. S.A. Native Affairs Commission 1903-5, Vol. V, p. 380, and see Law 4 of 1885 (S.A. Republic).
7. Memorandum dated 1880 by T. Shepstone, Jnr., c.m.g., published in 'Papers relating to Native Custom in Natal, 1881', p. 5.
8. Draft report by S. O. Samuelson, Under Secretary for Native Affairs, Natal, dated 21st December 1904.
9. Memorandum of A. F. Fynn, a.r.m., Pietermaritzburg, published in Supplement to Natal Government Gazette, 1st March 1853.
10. 'Code of Native Law as at present administered', Pietermaritzburg 1878, Preface, p. 6.
11. Maine, H. S. 'Ancient Law', (10th Edition), London, John Murray, 1906, p. 207.
12. Laurence, T. E. 'Principles of International Law', (6th Ed.), London, MacMillan, 1898, p. 15.
13. Institutes, Lib. I, Tit. ii.
14. See Report of S.A. Native Affairs Commission 1903-5, para. 297 (i), 'Polygamy generally is on the decrease throughout South Africa; this is due amongst other things to the increased cost of living, the loss of cattle and the consequent increase in obtaining lobolo consideration, and the increase in the proportion of men marrying.
15. Report of Power Leary, r. m. Mount Frere, in Cape Native Blue Book 1899, p. 55.
16. Report, para. 90.
17. Pp. 12-13.
18. P. 23.
19. S.A. Native Affairs Commission 1903-5, questions 29416-29442, 39449-39500.
20. Report, para. 297 (2).
21. Native Laws and Customs Commission (Cape) 1883, Report Vol. I, p. 30, a definition taken over *verbatim* by the S.A. Native Affairs Commission 1903-5, Vol. I, pp. 59-60.
22. Report of Rev. H. Calderwood, Special Commissioner, to report on Fingo Locations, dated Alice, 22nd January 1855.
23. This is probably the explanation most acceptable to social anthropologists today.
24. Papers relative to Native Custom in Natal, 1881, pp. 5-6.
25. Zulu.
26. Vol. V, p. 388.
27. Vol. V, pp. 63-4.
28. Report, p. 23.
29. Published in Supplement to the Natal Gazettes of 22nd February and 1st March 1853.
30. S.A. Native Affairs Commission 1903-5, Vol. V, p. 388.
31. Cape Native Laws and Customs Commission 1910, Report, para. 69.
32. Vol. V, p. 296. The italics are mine.
33. Section 35.
34. Appendix C, p. 259.
35. Gaius: Inst. I, 113.
36. Natal Native Commission 1881-2, Report, p. 18.
37. Natal Native Blue Book 1879, p. 19.
38. Report of Rev. H. Calderwood, Special Commissioner on Fingo Locations.
39. Cape Native Affairs Commission 1910, p. 41.
40. Report, para. 308.
41. Tryphoninius D 126 De Condict. Indeb. 64.

CHAPTER X

The Recognition and Codification of African Customary Law

After Union, it became the practice that cases arising out of African customary law could be taken in every part of the country to such special tribunals (Bantu Affairs Commissioners' Courts, Native Appeal Courts) as were available. There thus came to be complete recognition of African customary law in the type of case to which it could apply. But this had not always been the case in the period covered by this book (1830-1910) and it will be a necessary and useful task to make an historical analysis of the policies of the various South African governments in this matter.

Beginning with the Cape Province proper, we find from the very earliest days of European rule an almost inexplicable aversion to any formal recognition of African customary law. From the first the legal authorities held that Colonial laws applied to the Africans in default of legislation to the contrary – a principle as indefensible in theory as it was unfortunate in practice. For the Africans, to whom it was considered right that the Roman-Dutch law of marriage and inheritance should apply, were polygamists, habitually marrying with *lobolo* and following habitually the law of primogeniture as regards succession. Thus the effect of not recognising African customary law was not to assimilate African social practices to those of Europeans but merely to impair the authority of the recognised courts, and of law and government generally.

Practical administrators on the eastern frontier and in British Kaffraria felt themselves unable to follow the instructions of the legal pedants at Cape Town, who with a show of learning, violated all the soundest principles of jurisprudence. As early as 1849 Mr. Calderwood, the Civil Commissioner of Victoria East, found it necessary to recognise the African customary law principle of communal responsibility in connection with stock theft;[1] this marks the origin of numerous 'spoor laws' in various parts of South Africa. In British Kaffraria it was found quite impossible to attempt to apply European law, though a few practices such as *Tsiko* (the forcible distribution of unmarried girls among the chief and his principal men) and 'eating up' (the forcible sequestration of a man's goods by the chief) were discountenanced and, if the Government resources at the moment permitted, punished.[2]

129

When it became possible to make permanent rules regarding British Kaffraria, the authorities were in a quandary. The Law Department at Cape Town would not consider the recognition of African customary law; the magistrates on the spot could not apply any other system unless indeed they were to refuse to hear ninety-nine per cent of the cases brought before them. To allow magistrates to do what common sense and sound jurisprudence required them to do, it was thought necessary to retain martial law after the conclusion of peace[3] – fully as grave an infringement of Colonial law as a formal recognition of African customary law would have been. Until 1859 therefore martial law prevailed in the territory of British Kaffraria. 'No man could complain that we abused our power under martial law. The Attorney-General said that it was no law; and that martial law amounted to nothing; still I went on because it was necessary for the safety of the country and there was no objection raised.'[4]

The result of the changes of 1859-65 was that the Cape itself and British Kaffraria were both assumed to come under the Colonial law. For a short period in 1860 the Kaffrarian courts actually refused to entertain *ikazi (lobolo)* cases, but this attitude was reversed in the same year.[5] For years thereafter theory and practice had to be divergent. The courts of the Ciskei have never ceased to administer certain parts of African customary law from 1860. The theory was brought more into line with practice by the Native Succession Act of 1864 (Cape) and Ordinance of 1864 (Kaffraria). Still there were vast tracts of African customary law which the Colony's legislature did not recognise while the Colony's subordinate judiciary did – and had to. Take, for example, the purely tribal district of Herschel. The magistrate (Mr. D. B. Hook) reported to Government on the 26th December 1882, as follows:[6]

'Although Herschel is in the Colony and strictly speaking, altogether under the Colonial Law, it has been found absolutely necessary to settle most of what we call Native civil cases, such as dowry, etc., by Native Law and custom. So far there has been no hitch in particular, the magistrate sitting as arbitrator generally and having the assistance, in many cases, of headmen. But of late, Law Agents have come into court and caused some difficulty by asserting their dictum in opposition to the judgment of the magistrate and headman in Native cases, urging as a last resort that the whole thing is illegal, and every case must be settled by Colonial Law. I need scarcely say that it would be fatal to allow law agents to upset a rule that has been found to work so well in the district. As I am responsible to Government for my charge, and in order to prevent confusion in Court, I have intimated that I will hear no Agent who brings a suit into court other than through the form of Colonial Law, and maintain the right as arbiter in my district for the convenience of the people, to deny the rights of these Agents to dictate unduly or cause confusion, while I am acting reasonably and in the interests of the Government and the people, in the absence of any codes of Native Law like those in the Trans-Colonial Territories.'

Mr. Hook's action received the tacit approval of the Colonial Government. In the following year the Native Laws and Customs Commission issued its report, in which it, too, pointed out the divergence between theory and practice in this matter.

'It has been fully brought out in evidence,' they say,[7] 'that in several of the Frontier districts the mass of the inhabitants of the Native Locations, though equally subject to Colonial Law, have been only nominally so; and to a very considerable extent they are still actually under their own traditional laws and usages, to which they appear to be attached by habit and familiarity, as well as by the fact that their mode of procedure is simple and inexpensive.

'In the divisions of King William's Town and Queen's Town more particularly, the Special Magistrates and Superintendents of Natives, without any judicial authority under statute, have continued to administer Native customary law, and in some Locations and Villages, the Native Headmen deal with petty cases and disputes brought before them for arbitration and settlement, although there is no provision whatever for the enforcement of their decisions. This was the condition of things which the Commission found existing within the Colony at the time of its appointment.'

Although the matter was brought to its notice in so official and definite a way, the Government neither interfered to stop the magistrates' unauthorised action nor adopted, except for the Transkeian Territories, the Commission's recommendation that African customary law should be recognised as a system of uncodified common law. It may be argued that recognition of a system of law is not a matter for legislation. It exists *proprio vigore*. With this statement the writer is in the very heartiest accord; but unfortunately only the inferior courts worked on it. An appeal lay to the Supreme Court of the Colony and the Supreme Court refused to recognise Native Law or any part of it, in the absence of statutory authority for such recognition. Thus in 1893 in the case of *Ngqobela* vs. *Sihele*,[8] the Chief Justice stated:

'Provision is made by Act No. 16 of 1860 for the appointment of marriage officers for solemnizing the marriage of persons professing the Mohamedan faith according to the Mohamedan customs and usages, but *no similar provision exists for marriages according to Native Customs and usages*. The only mode in which a valid marriage can be contracted between Natives in this Colony is before a minister of religion, or a lay marriage officer, with previous publications of banns or notice, or failing these by special licence. A union, therefore, founded only upon Native customs and usages within the Colony proper is not a marriage, whatever rights may by special legislation[9] have been given to the offspring of such a union in respect of the distribution of property left by their parents upon their death. In the absence of special legislation recognising such a union as a valid marriage, the courts of law are bound – however much they may regret it – to treat the intercourse, *I will not say as immoral, but as illicit.*'

No argument could be stronger for the recognition of African customary law than the fact that in that part of South Africa where it was theoretically unrecognised the only methods of satisfactory administration should have been nine years of martial law in time of peace, followed by a deliberate and considered departure from the theory of the Government by the magistrates – a departure unreproved by Cabinet or Legislature, but reversed by the Supreme Court whenever an appeal was made.[10]

Coming next to the Transkeian Territories, we may observe that the occupation of Lesotho (1871-84) furnished the Cape Government with the principles and practice which form the groundwork of the Transkeian system today. African customary law was fully recognised in Lesotho from the beginning, even before its annexation to the Colony.[11] On the 6th November 1871[12] a set of regulations was promulgated for the Government of British Basutoland, in which marriage by African custom was recognised as legal[13] and provision was made for the entertainment of *bohadi* (*lobolo*) suits,[14] while the African customary law of succession was also recognised with a modification to the effect that a widow should exercise guardianship over her minor children.[15] Many points of African customary law are, however, specifically excluded from recognition.

In March 1877 a much improved set of regulations was drawn up,[16] and it was this revised scheme which was the basis of the regulations applied to the Transkeian Territories and Griqualand East by Proclamations 110 and 112 of the 16th and 17th September 1879. These proclamations decidedly recognised substantive African customary law – with certain limitations, it is true. The crux of the whole matter is to be found in section 23 of each proclamation (the wording being identical), which provides that 'where all the parties to the suit, or proceedings are what are commonly called Natives . . . it may be dealt with according to Native Law, and in case of there being any conflict of Laws by reason of the parties being natives subject to different laws, the suit or proceedings shall be dealt with according to the laws applicable to the defendant.' It will be noticed that this section as it stands is permissive only, but in 1900 the Supreme Court of the Cape of Good Hope ruled that in certain classes of actions at least the word 'may' must be taken to mean 'shall'.[17]

African customary law was administered in the Territories subject to the proviso that it be 'compatible with the general principles cf humanity observed throughout the civilised world.' Before the Native Laws and Customs Commission of 1883, Messrs. W. T. Brownlee and Newton O. Thompson described the system in working variously as 'natural law', 'justice' and 'equity'. To illustrate some of the changes made, it may be noted that *Abakweta* and *Intonjane* dances were strictly prohibited as early as 1878.[18] Witchcraft was refused recognition as a legitimate accusation from the first, but it is noteworthy that one chief had on his own initiative fined the members of one of his kraals for employing a 'witch doctor' in 1881.[19] Practice varied with regard to *Ukungena* (the taking over of a deceased brother's widow by a surviving brother) but in 1883 the Native Laws and Customs Commission refused[20] to recognise this practice in any way whatever. Sentence of death for murder – a further departure from the old ideas – was passed for the first time in 1880.[21] The change was softened by the employment of *amapakati* as 'jurors' in some areas without authority – under such sympathetic magistrates as Mr. C. J. Levey.[22] In the Xesibe Territory, not formally annexed until 1886, a magistrate resided administering African customary law as early as 1888.[23]

The Cape Native Laws and Customs Commission of 1883, which drew up the famous Penal Code for the Territories, approved of the recognition of African civil law, subject to the modifications of the 1879 proclamations and some fresh ones which it added. Thus the system operative in the Transkei after Union – recognition of African customary law as an uncodified system, differing in detail occasionally from tribe to tribe and determinable as a matter of fact in each case – was fully established by the year 1883. All evidence points to the satisfactory nature of its working.[24]

The penal code introduced certain rules of African customary law regarding procedure, e.g. section 263 allows the examination of an accused person and of his wife or her husband, as the case may be, as an ordinary witness – a common principle in African trials. It also introduced one great principle of substantive African customary law – communal responsibility – though confined in the code to stock theft. The original section of the Code (No. 200) was replaced by a slightly different one in section 1 of Act 41 of 1898, which is quoted here at length. The provision is commonly known as the 'spoor law':

'When the spoor of any stolen animal is traced to any kraal or locality, responsibility in respect of value of such stolen animals shall be determined as is hereinafter provided, that is to say:

'(1) The head of any kraal (*umninimizi*) shall be responsible for the value and damages of any stolen animals, the spoor of which is traced to such kraals.

'(2) The owner of any stolen animals, the spoor of which has become lost or obliterated, has a right of search for any traces of such animals, in any hut, kraal, enclosure or lands in that neighbourhood; any person refusing to permit such search is responsible for the value of the animal stolen.

'(3) When the owner of any animal is on the spoor of such animal, it shall be lawful for the owner to demand from the persons living in the neighbourhood all reasonable assistance in following up such spoor, and whoever neglects or refuses to give such assistance and by such neglect or refusal causes the loss or obliteration of such spoor, or whoever by wilful obstruction or malice causes the obliteration or loss of such spoor, is liable for the value of the animal stolen.

'(4) When such spoor cannot be traced to any specific kraal or kraals, but is lost or becomes obliterated on any lands, then the responsibility for the value of such stolen animal shall devolve upon the heads (*abaninimizi*) of the kraals adjacent to and surrounding the spot where such spoor has been lost or obliterated; and for the purpose of compensating the owner of such stolen animal, it shall be lawful for the resident magistrate so to fix such responsibility by an assessment not exceeding two head of cattle (or their money value) to be by such magistrate levied on each kraal, to make up the whole value, or as near as possible the whole value, of the stolen animal or animals.

'(5) Whenever a spoor is traced to, or within the confines of any locality occupied by any kraal or kraals, or to or within any area occupied by any community or section of a tribe, if the persons occupying such kraal or kraals, or locality, or constituting such community or such section of a tribe, without lawful excuse, neglect or refuse to receive to take over and follow over such spoor, they are responsible for the value of the stolen animal whose spoor shall have been so traced, and are to be compelled to make good such value to the owner in like manner as is provided for with reference to "lost spoor" cases in the preceding sub-section.'

How do provisions like these work in practice? To some they perhaps savour of injustice. But it is a mistake to read our own legal and ethical ideals into the minds of other people. The following report made by Mr. W. E. Stanford, then resident magistrate of Engcobo (later Senator Sir Walter Stanford), will furnish a very interesting comment on the spoor law.[25]

'I cite an instance or two. Three horses were stolen in May last from a European farmer on the border. He found the spoor, and I sent a Native policeman to his assistance. It was traced to a locality south of the Ulandudu Mountains, but it was not brought direct to any kraal. I held the owners of the kraals in the neighbourhood of the last point at which the hoof marks of the horses were seen, responsible for their values; and the horses were found at once. A clue to the actual thief was afterwards obtained, and he was arrested. He then told me that he had brought the horses back himself. No doubt the others had intimated to him that they were not prepared to pay for his misdeeds. In another case, five head of cattle were traced to the Chief Umgudhlwa's location and the spoor lost in the veld, having been obliterated by rain. This to our minds would seem a hard case in which to hold a community responsible. To the Native headman and their own chief, who sat as assessors in it, there was no injustice. "Why did they let the thief pass through with the cattle?", they said. "They must pay," and accordingly the usual fine was imposed and the farmer was compensated for his loss. Some time afterwards one of the men fined came to me privately and said he could tell me where the cattle were. I sent for the owner and by this means the missing cattle were recovered, the thieves arrested and ten other cattle previously stolen were also found. The cattle paid by Umgudhlwa's people were of course refunded. I could mention other cases where collective responsibility has resulted in the disclosure of thieves and recovery of stolen property. Natives can nearly always prevent thieves from getting through their country with stolen stock if they wish to do so.'

If an application of a cardinal principal of African customary law applies in one case, why should it not in others? In the Territories, collective responsibility was only applied in cases of stock theft, but the Natal Code imposed it as a general principle. A hierarchy of persons working up from the head of a family to the chief of a tribe was made responsible for an ever-widening circle of dependants and inferiors, who according to African custom should not do anything of importance without the cognisance of the superior concerned. It is the defect of our administration of African customary law that we have tended constantly to be wiser than nature, and to cut out points of the customary law not because they are contrary to the *jus naturale* but because they conflict with what Coke called the 'artificial and acquired reasoning' of our own advanced legal systems.

In Natal, African customary law is still applied to every African not specifically exempted therefrom under Law 28 of 1865. The full recognition of African customary law was one of the outstanding points of the Shepstone system and was adopted from the very beginning. The 1846-7 Commission recommended that the Diplomatic Agent to the African tribes should 'adapt his decisions to the usages and customs of the Native law where such accommodation can be effected without violating the requirements of justice.' 'We are of opinion,' the Commissoners continue, 'that it would be productive of no good result suddenly to abrogate the laws and usages they have practised from time immemorial, except such as are connected with their ideas of witchcraft and which affect the lives of the accused.' Earl Grey, in his despatch commenting on the report dated the 10th December 1847, lays down as a definite principle that the customary law is only to be abrogated where against 'the universal principles of humanity and decency.' On the 23rd June 1849, an ordinance of the Lieutenant-Governor-in-Council formally accorded full recognition to African customary law, but it had been recognised and acted on by the court of the Diplomatic Agent *proprio vigore* since 1847.

African customary law was given a fuller recognition in Natal than elsewhere, and even the imposition of European criminal law was carried through with great care and as far as possible by steps familiar to the Africans' own conceptions.

It was no part of the Shepstone policy to codify the African customary law, which up to 1875 was in Natal a matter of fact, varying from tribe to tribe, as in the Transkei. But in 1875 the codification commenced culminating in Law 19 of 1891. Today if one asks, 'What is Native Law as administered in Natal?' the answer is simple: 'The Schedule to Law 19 of 1891, as subsequently amended from time to time.'[26] Giving evidence before the South African Native Affairs Commission of 1903-5, S. O. Samuelson declared that the Natal Government 'has not gone so far as to say that the Code of Native Law is to be the entire Native Law on which the courts are to act. The Native High Court can go outside the Code, and upset the decisions of magistrates or chiefs on points of law which are not in the Code.'[27] But in practice the Code ruled.

The Code applies to Africans generally (not being necessarily domiciled in Natal) so long as they sojourn or reside in Natal (section 2, Law 19 of 1891).

It will be seen that the Natal system in one sense was the Transkeian system worked out more logically. It has worked well, though with better personnel it could have worked better. An examination of its functioning tends to confirm the view that African customary law should be fully recognised. In another sense, the Natal system can be usefully contrasted with the Transkeian system. It is a written Code of Law compared with a body of unwritten common law. This point of comparison is so interesting and important that it has been thought desirable to devote further attention to it later in this chapter. At any rate Natal deserves our thanks as having been the pioneer in recognising African customary law frankly. It grieves one to consider that it was a young layman who advocated and a doctor of laws who opposed, a step which is in full accord with all the best traditions of legal science.[28]

In the Transvaal African customary law was recognised 'so long as . . . not inconsistent with the general principles of civilisation.' 'All matters and disputes of a civil nature between Natives shall be dealt with according to the provisions of this law and not otherwise, and in accordance with Native laws *at present in use*, and *for the time being* in force.' The italicised words bring out one important fact in the Transvaal system – African customary law is not a stereotyped or single system. It is the law of the tribe to which the African belongs and its determination in the Transvaal becomes an enquiry as to fact at the present day, not as in Natal an interpretation of a Code.

In one respect the Transvaal differed tremendously from the Transkeian Territories and Natal. Up to 1911 the Transvaal courts took no cognisance of *lobolo* cases. Before 1897 this was a matter of usage, but Law 3 of 1897 made the non-recognition of *lobolo* cases binding on the courts. The courts recognised only 'lawful' marriages, and a 'lawful' marriage was a Christian or civil marriage. 'There was absolutely no legal redress for unions entered into by people under their natural and inherited ideas.'[30] The case of *Sigcolo* vs. *Mokau* (May, 1911) afforded some relief in deciding that a marriage may be presumed to be 'lawful' in default of evidence to the contrary. But even in the case of a 'lawful' marriage there was no real redress. The situation has, of course, been rectified since then.

In the Orange Free State, African customary law as a system cannot be said to apply at all. In the annexed Baralong Territory (Thaba 'Nchu Reserve), African customary marriage was fully recognised.[31] Otherwise marriages were not recognised until a modification of the law was introduced by Law 26 of 1899. This provided[32] that the offspring of 'heathen marriages' should have their right of inheritance recognised as if legitimate children, and the paternal power of the father was recognised also, 'when it shall be proved that the parents regard one another as husband and wife.'

For Africans outside the Thaba 'Nchu Reserve there was a most absurd law of intestate succession, which, flying in the face of African legal conceptions, provided that community of property should be considered to exist as between husband and wife, and that in the case of polygamy one half should belong to the husband and the other half to the wives jointly![33] This was absolutely inexcusable, for the African customary law of intestate succession is better worked out than the Roman-Dutch law itself. In the Orange Free State there is an extraordinary provision that, where no provision of law exists, the High Court may order an 'equitable' distribution of the estate. So far as the writer knows it has never been acted upon. No judge who had any vague sense of the rudiments of legal history would or could act upon it. In 1803, Sir Frederick Pollock tells us, the judicial officer of the island of Penang 'reported that the Law of Nature was the only law he could find to guide him. He found its guidance *inadequate for determining questions of succession and administering estates*, which, indeed was exactly what any mediaeval doctor (not to say Aristotle) would have told him to expect.'[34] Yet to the Law of Nature the unfortunate High Court of the Orange Free State was referred for this very class of case!

To what preliminary conclusion can we now come? Surely the preceding inquiry has led us quite irresistibly to the conclusion that practical exigencies combine with sound theory to favour the full recognition of such portions of African customary law as are not repugnant to the *jus naturale*.

There is not an experienced magistrate in any tribal area of the Republic who could give a different opinion. And surely there should not be a Doctor of Laws in South Africa who could argue against the formal recognition of existing systems of law.

The main argument for the recognition of African customary law is that the courts should take cognisance of existing facts. But this same principle leads us to the conclusion that in those parts of the Republic where African customary law is recognised there are certain Africans to whom it could not in fairness be fully applied – Africans who have become detribalised, monogamists, often town-dwellers, to whom the application of the principle of collective responsibility would be the height of injustice, and the failure to treat polygamous marriage as a crime a condonation of immorality. By all the arguments which support the recognition of African customary law, there must be a system also of exemption from it.

There are, today, two systems of exemption from African customary law in force in the Republic – the Transkeian and the Natal systems. Elsewhere, while exemption is granted from specific statutes (e.g. the pass laws) there is no provision for exemption from African customary law as a whole.

In the Transkeian Territories, by Act 39 of 1887 (Cape) any duly registered parliamentary voter was completely exempted from African customary law and from all laws differentially affecting Africans. The parliamentary franchise involved a small property[35] or wage qualification, *plus* the ability to sign one's name and write one's address and occupation. Partial exemption – including exemption from the African customary law of marriage and succession – was granted to Africans who (1) held a certificate from the Education Department of qualification as elementary teachers, or (2) held an Inspector's certificate that they had reached the 'fourth standard' or any higher education certificate, or (3) were graduates or under-graduates of a South African university, or (4) were ministers of the gospel duly admitted as such into any Christian church.

Exemption was not heritable, but it flowed automatically from the possession of the qualifications above referred to. No special application was necessary. The Government had no discretion. With the complete abolition of the Cape African franchise the general exemption referred to above has, of course, fallen away.

In Natal, exemption is based on Law 28 of 1865. There is reason to believe that Shepstone was opposed to this law and omitted to make its terms known to the Africans. From 1865 to 1876 (the date of his retirement) there were no applications for exemption at all. But between 1876 and 1880 there were no fewer than one hundred and forty-nine letters of exemption granted.[36]

The law is still in force but is obsolescent, few general exemptions of this kind having been granted in recent years. Any African male or any unmarried African female may apply for exemption. In the latter case a European of good standing must come forward as guardian. The qualifications are seven years' residence in Natal, monogamy, ability to read and write, and a furnishing of a recommendatory certificate by a resident (not being an African) possessing a juryman's qualification. Particulars of the applicant's chief, family, etc., must be furnished and the oath of allegiance must be taken.

All this does not entitle an African to exemption, but merely to apply for exemption. The State President may or may not grant the application. Exemption was only granted sparingly in Natal before Union,[37] and the policy in 1909, on the eve of Union, was strictly to discourage it.[38]

The exemption of a married man carries with it the exemption of his wife and of children beneath the age of sixteen born at the time of exemption. But children born *after* exemption do not take their father's exempted status and must apply for exemption afresh on reaching majority.[39]

Every exempted African is expected to have, and to be able to produce, Letters of Exemption. But there is no provision for the issue of letters of exemption to the offspring of Africans, born before their father's exemption, who are, however, automatically exempted. Once the letters have been issued, although the holder may revert to barbarous habits or be convicted of a crime, there is no provision for their revocation.

Exemption confers relief from the Code only, not from other laws differentially affecting Africans. The exempted African is thus not legally a European, but an unhappy *tertium quid*. 'While asking for bread, he has been given a stone by being denied the full privileges of the European.'[40] So generally unsatisfactory was the law that a critic as restrained as the late Mr. S. O. Samuelson described it as a 'blot on the Statute Book' and declared that it 'should never have been enacted.'[41]

It is natural to ask why no attempts were made after 1865 to amend this law. The answer is that attempts were made, but none of them actually became law. A special Bill was drafted in 1905 to amend Law 28 of 1865. It demanded, in addition to the 1865 qualifications, the occupation of a house as distinct from a hut, and the ownership of immovable property to the value of £50 or the hiring of immovable property to the value of £50, or the hiring of immovable property of the annual value of £10 on a lease of not less than five years. Children of an exempted African, whether born before or after exemption, were to be exempted automatically up to the age of eighteen years; at any time after reaching the age of sixteen they might formally apply for letters of exemption. If these were refused, or if they failed to apply, they reverted at eighteen to African customary law. Provision was made for the revocation of letters of exemption in the case of crime or proved reversion to barbarous habits.

This Bill never became law.

A Bill 'to amend the Code of Native Law and to extend the same to the Province of Zululand' of approximately the same date struck at another difficulty by providing that a chief might receive letters of exemption but, so far as he was a chief, should be governed by the provisions of the Code in the exercise of his powers. This Bill, too, remains a Bill.

The Natal Native Commission of 1906-7 reported as follows:[42]

'The Commission is of opinion that the standard for acquiring the privilege should not be exacting, a reasonable degree of learning, such as reading and writing either in English or Zulu, good character, and conformity to civilised customs, being all that should be necessary, and, further, that the benefits conferred should descend to children.

The opinion is also expressed that exemption should be granted by operation of law and not depend upon the will of an official, that is, the legal tests should be plain, official interference determining only whether the required standard had been reached. The exempted Natives feel very strongly the position in which children born subsequent to the issue of their parents' letters have been placed by recent decisions of the courts, and there is much force in their plea for uniformity in the family. There was some divergence of opinion amongst witnesses with respect to the withdrawal of the certificate of exemption for any criminal act or for reversion to tribal life and custom. After consideration, it appeared to the Commission that letters should only be revoked for fraud in their obtaining, leaving the offender upon conviction for any other crime alone answerable to ordinary judicial sentence. To avoid the implication of innocent wives and children, the punishment for any crime (save the fraud mentioned) should be personal to the offender.'

Absolutely nothing came of these recommendations.

Coming to the general principles underlying the Natal law, there seems certainly a tendency to make exemption unduly difficult and to place many restrictions in the way. It would appear that exemption should be a comparatively easy and, so far as may be, an automatic thing, if our main end of recognising facts in our laws is to be attained.

Again the tendency in Natal has been to widen the gulf between exempted and unexempted Africans. The former are treated as having 'come out from the unclean thing,' and made themselves separate. It is suggested that a better plan is not to accentuate these differences unduly and to make the transfer from one class to another as easy as possible. *The differentiation is one of legal justice and need not be used as a political test.*

It will be noticed that there are two great differences between the Transkeian and Natal exemptions. In the first place exemption in the Transkei flows automatically from the possession of certain qualifications: in Natal it was a matter for the Governor's discretion. It will be remembered that the 1906-7 Commission, in the paragraph quoted above, gave its opinion in favour of the Transkeian system. On the whole, though there are arguments on both sides, the Transkeian system seems the better.

Secondly, exemption in Natal is merely from African customary law, not from laws differentially affecting Africans. In the Transkei exemption is from both, and here again the Transkeian system is the better.

The qualifications for exemption could be any of those required to confer partial exemption in the Cape. The suggestion of Dean Green[43] that monogamic marriage by Christian rites should *per se* exempt the African so marrying is worthy of consideration. The suggestion of Mr. Charles Barter[44] that all African urban dwellers should become *ipso facto* exempt is one which, to the writer's mind, goes too far.

Coming back now to the majority – the Africans who remain subject to African customary law – we naturally ask ourselves: 'What is the future of African customary law?' Will it remain stationary, will it ultimately become coincident with European law, or will it develop into a civilised but distinct legal system?

In trying to answer this question, we must bear in mind that a law which does not reproduce the ideas and customs of those to whom it applies is worse than no law at all. The manipulation of Codes and judicial decisions in order to bring about changes in African life is reprehensible, impolitic and unscientific. Changes in fact must among a primitive people precede changes in law. The proper sphere in which to discourage polygamy is that of the Church and the School, not of the Statute Book. When polygamy has been practically brought to an end, it is the turn of the legislator to step in, bring law into line with fact and round up the defaulting minority who are lagging behind the social progress of the majority.

Unfortunately ever since Europeans have been responsible for the government of Africans in South Africa there has been a tendency to use the Statute Book as a means of reform, sometimes real, sometimes alleged. And, very frequently, European authorities have expressed their opinion openly that the end to be aimed at is the amalgamation of African with European law. Thus the Inter-Colonial Commission of 1903-5 says[45] 'the object of improvement, and, so far as may be, assimilation with the ordinary Colonial law should be kept in view as the ultimate goal.'

Other authorities have, however, realised that, just as the systems of civilised countries such as France, Germany and the Netherlands differ from one another, while all alike partaking of civilisation, so the gradual evolution of African customary law to a more civilised status need not and ought not to involve its amalgamation with the Roman-Dutch law. Thus Mr. John W. Shepstone before the Natal Commission of 1881-2 said: 'I think in course of time the Native and Colonial Laws could be assimilated; but I could not say with regard to amalgamation . . . They should be administered separately and distinctly . . . I do not see any objection to the continuance of Native Law if it is administered in the pure and simple manner it should be, because there is a great deal of good in it.'[46] About the same time Sir George Pomeroy Colley wrote: 'The Native has already discovered that our processes are more complicated, more costly, and more uncertain in results, than his own. It is hardly a matter of surprise, therefore, if these people cling to their own ruder but simpler forms.'[47] And one of the best known African leaders of his day reminded his people that, in their departure from the old, they should not fling away everything, but rather examine closely into all things afresh and convince themselves of the soundness of the reasons why they elect to retain or reject this or that custom.[48]

African customary law cannot remain stereotyped in its present state if we do our judicial work properly, unless African progress is absolutely checked. Law is the index of civilisation. The day will undoubtedly come when the majority of Africans will look on polygamy as anomalous and abnormal, if not criminal. The day may come – though this is far more doubtful – when they will take up a similar attitude as regards *lobolo*. It would be idle to pretend that African customary law is a perfect system, or that African society will never change from its present state. And even if Government does nothing to encourage change, yet the influence of the missionaries, the example of European institutions and customs, and the slow process of natural growth will undoubtedly effect important changes.

But at the same time, there is no great reason why African customary law should be assimilated in all points to, or amalgamated with, European (i.e. Roman-Dutch) law. With regard to intestate succession, it is extremely doubtful whether the Roman-Dutch system is as good as that of African customary law. The law of primogeniture, universally observed among the Africans, will, if property in land becomes more individualised, be productive of more beneficial results than the equal division of land among all the children. The latter system tends to produce a miserably poor peasantry, the former a class of respectable peasant-proprietors, *plus* a sufficiency of agricultural labourers. When the 1903-5 Commission therefore tells us that it is of opinion 'that in the case of a Native dying intestate, the succession and inheritance to all land in his estate held under title in the form customary in South Africa should, unless otherwise provided in such title, be determined in accordance with ordinary Colonial law,' we can only express surprise and disappointment at such an attitude.

The conclusion to which we are led is, then, that African customary law will gradually advance as African social life changes, but that it is quite unnecessary that it should in all points coincide with European law. We may safely leave the issue to the future.

The question of the codification of African customary law is raised in a very practical form by the existence of the Natal Native Code, and less fully by that of the Transkeian Penal Code. We must examine firstly the history of codification in the Cape leading up to the Penal Code, and secondly the history of codification in Natal (codification is unknown in any form in the two remaining Provinces); then briefly to place our Codes against the background of the general history of codification.

The idea of codification in the Cape appears to have originated with Sir Benjamin D'Urban and Sir Harry Smith (then Colonel Smith). In a despatch to Lord Glenelg dated the 7th November 1835 Sir Benjamin D'Urban writes: 'It is sufficiently obvious that, for a considerable time to come, the law martial must continue in force in the new province, acting, with regard to His Majesty's new subjects, upon the basis and principles, and according to the spirit, of the treaty by which they have been received as such, and by the obligations of which both they and the Governor in the King's name are bound; and the judges of the Colonial bench may be called upon to prepare drafts of such ordinances, to be proposed by the Governor for the consideration of the Legislative Council, as may be specially adapted to the condition of these people, still keeping in view the principles of the treaties; by which ordinances the law martial may be replaced, when it may become expedient to remove it.'

Lord Glenelg replied on the 17th February 1836: 'I perceive that you intend to frame a detailed Code for the government of the Caffres; and in the meantime to leave them under martial law. The plan has not been very fully digested, but I fear that it would be found in practice scarcely possible for the legislature of a civilised country to devise and promulgate a Code fit for the government of a barbarous people. If not accommodated to their habits of thought and action, it would be at once unjust and inefficient; and if so accommodated, it must involve a compromise of many principles which we justly regard as sacred.'

This reply put an effectual 'wet blanket' on Sir Benjamin D'Urban and also on Colonel Harry Smith, who had written to Sir Benjamin on the 18th April 1836 to the effect that 'magistrates are alone required, and a Code of Laws ably compiled to work progressively from the Caffre up to the British law.'[49]

While much was done with regard to African customary law in the interim, the question of its codification remained in abeyance until 1856. In that year 'Maclean's Compendium', as it was familiarly known, was produced for use in British Kaffraria. It was not a Code, but a handbook for the guidance of magistrates, specifying conflicting customs and usages where such existed and leaving the magistrate to decide which was prevalent in his own area, or applicable to the parties to a suit – in short, the kind of handbook we should like to see compiled for the Republic today. The compiler and editor was Colonel Maclean, Chief Commissioner for British Kaffraria, who had the able assistance of the Rev. H. H. Dugmore, Mr. J. C. Warner, 'Tambookie' Agent, Mr. Charles Brownlee, 'Gaika' Commissioner, Mr. John Ayliff and other less important authorities. This handbook was approved by Sir George Grey, and guided the decisions of magistrates in cases tried under African customary law up to the report of the 1883 Commission and in some points after that date.

In 1865 a large number of Mfengu, estimated as 40 000, were settled in the present Transkeian Territories. On the 21st August of that year, Sir Walter Currie presented a memorandum to the Government at Cape Town, in which he stated that 'Kafir law was to prevail in so far as not repugnant to the feelings of humanity. The book published by the British Kaffrarian Government entitled "Kafir Laws and Customs" [i.e. Maclean's compendium] to be the text-book in law proceedings.'

In the same memorandum Sir Walter Currie included what he terms the 'Outline of a Code'. It consisted of nine short paragraphs dealing with Stolen Property, General Collective Responsibility, Disputes between

143

different Locations, Duties of Chiefs and Headmen towards Magistrate, *Izizi* (i.e. fines in civil cases), Strange Live-Stock, Settlement of Strangers in Locations. This 'Code' was approved with some slight alterations by Colonial Secretary's minute of 12th September 1865. It was concerned mostly, as will be gathered, with jurisdiction and procedure, but embraced some points of substantive law, e.g. the section dealing with Collective Responsibility which reads: 'The individual residents of each location and kraal to be held *collectively* responsible for the acts of its individual members (according to Kafir law).'[50]

It must be realised that Sir Walter Currie's 'Code' was not a code in the ordinary sense of the word – that is, it lacked statutory recognition and decisions of magistrates under it were liable to be reversed on appeal to the Supreme Court.

When Lesotho was taken over by the Cape in 1871 a set of regulations was drawn up, and this was followed by a revised and more complete compendium drawn up in 1872-3, but not promulgated until 1877.[51] This, too, was a compendium, not a legislative Code, and with the retrocession of Lesotho in 1884 it passes beyond our scope.

Such was the experience on which the Native Laws and Customs Commission of 1883 had to work. The result of its labours was the recognition of Native Civil Law, coupled with a definite refusal to codify[52] it; and the preparation of a Penal Code specially for the Territories.

That a Penal Code was necessary was agreed upon by all the important witnesses who appeared before the Commission, particularly by Sir Theophilus Shepstone by whom the Commission was 'much assisted and guided'.[53] Shepstone, while supporting a penal code, was against a civil code, fearing sterilisation as a result of it, and his view was adopted by the Commission, which agreed with him that this danger of sterilisation was of little weight with regard to a criminal code.[54]

The Transkeian penal code is almost entirely the work of Sir J. D. Barry, chairman of the Commission. It is not African customary law, but Colonial law with certain modifications.[55] The Commission gave as its reasons for taking Colonial law as a basis (i) that the distinction between civil and criminal law in African customary law is very vague; (ii) that such criminal law as there is, is based upon the assumption that all members of the tribe belong to the chief and that injury to them is injury to him. On the other hand Colonial law alone was insufficient, because (i) it did not concern itself with imputation of witchcraft, with which so much African crime is bound up; (ii) its law of procedure offended the African sense of justice by failing to exhaust every source of information, including the examination of the accused and other persons who are able to throw light on the subject under investigation; (iii) it did not recognise the principle of communal responsibility.

The penal code deals with witchcraft in sections 171 to 175 (in the original draft, 177 to 181). The imputation of witchcraft is an offence punishable by a fine of forty shillings or in default of payment, imprisonment for fourteen days. The imputation of witchcraft *plus* habitual practice as a witch-finder (*isanusi*) is punishable by imprisonment with or without hard labour, for a term which may extend to two years, or with fine, or flogging, or any two or more of such punishments.

The 'illustration' of the last-mentioned crime – one of the many excellent 'illustrations' in the original draft – is as follows: 'B is employed by A, the owner of a kraal in Griqualand East, to tell him why his child C is suffering from measles. B accuses D of having bewitched the child by means of a charm which D has received from a baboon. B is proved to be by habit and repute a witch-finder (*isanusi*). B is liable to imprisonment under this section. Employing a witch-finder and supplying or using "witch medicine" with intent to injure are also criminal offences.'

The main departure from Colonial law as regards procedure is to be found in section 263: 'In any proceeding under this Code the accused person and his wife or husband as the case may be may, if such person thinks fit, be called, sworn, examined and cross-examined as an ordinary witness in the case.'

Communal responsibility was recognised by the Code only in respect of stock-theft (section 200).

One very interesting feature of the code, as orginally drafted, was the excellent 'illustrations' following each clause, modelled on the famous Indian Penal Code drawn up by Lord Macaulay's commission. With characteristic distrust of novelty and lack of imagination, the Government dropped these from the Code as ultimately enacted. Two examples are quoted. (The numbers follow the original draft):

'Section 143. Acceleration of death

'Every one who by an act or omission causes the death of another shall be deemed to kill that person, although the effect of the bodily injury caused to such other person be merely to accelerate his death while labouring under some disorder or disease, arising from some other cause.
'*Illustration*
'A strikes B, who is at the time so ill that she could not possibly have lived for more than six weeks had she not been struck. B dies earlier than she would otherwise have died in consequence. A has killed B.

'Section 144. Causing death which might have been prevented

'Every one who by an act or omission causes the death of another shall be deemed to kill that person, although death from that cause might have been prevented by resorting to proper means.
'*Illustration*
'A injures B's finger. B is advised by a surgeon to allow it to be amputated, refuses to do so, and dies of lockjaw. A has killed B.'

The code is a territorial, not a personal one, i.e. every resident of the Transkeian Territories, African and European alike, is subject to it – a contrast to the Natal Code which is personal.

A judicial commission to revise the Code periodically was suggested by the Commission,[56] but Government did not accept this excellent suggestion.

The Code, in an amended form, was enacted as Act 24 of 1886 and came into force on the 1st January 1887.[57]

The magistrates were asked to comment on the working of the Code in their reports for the year 1887. The following extracts from their reports will assist the student in forming his conclusions:

Captain Matthew Blyth, Chief Magistrate, Transkei: 'The Code seems admirably adapted to the conditions existing in these Native Territories.' (Cape Native Blue Book, 1888, p. 34)

H. G. Elliott, Chief Magistrate, Tembuland: 'The Code and its method of administration is now accepted as being fair and equitable, which is, I think, in no small measure due to the presence of Councillors as Assessors. These men are selected from the most astute and trusted Councillors of the tribes. They watch the proceedings with much interest and intelligence and from their intimate acquaintance with all the wiles and tricks of their people frequently put questions that materially assist the court in eliciting the truth, and after their work is over they explain to the chiefs and people at their usual gatherings what took place.

'I attribute the total absence of political unrest and intriguing among my people during the past year to their acquiescence in the Penal Code, and the mode provided for its administration. The Code, in my opinion, works well, and is admirably adapted to the present condition of the people. A more elaborate and intricate Code of Laws would neither be understood nor appreciated by them.' (Ibid, p. 45)

W. E. Stanford, Chief Magistrate, Griqualand East: 'The Code has worked well. The rules of law laid down for the guidance of magistrates are instructive, and the procedure is simple and effective. The Natives appreciate highly the privilege of sitting as Assessors.' (Ibid, p. 61)

It will be seen that the three chief magistrates were in agreement in reporting favourably on the Code. Of the district magistrates whose reports are available, those of Engcobo, Umtata, Saint Mark's, Xalanga, Elliotdale and Mqanduli report in favour of the Code, and only those of Umzimkulu and Mount Ayliff against it. The magistrate of Tsolo takes up a non-committal attitude. The reports of 1888 (Blue Books of 1889) were almost unanimously favourable; and there is no general discussion of the Code in subsequent Blue Books.

It is not to be supposed, however, that this consensus of opinion warrants the impartial investigator in recommending the enactment of a similar code for the Republic or of similar codes for other African territories. Reading through the magisterial reports carefully, one is led to the conclusion that the system of Assessors (the old *Amapakati*) is what presents itself most favourably to the magisterial mind. In spite of an overwhelming preponderance of favourable reports on the way in which these assessors performed their duties, the system was abolished as regards the more important cases in 1889 after only two years' trial and replaced by circuit courts and juries. This was the subject of some adverse magisterial comment at the time, and shortly afterwards the annual reports show a retrogression towards heathen customs in the Territories. *Post hoc* is not always, of course, *propter hoc*, yet we cannot but feel that the change was ill-advised.

Can we draw any general lessons from the Transkeian Penal Code? At this date, when Africans all over the Republic have been subjected to European criminal law for over a century, it is perhaps merely pedantic to argue with Mr. John Ayliff[58] that the Code should have mirrored existing African practice instead of laying down a foreign system. It is quite impossible to hope that our Legislature and our courts will be persuaded to substitute for the useless and expensive penalty of imprisonment,[59] the old African customary penalties of fines, preferably in kind, and, under stringent restrictions, of corporal punishment.

Accepting in practice the position that criminal law for Africans must be the European criminal law, at any rate in the main, we arrive at the position that the Transkeian Penal Code, so far as it is successful, is an argument not for African codification, but for the codification of European criminal law. As such the writer accepts it whole-heartedly. A general code of criminal law would be an inestimable boon to magistrates, and would not be productive of those dangers which threaten societies that codify their civil law. Such a criminal code could contain, with advantage, certain modifications of substantive law and procedure applicable when the defendant is an unexempted African.

More than this the history of the Transkeian Code does not prove. It is not a code of African customary law in any real sense of that term. It is a code of advanced, refined, and occasionally modified, European law. That it has been on the whole successful does not prove that a code of civil law (such as the Natal Code) is desirable.

The Transkeian Code is a territorial one; any civil code would, quite obviously, have to be a personal one. The importance of this difference may be exaggerated, but it is well that we should note it.

We are driven, then, to the examination of the Natal Code, as being of more direct value for our purposes. Codification in Natal was no part of the original Shepstone policy, and its adoption marked the passing of Sir Theophilus Shepstone's rule. We know, from his evidence before the Cape Native Laws and Customs Commission of 1883[60] that Sir Theophilus Shepstone was against codification, though curiously enough Mr. Henrique Shepstone was a thorough-going believer in it.[61] In the Native Administration Law of 1875 provision was made for the constitution of a Board of Native Administration which *inter alia* was to draw up, for the guidance of magistrates, a code of native law. This code, consisting of sixty-eight clauses, was promulgated on the 28th February 1878.

Not many years elapsed before it was thought desirable to revise the

Code and give it a more definite form. Accordingly by Law 44 of 1887 the Executive was given power to issue a Code. Operations were begun at once, a draft code being drawn up by Mr. W. Y. Campbell, of Durban, and printed in 1888. This formed the basis of the 1891 Code. As finally worked out it was presented to Parliament in 1891 – the Executive having thus tacitly surrendered its power of legislating– and passed *en bloc* as Law 19 of that year. The Law contained no provisions authorising the Executive to amend it.

In Zululand the 1891 Code was not applied on the annexation of that province to Natal, except one section relating to the appointment of chiefs and another making the Governor of Natal Supreme Chief.[64] Otherwise the earlier code applied. Natives in Zululand may be exempted from 'Native Law as administered therein.'

The Code consists mainly of ordinary civil law, but a few points of procedure and of public law appear. In addition to permitting an accused person to be examined and cross-examined as an ordinary witness, the Code permits the obtaining of witness by commission and does not necessarily exclude hearsay evidence. The position of the Governor (now the State President) as Supreme Chief is defined and a hierarchy of responsibility is set up – chiefs are responsible to the Supreme Chief, heads of kraals to their chiefs, heads of families to their kraalheads. Communal responsibility is fully established. With regard to property, there is a rule that prescription is not recognised. Any refusal, express or implied, of a chief to obey a lawful order of the Supreme Chief is treason. The main part of the Code is concerned with marriage, *lobolo* and inheritance, and these are dealt with in great detail. Indeed it has been a peculiarity of the Natal system to reduce the most minute customs to writing and this is illustrated, even more clearly than in the Code, by subsequent regulatory legislation regarding beer drinks, e.g. 'The superior position and rank of the men (*amadoda*) must be recognised and respected by the young men (*izinsizwa*) who will be guilty of a contravention of these regulations should they sit down and drink beer in company with the men (*amadoda*) unless specially invited to do so by the principal man of the hut, with the approval of the others present.'[65]

How has the Natal Code worked and is it possible to get an answer from the experience of its working to the question whether codification is generally desirable?

It is most difficult to answer these questions. We do know that the fixing of the number of *lobolo* cattle and the provision that *lobolo* must be paid over in its entirety before the marriage have seriously affected the African view of what in iself is a laudable institution, and tended to emphasise more the conception of barter or sale.[66] This, however, is only to argue that a code should reproduce the actual structure of the society for which it is enacted, not the structure which the codifier thinks ought to exist – a very elementary point. Most of the Natal evidence before the 1903-5 Commission was in favour of a code, though not necessarily of *the* Code. Mr. J. Y. Gibson, the well-known writer on Native Affairs, was in favour of the Code as it stood.[67] Mr. H. C. Shepstone favoured its extension,[68] Mr. Justice Boshoff,[69] Judge President of the Native High Court, and Mr. Justice (later Sir William) Beaumont[70] were ready to support the principle of codification but wanted to see the existing Code amended. The Natal Commission of 1906-7 reported that 'there was an almost unanimous expression of opinion by magistrates and others that there should be a code'[71] but also stated: 'That there is need for amendment is abundantly established by the evidence.'[72] It is noteworthy that the 1903-5 Commission, after duly considering evidence from every part of South Africa, reported: 'The weight of the evidence adduced before the Commission is against the enactment of a statutory code based on Native Law.'[73]

We are therefore left in more or less of an agnostic position. Quite certainly, the Natal Code has not been a complete success: equally certainly, it has not been an utter failure. Whether things are better or worse for its enactment than they would have been otherwise it is not possible to say at all dogmatically on the evidence before us. Most Natal magistrates swear by the Code, but then Transkeian magistrates are often equally ardent for their own system of unwritten African customary law. There is always a certain conservatism in people who administer justice. The only verdict we can come to as regards the Natal Code is 'not proven', and to arrive at a definite conclusion relative to the problems of codification generally we must pass from the concrete history of codes in South Africa, to the consideration of the general causes and characteristics of codification.

For a code to arise naturally among peoples in a primitive state of legal development, Maine has shown us that one or both of two factors must be present, viz.: (1) The discovery of the art of writing; (2) the desire to take law out of the hands of a professional or oligarchal class, and make it 'cognoscible' to the people at large.[74] Now neither of these reasons was or is of effect among the Africans. The art of writing has only been instilled from outside by Europeans. The knowledge of law has never been, among the Africans, the monopoly of any given class. Trials were always public, and any one not afraid of making a fool of himself might speak as a councillor. African customary law has not reached into the early stages of codification of which the Law of the Twelve Tables is so excellent an example. African codes today are not natural but artificial: they are imposed from without, not evolved from within.

Now if the Twelve Tables or the Code of Manu were – as they admittedly were – premature, it must be clear that *a fortiori* the codification of the yet more archaic laws of the Africans would be premature. It does seem therefore that the *onus* lies on the supporters of a Republican Native Code to prove their case. The Code of Manu has been the tragedy of a whole civilisation: it behoves us, then, to look warily on premature codification.

We know that the Romans, with their unerring legal instinct, found a remedy for their too early codification. They — and *a fortiori* the Africans — had not reached that stage of self-consciousness which produces the modern 'legislation-state'. The remedy which they discovered was that of legal fiction. Thus, for example, the Code of the Twelve Tables, as is well known, provided for one means only of terminating the *patria potestas* — that is that a father who sells his son thrice into bondage shall be punished by forfeiting his *potestas*. In later days the emancipation of a son on attaining his majority took place as a matter of course by a fictitious sale of the son to a collusive friend thrice in rapid succession, followed by a formal *mancipatio*'[75] In parts of South Africa where the African customary law is not codified legal fiction is often used to meet the necessity of *lobolo* payments in a time of scarcity — baskets of corn and even stones being passed as a token in place of the customary cattle. But where we have codified this is no longer possible. As our codification of African customary law is not natural, the natural remedy does not come into play. The courts which administer our Codes have got beyond the 'legal fiction' stages.

Our Native Codes, therefore, having been imposed from without, and being incapable of amendment by the natural means of legal fiction, must be amended from without by the method of legislation. Otherwise progress becomes sterilised and the Code is rendered definitely a curse.

Can we rely on the legislative remedy being applied? The experience of the past in Natal leads us to a quite distinct negative. Our legislatures, as a whole, have had neither the time, the inclination nor the expert knowledge to revise the existing Codes adequately. The post-Union system of allowing amendments of the Code by regulation has made amendment easier, but the Codes will still lag behind the facts.

The great argument against codification has already been brought out clearly — the danger of imparting rigidity to an archaic and imperfectly developed system. Here it is perhaps only necessary to requote the opinion of Sir Theophilus Shepstone expressed before the Cape Native Laws and Customs Commission of 1883:[76]

'Q: I don't know if I am right in gathering that you are not much in favour of codifying Native Law?

'A: I have an objection to making Native Law too technical. I recognise the necessity of having a text book for magistrates to be guided by and laying down and exemplifying principles to be observed in different cases.

'Q: Your objection to the proposal to codify the Native Law is based upon the possibility that the very codification of the Native Law will make it too rigid, and so absolutely check the improvement you wish to bring about?

'A: That is the danger which I fear.'

NOTES TO CHAPTER X

1. Instructions to Superintendents of Fingoes, dated Alice, 29th January 1849.
2. Col. Mackinnon to Sir Harry Smith, 25th February 1849 and 1st March 1850.
3. Sir Geo. Cathcart to Sir G. A. Pakington, 20th May 1852.
4. Evidence of Sir Walter Currie before Select Committee of the Cape House of Assembly, 1859, pp. 2-3.
5. Cape Native Laws and Customs Commission 1883, p. 9.
6. Cape Native Blue Book 1883, p. 9.
7. Report, pp. 17-18.
8. 10, Juta, p. 346.
9. e.g. The Native Succession Act of 1864.
10. See further Cape Native Affairs Commission 1910, pp. 35-9.
11. See Sir Philip Wodehouse's despatch No. 31 of 2nd May 1868.
12. Proclamation 74 of 1871.
13. Reg. 1.
14. Reg. 4.
15. Reg. 6.
16. Proclamation 44 of 1877. This involved a flexible acceptance of 'Native Law' but Cape Law was often applied.
17. *Sekelini* v. *Sekelini* 21 S.C.R. p. 118.
18. Cape Native Blue Book 1879, p. 109.
19. Cape Native Blue Book 1883, p. 41.
20. Report, para. 100, p. 38.
21. Cape Native Blue Book 1880, p. 103.
22. Ibid., p. 18.
23. Colonial Secretary's (Cape) minute No. 1851 of 3rd December 1881.
24. For a general résumé of the Transkeian system in this respect *vide* S.A. Native Affairs Commission 1903-5, Report, Vol. I, Appendix p. 6.
25. See Cape Native Blue Book 1884, p. 127.
26. Before Union the most important amending enactments were Law 25 of 1892 and Acts 40 of 1896, 8 of 1897, 1 of 1901, 47 of 1903 and 7 of 1910. The Code may now be amended by Proclamation and revisions of the whole Code were made by proclamation in 1932 and again in 1967.
27. Evidence of S. O. Samuelson, Under-Secretary for Native Affairs, Natal, before S.A. Native Affairs Commission 1903-5, Q. 41315 (Vol. IV, p. 569).
28. Theophilus Shepstone and Dr. Henry Cloete.
29. Law 4 of 1885 (S.A. Republic), Sec. 2.
30. S.A. Native Affairs Commission 1903-5, Evidence, Vol. IV, p. 435, Vol. V, p. 297.
31. Wetboek van die Oranje Vrystaat, Hoofstuk IV, 1.
32. Section 28.
33. Wetboek van die Oranje Vrystaat, Hoofstuk IV, 3.
34. The Law of Nature: A Preliminary Study (in Journal of the Society of Comparative Legislation, December, 1901).
35. Property held on communal tenure or under the Glen Grey system of tenure was not counted for purposes of the franchise.
36. Blue Book: Papers relating to Native Custom in Natal, 1881.
37. Memorandum of S. O. Samuelson, Under-Secretary for Native Affairs, Natal, dated September 1907; Report of Natal Native Affairs Commission 1906-7, paras. 13-14, p. 4.

38 Circular S.N.A. 23/1909 dated 28th April 1909.
39 Ibid.
40 Natal Native Affairs Commission 1906-7, Report, para. 14.
41 Memorandum dated September 1907.
42 Report, para. 64.
43 Minority report, Natal Native Commission 1881-2, p. 21.
44 Natal Native Blue Book 1881, p. 157.
45 Report, para. 233.
46 Natal Native Commission 1881-2, Report and Evidence, Vol. II, p. 96.
47 Sir George Pomeroy Colley to the Earl of Kimberley, 16th July 1880.
48 Address of D. D. T. Jabavu at the 'King Teachers Association' at Debe Nek, C.P., November 1919.
49 Confidential notes by Col. H. G. Smith on the Treaties of 17th September 1835, with the Native Tribes.
50 Correspondence with reference to the Principles, Conditions and Detailed Arrangements in which the Fingo Exodus has been carried out, Cape Town, 1867.
51 See Cape Native Blue Book 1878, p. 18.
52 Report, para. 61. Certain regulations were, however, drawn up with regard to marriage, *lobolo* and inheritance.
53 Report, pp. 14 and 20.
54 Ibid., p. 20.
55 Ibid., p. 23.
56 Ibid., p. 41.
57 Cape Native Blue Book 1887, p. 55.
58 Minority Report to the Report of the Cape Native Laws and Customs Commission 1883.
59 It is, perhaps, unnecessary to say that this punishment was unknown among Africans before the introduction of European rule. (See also the handling of the subject in Richmond Haigh's able little book 'Otai'. (Cape Town, Juta, 1922)).
60 Minutes of Evidence, Questions 151, 259, 326, 435, 436, 437.
61 See the evidence before the S.A. Native Affairs Commission 1903-5, Questions 19172-19174 (Vol. III, p. 86).
62 Report of Natal Native Affairs Commission 1906-7, para. 44.
63 Minute of Henry Escombe, Attorney-General of Natal, dated 8th April 1895.
64 Evidence of Mr. (later Sir) Charles Saunders, Chief Magistrate of Zululand before the S.A. Native Affairs Commission of 1903-5.
65 Government Notice (Natal) 620 of 1898, dated 23rd October 1898. See also S.N.A. Circulars of 11th October 1884 and 15th April 1893.
66 This point is brought out *inter alia* in the report of the Natal Native Affairs Commission of 1906-7, paras. 61 and 62.
67 Evidence, Vol. III, p. 41.
68 Ibid., p. 86.
69 Ibid., p. 348.
70 Ibid., pp. 16-17.
71 Ibid., Report, para. 63.
72 Ibid., Report, para. 61.
73 Ibid., Report, para. 232.
74 Maine, H. S.; 'Ancient Law', London, John Murray, 1916. Chapter I.
75 *Vide*, e.g. Sohm, R. 'Institutes of Roman Law', 3rd Edition. (Oxford at the Clarendon Press, 1907). Translated J. C. Ledlie. pp. 482 and 486-7.
76 Questions 435 and 437, p. 24.

CHAPTER XI

Local Administration

The natural administrative unit for Africans living in rural reserves was the tribe, and the tribe was normally governed by an hereditary chief. The chief, as a rule, was a limited monarch and in exercising his functions he consulted with his uncles and other senior relatives and with men of consequence in the tribe, and on vital matters such as war he tried to carry the whole tribe with him. Absolute large-scale monarchies, such as that of Shaka, were unusual and no more typical of normal African government than that of Hitler was of normal European government.[1] Lesotho, with its active national monarchy coupled with regular pitsos or assemblies of the people, formed yet another system.[2]

With scarcely an exception the chief was retained in tribal areas as the local unit of administration and minor judicial activities, always, however, with an appeal to the white magistrate or native commissioner in charge of the district. On the whole the people accepted this arrangement gladly and appeals were the exception, not the rule.

In the Cape these local functions were entrusted to Government headmen, but as chiefs were usually appointed to these posts the difference was more apparent than real. In Natal, due mainly to the break-up of tribes under Shaka's invasions, hereditary chiefs were not always discoverable, and there were occasions when Shepstone appointed men, sometimes his own personal attendants, as chiefs. In the course of four or five generations the successors of these men have become accepted as chiefs, notwithstanding their somewhat ignoble origins.

Paramount chiefs have been acknowledged both in the Cape and Natal but their posts have been purely honorific and they have not in fact been given legal powers over ordinary tribal chiefs. In Eastern and Western Pondoland the respective paramount chiefs were given the power to nominate members to the local councils.

Such was the position of the chiefs at and just after the time of Union.[3] Since Union the tendency has been to increase their powers in practice, though not in legal theory. They are more consulted by the magistrates (Bantu Affairs Commissioners) than used to be the case. While the Natives Representative Council existed, the four nominated posts were usually filled by paramount or other powerful chiefs. Attempts have been made to give chiefs some sort of voice in urban locations – something never attempted before Union. It is no part of the plan of this book go into details of policy after 1910, but these remarkable and very

153

unexpected changes should be mentioned if only in outline.

Chiefs, then, remained after annexation, the basis of local administration, but their powers were limited by the introduction of the council system[4] and by the appointment of magistrates. Except in Pondoland the chiefs were not legally a part of the council system *qua* chiefs, though more often than not they were either elected or nominated as members. In very recent years the development of legislatures in the 'homelands' has tended to relegate 'paramount' chiefs to ceremonial functions and to make the really powerful figure the Minister who heads the 'homeland' executive.

Actually until 1910 – though in this again there have been very significant post-Union changes – the most important figure in African administration was the magistrate or similar white official. This was certainly colonial paternalism but, in a very large number of cases, benevolent paternalism. Magistrates were not trained as African administrators, although of course they were required to have proper qualifications for their judicial functions, but many did possess knowledge which fitted them to understand and, where necessary, to administer tribal affairs. Among the most successful were sons of missionaries who had grown up among the people and spoke their language. In spite of current outcries against 'colonialism' and 'paternalism', it would not be right to withhold their due praise from the many unselfish and capable men among these magistrates.

The greatest difference between the pre-Union systems of African local administration was the departmental control of the district officer, and the study of this matter is complicated by the inconsistency of nomenclature, as, e.g. a 'magistrate' in the Transkei is a Native Affairs official, and in Natal an official of the Department of Justice. We shall have to find our way through this labyrinth with some care.

In the Transkeian Territories, with the exception of two outlying white farming areas, the system was clear and comprehensible and has worked well. Every district was headed by a magistrate who was, with all his staff, a member of the Native Affairs Department. They were presided over by a chief magistrate who combined judicial with administrative functions and was also an official of the Department of Native Affairs. Such white people as lived in the area had to accept the authority of these Native Affairs Department officials even as regards disputes *inter se*.

Beyond the confines of the Transkei, the Cape magistrate was an official of the Department of Justice, except in the overwhelmingly African districts of Herschel and Glen Grey. In certain mixed but preponderantly African districts (e.g. King William's Town) the Department of Justice magistrate was assisted by subordinate officers termed Superintendents of Natives. These were officers of the Native Affairs Department but were attached to the staff of the magistrate, through whom they corresponded with their Department.

We cannot say that the magistrate was a Native Affairs official when

Africans were in the majority, and a Department of Justice official when Europeans were in a majority: it is not as simple as that. An overwhelming proportion of Africans (the percentage never legally defined) was required for a Native Affairs magistracy. There has been no serious complaint by whites placed under Native Affairs officers, nor by blacks placed under Department of Justice officers. The personality of the magistrate rather than his Departmental connection is what really counts.

In Natal in all districts (even in the purely African areas of Northern Zululand), the magistrates were officers of the Department of Justice. The only local officials under the direct control of the Native Affairs Department were a number of superintendents of locations, dipping supervisors and forest officials. Although it is possible to exaggerate the disadvantages which the Native Affairs Department experienced in carrying out its functions locally through officers subject to the jurisdiction of another Departmental head, the system was not really defensible. From the practical point of view there was the danger of the appointment of magistrates with no experience of the African people and their ways, and sometimes the selection of men on the basis of their acceptability to the white community.

Natal entered Union with a Chief Native Commissioner and four local Native Commissioners under the Native Affairs Department.[5] These officers exercised no judicial functions. Their posts were abolished within two years of the coming into force of Union. Considerable changes, of course, have been made in other directions since Union.

The dominating principle of the Transvaal system was the provision of separate local officers for all African work as far as practicable. Every magistrate was *ex officio* a Native Commissioner and, as such, had nominal administrative and judicial control of the Africans in his area. In some cases where the African population was comparatively sparse, his nominal control became actual. All magistrates in the Transvaal were officers of the Department of Justice. In certain districts where there was a substantial African population, officers known as Native Sub-Commissioners[6] were stationed. The Native Sub-Commissioner was theoretically, of course, an assistant to the magistrate (Native Commissioner) but practically he dealt with most of the African work of his district. His activities were both administrative and judicial, and he dealt with Africans only. All Native Sub-Commissioners were officers of the Department of Native Affairs.

Though the Transvaal system was fruitful in suggestion, it is open to one or two criticisms. If the principle of one set of officers for Europeans and one for Africans be adopted at all, why was it not carried out in its entirety? Could not some of the less densely populated African areas have been combined, two or more, into one Native Sub-Commissionership; and the expense of the additional posts be counterbalanced by the combination in the same way of two or more areas with a sparse European population into a single magistracy? Up to 1910 there was the distinct defect, as in Natal, that officers with direct responsibility for Africans were in some cases not officers of the Native Affairs Department.

Secondly – though this may be chiefly a theoretical objection – why the suggestion of subordination in the case of the Native Affairs officer? Why not have defined his jurisdiction and made him independent of the magistrate?

The courts of Native Commissioners and Sub-Commissioners were the kernel of the judicial system. But chiefs 'appointed by the Government' had petty civil jurisdiction over their own tribes.[7]

The policy of the Republican Government – doubtless influenced by the work of Mr. Henrique Shepstone as Secretary of Native Affairs during the British occupation (1877-81) as it bears the strong impress of the original Shepstone system – was to concentrate all functions of African government nominally in the President as Paramount Chief, actually in the Superintendent of Natives, the permanent head of the Native Affairs Department. An appeal lay to the Superintendent of Natives from all commissioners', sub-commissioners' and chiefs' decisions. The President had a general power to review decisions and might also fine a tribe. (Law 4 of 1885, sections 4, 7 and 10). These powers descended to the Governor and Commissioner of Native Affairs respectively after the annexation of 1900. By Act 29 of 1907, however, they were abolished and appeal thereafter lay to the Supreme Court of the Province.

The history of the evolution of Transvaal African administration is full of interest. In the early days of struggle there was no special Native Affairs Department. The concern of the Republic with African tribes was chiefly its defence against them: naturally enough, one has to look for archives dealing with African policy among the papers of the Commandant-General. Locally, so far as jurisdiction was extended to Africans, the Landdrost (magistrate) was the responsible officer.

The years 1877-81 are of great importance in the history of African administration in the Transvaal. The British Government, on the annexation, created a Department of Native Affairs and staffed it entirely with Natal officers, Mr. Henrique Shepstone, C.M.G., being the first Secretary. This department did much useful spade-work and drew up draft legislation, some of which, improved upon or otherwise altered, was enacted by the restored South African Republic (1884-1900).

On the retrocession (1881), the principle of a separate Department was retained, and shortly afterwards a Superintendent of Native Affairs (later termed Superintendent of Natives) was appointed as its head. By Law 4 of 1885, a definite system was introduced. Some of its most useful features have disappeared, but the idea of separate officers for Africans can be traced to it. Under its provisions, commissioners were to be appointed over Africans in districts where the Volksraad considered such a step necessary, the landdrost serving in other districts. Ordinance 3 of 1902 modified this provision, not altogether happily, into the immediate pre-Union administrative system.

Although this book limits its scope to the years 1830-1910, it would have been useful to consider the alterations brought about since Union. But the changes made as the 'homelands' are being developed are so far-reaching and at the same time so incomplete that any summary of post-Union administration could be positively misleading. In all fairness it must be said that the promotion of Africans to magisterial office, though still exceptional, has opened up opportunities never known before.

In so far as it may be desirable, or inevitable, to have separate administrative arrangements for Africans, it is desirable to have men specially trained for this work, though indeed it is qualities of personality which count most. The vital thing to every African, and indeed to every human, is to be treated as a *person*, not as a case or a statistic. It is remarkable that right up to 1910 no university course existed in any part of the subsequent Union dealing with African studies.

However much it may be necessary for men working mainly among the Africans to possess qualifications such as these, it remains true that any African in day-to-day life is bound to be attended to by railway ticket-sellers, conductors and porters, drivers of Railway buses, and a host of lesser officials who cannot in practice be expected to be specially trained in African studies. Though we should be keen supporters of separate development, we should be bound to admit that there are vast areas of common life, and though we should be convinced liberal integrationists we should have to face the reality of such things as *lobolo* cases between Africans unable to speak the official languages.

Unfortunately the contacts of the average African with junior clerks, ticket-collectors and the like are much more frequent than those with magistrates or other high officials. The magistrate will be courteous in the vast majority of cases, but it is the discourteous minor official with whom the African has most to do. There is the further point that a poorly-educated white man, especially if he is dealing with a highly educated man of colour, tends to feel an inferiority complex which he often counters with aggressiveness and the stressing of the one asset which cannot be taken away from him – his white skin. Immeasurable harm is done to the human personality and to racial harmony by this sort of thing. It is a product of the colour bar, and while this remains, it can be countered only by better education in primary schools, homes and churches, not by specialist university courses in African studies.

A word should be added about the administration of urban locations or villages. This began to receive general and systematic attention only in 1923 with the passing of the first Natives (Urban Areas) Act, and has since become a matter of almost infinite complexity, in which municipalities are closely – too closely – supervised by the Department of Bantu Administration and Development. But before 1910 African urbanisation was a small, irregular and inadequately supervised development. If a good manager was appointed (and some were) it was a happy chance: there was no system and poor appointments were all too common.[8]

NOTES TO CHAPTER XI

1 See Report of the S.A. Native Affairs Commission 1903-5, paras. 420-422.
2 See views of Col. C. D. Griffith, Governor's Agent, in Cape Native Blue Book 1875, pp. 2-3.
3 Detailed notes have not been given here, but the reader is referred to the notes under the Territorial heads in the earlier chapters.
4 See Chapter XII.
5 See Chapter VI.
6 Frequently, but indefensibly from a linguistic point of view, referred to as 'Sub-Native Commissioners'.
7 Law 4 of 1885 (S.A. Republic), sec. 4. Appointments, as contemplated by the Law, were only made for the first time some years after. Chiefs had exercised temporary jurisdiction in the interval under section 1 of the Law.
8 Dr. H. J. van Aswegen's 'Die Verstedeliking van die Nie-Blanke in die Oranje Vrystaat 1854-1902' (in S.A. Historical Journal of November, 1970) could be read with advantage.

CHAPTER XII

Land Distribution and Land Tenure

With a few exceptions the different areas of South Africa between 1830 and 1910 practised what was called loosely, and somewhat offensively, 'segregation'. This was not complete residential separation, since white South Africans not only permitted but encouraged Africans to come out of the areas allocated to them to work in white homes, shops and industries. It is what has sometimes been called 'possessory segregation', that is, separation based on the ownership or lawful occupation of land.

The exceptions were, during the whole period, the Cape Colony west of the Great Fish River, and for varying lengths within the period, Natal and the Transvaal. In Natal from 1845 to 1910, and in the Transvaal from 1905 to 1910, Africans were permitted to buy land outside the reserves set aside for them. Most purchases of this kind took place between 1890 and 1910.

It never seems to have crossed the minds of white South Africans that there was any arrogance in assuming that all the land belonged to the whites except for those areas legally set aside for the blacks. But, considering the land hunger of the Voortrekkers and other early settlers, the putting of Africans into rural 'Reserves' was arguably the best way of preventing the erosion of all African land rights and the turning of all Africans into 'squatters' on white land. This was the sad experience of the Griquas in Griqualand East.

The principle having been accepted of marking out special Reserves for the Africans, the question arose of whether these were to be scattered small areas or large consolidated territories. Both in the Ciskei and in Natal the former system was preferred – in Natal against the wishes both of the Voortrekkers and of Theophilus Shepstone.[1] While undoubtedly one motive for this separation of the Africans into scattered small reserves was to prevent military combination, a strong motive was to facilitate the supply of labour to neighbouring European settlers. As Earl Grey wrote as early as 1849,[2] 'Permanent locations should be established within the Colony, and in selecting the sites of these locations, sufficient intervals shall be left between each of them for the spread of white settlements, each European immigrant would thus have it in his power to draw supplies of labour from the location in his more immediate proximity.'

This system seemed justifiable at the time – in the case of Natal almost forced upon the Government by the land tangle caused by Voortrekker land grants and the purchases of speculators – but has given many a headache to the Government of the Republic since the policy of self-governing homelands was adopted. For self-government is very difficult, indeed impossible, when it has to apply to a territory made up of twenty or thirty small areas separated by European-owned land. The Government of the Republic has sought to remedy the situation by expropriating land bought in freehold by Africans, which they have been pleased to call 'black spots', and moving the inhabitants, much against their will, to patches of land which adjoin reserves or may be used to link up reserves with one another.

Perhaps it was practical necessity rather than a deliberate change of theory that led to the building up of larger and more consolidated areas elsewhere. When Lesotho was annexed to the Cape in 1871, there was no question of permitting white farmers to own land within its boundaries, nor has that been permitted since. In the case of the gradual annexation of the lands east of the Kei River, the greater part of the Transkei was left to the Africans themselves. Except in the districts of Maclear, Mount Currie and Matatiele, a little segment round Port John's, and the recognised urban areas, European ownership of land was not permitted. It is thus very much easier in present-day conditions to make an autonomous 'homeland' out of the Transkei than out of Natal or Zululand.

Both the limitation of African possession to the Reserves and the general absence of freehold property in them have offered powerful obstacles to the development of agriculture by Africans, and the limited right to buy in freehold outside the reserves is today actively discouraged by the South African government.[3] Thus are raised two questions – the policy of 'segregation' and the influence of different forms of land tenure on African life.

Dealing first with 'segregation', it may be said that the will-o'-the-wisp of complete separation has been and still is what a leading Frenchman in 1870 described as 'une agonie dans l'impossible'. The economic facts were against it in the pre-industrial era of South African history and are still against it in the present-day industrial era. Theoretically the complete division of all South Africa into white and black areas might solve South Africa's problems. But this is only practicable if white South Africans are willing to accept the immense sacrifice of moving out of rich farming areas and prosperous towns and cities, if they are willing to do without black labour, and if the black states formed are to be economically viable. In the face of these practically impossible provisos, the theory of segregation, separation, apartheid, call it what you will, is a thick mist of unreality, preventing clear and honest thinking and evading the real choices in the South African situation.

So much must in all fairness be said, but the object of this book is to record historical facts, not to discuss political theories, and so, except for some references in the concluding chapter, we must leave this explosively controversial subject and pass on to the more humdrum but not unimportant question of land tenure.

Freehold ownership of land by Africans is all but unknown within the reserves. In a diminishing number of cases land *outside* the reserves is so held. It is not an unfair criticism to say that governmental policy today is against the extension of freehold and indeed favours the reduction even of the limited number of cases where it exists.

Within the reserves, there are but two forms of tenure, tribal communal ownership and the quit-rent system. Although these differ in many respects there is one point that they have in common – the restriction of the average tribesman's land to a small area – often not more than five morgen (approximately ten acres), plus a share in communal grazing rights. Save under exceptionally favourable conditions of well-irrigated land, no man can make a living on this small area. Tribal Africans before 1910, and even today, are not normally good agriculturists, their traditional interests being hunting and pastoral pursuits, and the cultivation of the ground having been largely the work of women. But there are Africans who, in increasing numbers, have shown an aptitude for and an interest in farming, and these are discouraged by the limitation imposed by the 'one-man-one-lot' tenures in the reserves and the difficulties placed in the way of freehold ownership outside them.

If we are to go into the question of land tenure in any detail we should first examine what African customary law has to say on the subject.

As usual in a primitive legal system, the conceptions of jurisdiction and ownership (*dominium*) were confused. The tribe – or the chief: an African would not draw the distinction between the two that we do – was sovereign over the land which it occupied, therefore it (he) owned the land. The individual in African customary law never held on any other tenure than occupation at the tribe's (chief's) pleasure: African customary law would never have recognised any sale of land by an individual, for an individual had nothing to sell but his right of occupation, the change of which involved the chief's consent.

Undoubtedly the chief's ownership, if we may apply our legal terms to a different society, was in essence a trust. He could not give away his people's land except as a tribal act, after taking counsel with his counsellors. He would not, for example, settle at his own will members of other tribes on the tribal land. The land was owned by a trust of which the chief-in-council was sole member. If you like, it was 'mandated territory'. All the legal incidents of a trust, as we understand them, were implicitly present. The individual tribesman had only the right to occupy a piece of land, and this right was neither transferable nor heritable, save at the chief's good pleasure.

This is virtually the present form of tenure, allowing for Government supervision over the chief, in all locations in the Orange Free State, Transvaal and Natal; and in the 'unsurveyed' reserves of the Transkeian Territories. As an illustration of the detailed working of it, we may quote from Natal Government Notice No. 49 of 18th January 1902.

'It shall be the duty of the chief of each location, subject to the approval of the magistrate, where a doubt or dispute exists, to allot within his recognised district to each inhabitant of such district under him whose name appears on the hut tax register, arable land sufficient for the requirements of the household of such inhabitant, if available, and any person who shall cultivate land not so allotted to him, or who shall enlarge the area or limits of his allotment, or who shall occupy, trespass upon or use land beyond the appointed boundary of his allotment without the approval of the magistrate first had and obtained, shall be deemed to have committed a breach of these regulations. Provided that it shall be lawful for any person, with the consent of his chief, to allow any relative or friend to cultivate his allotment. If any land shall be the subject of tribal dispute, the allotment shall be made by the magistrate or be by him referred to the Secretary of the Natal Native Trust, with his recommendations, for decision, and the decision of the Secretary to the Natal Native Trust shall be final.

'All lands which, at the time of the passing of these regulations, shall have been brought under cultivation shall be deemed to have been allotted to the person cultivating the same, unless proof to the contrary be adduced, and any person enlarging the limits of such allotment without the permission of the chief first had and obtained shall be deemed to have committed a breach of these regulations. The permission of the chief may be reviewed and set aside or varied by the magistrate of the division.

'In the event of any person removing from a location the land allotted to him for cultivation shall be at the disposal of the chief of the location who may allot the same, with the approval of the magistrate of the division first had and obtained, to some other person of his tribe. Provided that any person who shall remove from the division for the purpose of seeking service shall have the option of leaving his allotment in charge of some relative or friend.'

The growth of the reserve system has already been referred to. It is sufficient to say here that that system was forced upon the various governments of South Africa by the exigencies of the case. It was not so much the best system as, at the time, the only possible system. Moreover we have it with us today as the hugest vested interest in South Africa, possessing strong prescriptive rights. It would be madness to attempt to abolish it, however much reform may be desirable in details.

The reserve system in practical working is, except in areas where quit-rent has been introduced, simply the tenure familiar to African customary law. The tribe actually owns the land, and individuals occupy, as before. But in legal theory, grave difficulties present themselves. By a fiction of English law, very improperly grafted on to our Romanised system, all land in a newly-occupied territory has been held to vest in the Crown (in the Republican era, the State), not only from the point of sovereignty, which remains perpetually, but also from the point of view of unfettered and complete *dominium* (ownership) of which however the State may divest itself by sale, grant, or otherwise. Now this ownership of the State is not on all fours with the ownership of the chief in primitive African customary law. It is not, legally speaking, an ownership in trust; but an ownership entirely free of conditions, entirely unfettered by the conception of trusteeship or mandate.

How then, apart from public opinion, is the tribal African to be protected as regards his rights to occupy land? The State may be restrained by statute from alienating land.[4] This means that a discretionary power not on all fours with Parliament's theoretical right to confiscate private immovable property, vests in Parliament. What seems, legally, the more satisfactory method is that the State should alienate the lands to itself, an official or a board of officials *in trust*. This is the 'trust system' as understood in Natal and Zululand.

The Natal Native Commission of 1846-7 recommended that as the only means of giving the Africans legal right to any locations appropriated for their use, such locations should be vested in the hands of trustees, the Government reserving to itself the right to convert these lands, or portions of them, into freehold grants for Africans whose improved condition of life rendered such action desirable.

The original intention of the Native Affairs Department[5] was that legal titles should be issued to each tribe, and where a tribe was divided, to each section of a tribe, that the titles should be vested in trustees, one of whom should be the chief of the tribe, and that the trustees should have power to divide the lands into similar smaller tracts and apportion them among different sections of the tribe, and where practicable or expedient, into family holdings and unfettered titles. When any part of these location lands was alienated to families, a purchase price was to be paid at the rate of 2/- per acre, by yearly instalments extending over six years.

When the Natal Native Trust was actually constituted (under Letters Patent of 27th April 1864) most of these principles disappeared. Nothing was said, and nothing was subsequently done, with regard to alienation of the location lands to families or individuals; a general title was issued to all the location and mission lands (respectively 2 262 066 and 144 192 acres) to the Executive Council of the Colony of Natal in trust. But such trust embraced *all* the Africans concerned, that is, there was no separate trust for each tribe. Under the earlier system, the Trust could not have moved tribes, under the existing system it can. Admitting the conception of the Governor-in-Council as supreme chief, this does not seem to be an unreasonable application of African customary law – (of course the Trust system purports to be merely a legalising of African agrarian law). Naturally with the generalising of the Trust, the inclusion of chiefs as trustees had to be dropped.

It must be stated that, to the legal members of the Executive Council at any rate, the functions of the Natal Native Trust were fully recognised as separable from those of the Executive Council notwithstanding the fusion of personnel. Harry Escombe, Attorney-General of Natal, writes in a memorandum dated 5th April 1895:[6]

'The duties of the Natal Native Trust are separate and distinct from the duties of the Executive.

'The members of the Natal Native Trust (although they are also members of the Executive) are, as regards the location lands, nothing more or less than trustees with powers and under obligations wholly distinct from the powers and obligations of an Executive Council.'

The Natal Native Commission of 1906-7 reported adversely[7] on the work of the Trust during the forty-three years of its existence, pointing out that beyond some tree-planting, fencing, and the construction of a few water-courses and roads, no attempt had been made to improve the vast estate controlled by the Trust in order to make it more habitable or carry a larger population, and recommended a change of trustees, which was not effected. In the face of this recommendation, indeed, the whole vast area of Zululand was vested on the 6th April 1909 in the Zululand Trust – also the Executive Council of Natal.

A small 'Putili' Trust was constituted by indenture dated 18th September 1878, but transferred, as a separate trust, to the Trustees of the Natal Native Trust on 28th February 1908.

One exceptional trust still exists, which was created by indenture, dated 27th May 1858 – some six years before the Natal Native Trust came into existence. It exhibits the type of trust which was originally favoured by the Natal Government. The Umnini Trust consists of three trustees – the Chief Native Commissioner, the chief of the Amatuli tribe (the tribe occupying the Umnini location) and a non-official member.[8]

By Act 1 of 1912 the Governor-General was authorised to delegate to the Minister of Native Affairs the administration of all such matters as were administered by any legally constituted Native Trust. The delegation was made by Government Notice No. 1601 of 25th November 1912. As far as administration is concerned, therefore, there is no difference today between the locations owned by the State President-in-Council in trust and those owned by the State directly.

In view of the difficulties presented by the lacunae in the Roman-Dutch, as compared with the English, law of trusts, it would be presumptuous for anyone not being a skilled lawyer to endeavour to summarise the full legal powers and duties of the Government as trustees. So far as a layman may express an opinion, the Africans living in Trust locations are, in law, no better and no worse off as regards security of tenure than Africans living in State locations.

More than one attempt has been made to introduce the trust system in the Cape Province. It was definitely intended that the ownership of the locations laid out in the Victoria East, Fort Beaufort and Queenstown districts should be vested in Boards of Trustees containing 'the missionary' and the civil commissioner of each district,[9] but nothing ultimately came of this. The principle of trusts was also recommended by the Cape Native Laws and Customs Commission of 1883[10], again, however, without effect.

In the South African Republic it was at first held that Africans could not acquire the ownership of land. The legal position about the locations was not quite clear. They would not vest in the State President and they could hardly be said to be *res nullius*, though constantly treated as if they were such. One of the conditions of the retrocession of the Transvaal in 1881 was the appointment of a location commission, consisting of the State President (or deputy), the British Resident (or deputy) and a third person nominated by mutual consent.[11] This commission was responsible for laying out locations, the boundaries of which could not be altered without its consent, but ownership of the locations did not vest in the commission, in trust or otherwise. The Location Commission, however, laid down one important principle before it became defunct, viz., that only if all the people of a tribe or community agreed to sale could communal land be sold[12] – in other words, the commissioners virtually took up the position, in this regard, of trustees. However, the legal position as regards ownership remained in a certain ambiguity, until the annexation of 1900, since when the unfettered ownership of locations has been deemed to be vested in the State.

In view of the law prevailing in the Republic that Africans could not acquire landed property, the Pretoria Convention of 1881 contained another provision[13] to the effect that Africans who wished to buy land could do so, on condition that transfer was passed to the Location Commission in trust. When this body became defunct the *nuda proprietas* of such land vested in the Superintendent of Natives, whose legal successor today is the Minister of Native Affairs. Although by a Supreme Court decision of 1905[14] Africans were allowed to receive transfer direct and own their land personally this applied in practice only to new transfers, and, the Natives' Land Act of 1913 restricting these, the ownership of the bulk of African-occupied land in the Transvaal today, outside Government locations, vests in the Minister of Native Affairs in trust. It should be noticed that this is quite different from the Natal system. The normal case of trust in the Transvaal is that of a more or less detribalised African or group of Africans who, in Natal, had always been able (subject now to the provisions of the Natives Land Act, 1913) to get full ownership. The trust system in Natal applies only to tribal Africans, who, in the Transvaal, generally live in locations which are direct State property. Nevertheless there are cases[15] of private land bought by tribes and vested in the Minister of Native Affairs in trust.

It will be interesting to follow, in course of time, the exact working out of the legal aspect of African land tenure in South-West Africa. Under the Mandate, it is submitted that unalienated lands, at any rate unalienated lands occupied by Africans when the Mandate was issued, cannot be said to be the absolute property of the State President-in-Council but only to vest in the State President-in-Council in trust. There appears to be a tendency in the territory to disregard this point.

In the Cape Province the history of land tenure in locations is the history of the gradual introduction of quit-rent holdings. The first experiment in this direction dates from the famous Smith-Calderwood location scheme of 1849,[16] when the Mfengu in the Victoria East district were all granted individual title to their plots on the payment of £1 per annum quit-rent. From the very beginning, the scheme worked satisfactorily. The quit-rents were paid promptly and so successful was the whole arrangement that Sir Harry Smith proposed[17] to introduce it in Natal – a proposal which fell through. Similar tenure was gradually introduced among mission communities in neighbouring districts.[18] The report of Mr. Calderwood on the Mfengu locations dated 22nd January 1855 shows that, though his system had not been worked out as fully as he would have wished, it had proved up to that date a distinct success. By 1865 over 5 000 titles had been issued.

The Native Locations Act (No. 40 of 1879) introduced this as a permissive tenure generally (i.e. not limited to any particular African tribe or district). This Act is of great interest in comparison with the Glen Grey Act, and a summary of the differences is contained in an appendix to this chapter. Wherever possible, new title deeds for many years have been issued with the Glen Grey conditions or slight variants thereof, but there are still many instances in the Cape Province of land held under the original conditions of Act 40 of 1879.

The Native Laws and Customs Commission of 1883 recommended that where the majority of occupiers under tribal tenure in any area, or any section of any area, requested the issue of individual title, their request should be acceded to.[19] In the same year, the Port Elizabeth Native Strangers Location Bill gave the first instance of the adoption of quit-rent for a large municipal location.

Everything was tending towards the adoption of that far-reaching measure, the Glen Grey Act of 1894. The name of Cecil Rhodes is familiarly associated with this Act, but we must also recognise the great part played by the permanent public service in the evolution of the policy. All the more important provisions of the Glen Grey Act were foreshadowed in a memorandum of that distinguished administrator, Captain Matthew Blyth, chief magistrate of the Transkei, dated 13th January 1882:[20]

'I have strongly urged the Government to grant individual titles to those Fingoes who may desire to have them, fixing a certain standard, such as building a proper house, planting trees, enclosing, say from ten to twenty acres of land, and when these are fulfilled, then the title to be issued. Were this plan adopted an immense stimulus would be given to the people, and in a short time the whole face of the country would be covered with wheat, homesteads, with trees, etc.

'I trust and hope that shortly the Fingoes will agree to pay a voluntary contribution of, say, 5/- per man as a local tax for local wants, etc., and to be expended by themselves under the guidance and direction of the magistrate. In fact *that a sort of municipal council be formed in each district*.[21] This would be a step in the right direction, and be the beginning of local self-government in its simplest and safest form, which might be afterwards extended as education and civilisation advances.

'Every effort should also be made to induce the headman and people to take an intelligent part in their own government, acting as jurors or assessors, a public discussion of all laws affecting their districts, etc., so that they can feel that they have some voice in public matters. Then, and then only, are Native Affairs on a safe footing.'

Ten years later it was decided by Government to consider the feasibility of introducing such a scheme in the Glen Grey district, as an experiment, with a view to its further extension if successful. A commission was appointed to consider the question consisting of Mr. B. H. Holland, Civil Commissioner of King William's Town, Mr. John Frost, C.M.G., M.L.A., and Mr. W. H. Janse van Rensburg, M.L.A. As a result of its report, dated 27th May 1892, Act 25 of 1894, commonly known as the Glen Grey Act, was passed by the Cape Parliament. In addition to the improved quit-rent tenure (details of which will be analysed later) – which, be it noted, became compulsory within the district – was introduced, first, a council system of local self-government, and second, a labour tax on all Africans who did not go out to work for Europeans. The Bill, so drafted, proved a masterpiece of political strategy. Nine-tenths of the House were in favour of either the labour tax or the quit-rent tenure, though probably those whole-heartedly in favour of both could have been counted on the fingers of one hand, and so the Bill had a comparatively easy passage. In the Glen Grey district itself, the measure was anything but enthusiastically received: notwithstanding this it was in 1895 extended to many districts of the Transkeian Territories and the process of extension continued.

The labour tax nearly killed the whole system in the Transkei. In Idutwya district, the proclamation of the Act was regarded with the greatest apprehension by all the Africans of the district. It was felt by the Africans to be a most harsh oppressive measure, and it was productive of the greatest agitation. The magistrate attributed this opposition chiefly to the labour tax.[22] The same phenomenon, not quite so intensely exhibited, was noticed in the Butterworth district.[23] In the Tsomo district the magistrate was, for a time, apprehensive of open rebellion.[24] Only in Nqamakwe was the change received with tranquillity.[25]

Much of this opposition disappeared as the system became better known. In Tsomo, the very district where disaffection had been deepest, a very few months sufficed to bring about a complete change of front on the part of the more influential Africans.[26] The council system from the first worked admirably. The obnoxious labour clause, the withdrawal of which was recommended by a Select Committee of the House of

Assembly in 1898,[27] soon became a dead letter and was formally repealed for the Territories by Proclamation 6 of 1905, Mr. E. E. Dower, Chief Clerk, Cape Native Affairs Department, and subsequently Under Secretary for Native Affairs, repeatedly gave his opinion before the Inter-Colonial Commission of 1903-5, that the Act had proved most beneficial in practice,[28] and the Commission itself was warm, if discriminating, in its praises of the system.[29]

Let us now proceed to examine the details of the Glen Grey tenure. The first condition of the holding is the payment of perpetual quit-rent; but the transaction is not one of ordinary *emphyteusis*, for in addition to the payment of quit-rent there are certain statutory obligations resting on the occupier. One thing is certain: the occupier does not possess full ownership (*dominium*) in the ordinary acceptation of the term. We are really faced here with a nice legal problem. If the older form of *emphyteusis* were to apply, the ownership would be the State's and the usufruct the African's. In the later form of *emphyteusis* – the *erfpacht* of Roman-Dutch law – the ownership would be the African's, subject to certain perpetual servitudes of which the payment of quit-rent would be the chief. On the whole it seems probable that the Glen Grey tenure is rather the later type of *emphyteusis* than the earlier but there is nothing quite like it elsewhere, and probably it is safe to say that it adds another complex of rights and obligations to legal science.

The amount of quit-rent payable was 15/- per garden allotment (about four, not more than five morgen) plus 3/- for every additional morgen above five; and 5/- per building allotment ($\frac{1}{2}$ morgen on the commonage).

In practice, we can ignore the building allotment which was not widely taken up by the Africans, they preferring to retain their existing homes round which the garden allotments were grouped. What was done in the survey of a district was this. The district was divided up into garden allotments, the survey following the existing lines of occupation, subject to the limits of area prescribed. All the spare land in each location was treated as commonage, on which building allotments could be granted, on the applicants' satisfying the Government that they intended to erect substantial buildings thereon. The course of procedure was clearly laid down and provision for most contingencies made in the Acts and Regulations. The cost of survey in the first instance was payable by the applicant, but could be advanced by the Government. If so advanced, half of the advance was to be paid by the applicant within three months of receiving notice to do so; the title deeds were not issued until this half was paid. The balance was payable by four equal instalments, the ultimate remedy for non-payment being cancellation of title. The survey of allotments had been unduly expensive in the past, and the Survey Commission of 1920 (on which a member of the Native Affairs Commission sat) recommended a simpler and more common-sense mode of survey of African allotments than had previously existed. The Commission considered that only the simplest calculations were necessary for these small allotments and that the African's title deeds should contain a picture of the ground allotted to him.[30] Provision for the recovery of arrear quit-rent was given by the issue of a summary warrant on the occupier's movable property, and, in the last resource, by cancellation of title.

The Glen Grey system was one of *perpetual* quit-rent. The rent may not be compounded in a single sum, though quit-rent of lands held under Act 40 of 1879 may be compounded by the payment of $16\frac{3}{4}$ years' rent down.

We come now to the statutory conditions. In the first place the land may not be alienated without the State President's consent. This is frequently granted as between African and African, but has never yet been granted as between African and European, the policy of the administration being to keep these 'surveyed' districts purely African. Transfer, when consent has been given, does not involve expensive formalities. It is effected by a simple endorsement made on the title deeds by the magistrate of the district, at a fee of 2/6, the magistrate subsequently notifying the Registrar of Deeds.

The land may not be mortgaged. This is undoubtedly one of the finest features of the whole system. So far as legislation can do it, the African allotment holder is absolutely protected against the money lender.[31]

The allotments may not be subdivided except with the State President's approval, nor sub-let. Originally subdivision was impossible in any case, but Proclamation 300 of 1913, originally caused by errors in the allocation of plots in the Butterworth district in 1900, permits it with the State President's approval, provided that no garden allotment is reduced to less than three morgen and no building allotment to less than a half-morgen.[32]

The land may not be devised by will, but passes by intestate succession in a prescribed order contained in the Schedule to Act 25 of 1894, which is designed to reproduce the system of intestate succession in African customary law. By subsequent legislation[33] one important departure from African customary law – the grant of usufructuary rights to the widow – has been authorised.

The principle of 'one man, one lot' is laid down explicitly, and must be observed even in cases of succession. This preserves the rough equality of status which was so marked a feature of primitive tribal customs regarding property, but of course is a very serious stumbling-block to the progressive African farmer.

Precious stones and minerals are reserved to the State. The State may also make roads, railways, dams, etc., across or on allotments and take materials for the same from allotments without compensation, and may establish outspans on allotments.

The title may be forfeited for the following reasons in addition to non-payment of survey expenses or quit-rent, viz., (i) rebellion; (ii) stock-theft punished by imprisonment for a term of not less than a year; (iii) failure to occupy the land beneficially.

Beneficial occupation means the cultivation of, or growing of crops on, an allotment or portion thereof by the registered holder personally, or under his personal supervision or under supervision of a representative appointed by the magistrate, for a period of two years with subsequent extensions in the magistrate's discretion. The magistrate is authorised to grant such permission, at his discretion, when the applicant leaves (i) to seek work or (ii) to carry on any trade or occupation necessitating absence from the location, or (iii) to attend any educational or industrial institution, or (iv) for any reasonable purpose which in the magistrate's opinion, justifies temporary absence from the location. Three months' notice of the intention to cancel title must be given.

The control of the commonage is vested in a location board, though the *dominium* must be held to vest absolutely in the State.

The possession of land under the Glen Grey system was specially ruled out as a qualification for the Parliamentary franchise, which must have been qualified for in some other way. In the circumstances this was virtually a permanent disqualifiction of the majority of tribal Africans in the Territories.

To sum up, then, the kinds of tenure on which Africans hold in locations: Freehold tenure is unknown. The vast bulk of Africans – including those living on State Lands other than locations – hold their land either (i) on a semi-individualistic quit-rent tenure or (ii) on the basis of occupation at pleasure, in a communal system.

A further train of thought is this – that the communal location must not *necessarily* be condemned as against the quit-rent location because the population of the latter is often the more happy, contented and prosperous of the two. It has been exceedingly difficult, somehow, to get South African administrators outside the Cape Province to add to the amenities of life in locations. The Natal Commission of 1846-7, to which the Natal reserve system is due, recommended all kinds of measures for the improvement of the location Africans, but the then Colonial Secretary, Earl Grey, replied, in phrases that have haunted Natal reserve administrators ever since: 'It is my duty at once and distinctly to discountenance the expectation that any plans for the improvement of the Natal District which would involve large expense to be provided for by Parliament can be adopted.'

With the quit-rent system, on the other hand, went from the very beginning[34] the splendidly worked out details of the Smith-Calderwood scheme. Superintendents were appointed for each location. Schoolmasters were employed. Prizes were awarded for cleanliness of person and clothing, for neatness of residence, and for agricultural progress. In sixteen years the inhabitants of these first quit-rent locations had become the most progressive group of Africans in South Africa; but we should make an unwarrantable presumption if we stated, without further evidence, that this was due solely, or even mainly, to the particular form of tenure.

APPENDIX TO CHAPTER XII

Memorandum prepared by Mr. E. E. Dower, Chief Clerk, Native Affairs Department, Cape Colony, dated 20th October 1902, illustrating the difference between Quit-Rent tenure under Act 40 of 1879 and under the Glen Grey Act.
(Annexure I to the Report of the S.A. Native Affairs Commission, 1903-5.)

(1) Allocation of lands

Under Act 40 of 1879
A building as well as a garden lot is surveyed, the remaining extent of land being reserved as commonage. (N.B. – The building lots have generally speaking not been taken up.) There are no exact directions laid down in the law as to how the allocation of lands is to be carried out.

Under Glen Grey Act
A garden allotment only is surveyed in the first instance, the law laying down that the area of such shall be according to the then existing lines of occupation. Survey of a district as a whole is contemplated, the district is divided into locations and after survey of garden allotments in each the remaining extent is set apart as Commonage. The removal of homesteads which are on the Commonage is not contemplated; any registered holder of an allotment may obtain the grant of a building lot upon securing the concurrence of the Location Board and satisfying the Governor that he has erected or intends erecting a substantial building. The course of procedure is clearly laid down and provision made for regulations or directions.

(2) Cost of Survey

Under Act 40 of 1879
No directions.
In practice all approved applicants are required to deposit the full amount of survey expenses and therein lies one of the great difficulties. In every location some residents object to the survey and refuse to pay, causing long delay in the actual commencement of the survey. Then if their names are struck off the list no means are provided for dealing with them. Legal advice is to the effect that their original occupation being lawful such squatters cannot be removed unless registered owners in whom commonage becomes vested approach Supreme Court in order to obtain an Order. Apart from the cost of such proceedings no local body such as is contemplated for controlling commonage in the conditions of title is as a rule established in such communities.

Under Glen Grey Act
Costs are in first instance advanced by Government out of funds voted by Parliament, half to be paid by each applicant, within 3 months of notice so to do, this to be deposited before issue of title deeds, balance to be paid in four equal instalments. Means for dealing with defaulters (1) by legal process of summary warrant or (2) cancellation of approved claim.

Under Act 40 of 1879	Under Glen Grey Act
	(3) Quit-rent
2/6 for building lot. 10/- for garden allotment.	Not exceeding 5/- for building lot. 15/- four morgen garden allotment and 3/- every additional morgen above five.
	(4) Recovery of Quit-rent
No special means provided. Arrears can only be recovered according to ordinary process of law.	1st by summary warrant authorising seizure of movable property. 2nd by forfeiture upon continued default subject to necessary safeguards.
	(5) Transfer of Property
Not allowed without approval of Government, but no special means afforded for facilitating transfer. All deeds of transfer have to be passed through the Deeds Office. (Cost of conveyancing, etc., generally amounts to £5 or £6 at least.) N.B. – In later cases, viz., surveys in Guma, Zibi Zali and Mhlambisa's locations, King William's Town, the conditions of the Glen Grey Act have in this and other respects been incorporated.	Transfer effected by simple endorsement before R.M. (who notifies Registrar) upon payment of a fee of 2/6. Regulations may be framed by the Governor providing for cases in which formal transfer is not applied for.
	(6) Administration of Estate (Land)
Subject to ordinary law. In practice it generally happens that property passes in accordance with the principles of Native Law from father to son and so on, without formal transfer being effected. Hence the difficulty in respect of overlapping transfers and in addition Registrar of Deeds in most cases requires Order of Court to be obtained, cost prohibitive and often greater than value of land.	Landed property cannot be devised by will. Law of primogeniture applies under table of succession based on Native (unwritten) law and custom.
	(7) Control of Commonage
This is vested in a Committee or Municipality elected in such manner as the Governor may determine. No regulations have been provided, and there is no case of any such body being appointed. Power is vested in the Governor to make regulations but no provision is made for imposing any penalty for contravention thereof. In some instances communities have established Village Management Boards but the law relating to such Boards is largely inapplicable to the conditions obtaining in Native Locations. (*Vide* N.B. to (5).)	This is vested in a Location Board and Governor has power to make regulations.

LAND DISTRIBUTION AND LAND TENURE

(8) Forfeiture of land

Under Act 40 of 1879

No measure of forfeiture is provided.

Under Glen Grey Act
The measure of forfeiture is provided under certain conditions for:
1. Rebellion.
2. Stock theft.
3. Non-payment of survey expenses. (*Vide* (2).)
4. Non-payment of quit-rent. (*Vide* (4).)
5. Non-beneficial occupation.

(9) One man, one lot

The principle is not laid down in the law but the restriction in respect of transfer admits of its being carried out as a matter of policy. There are however a number of cases in which the rule has not been observed. Owing also to the general slackness in obtaining transfer there is no saying to what extent deviation from the principle actually takes place.

The principle is definitely laid down in the law and has to be observed even in cases of succession.

(10) Conditions of Title Deeds generally

These have been approved from time to time by Parliament as each survey has taken place. The conditions have gradually been added to so that in the latest surveys they almost coincide with those laid down in the Glen Grey Act. Generally speaking, there is however little uniformity in the conditions applying to various locations.

A form of title-deed is provided.

NOTES TO CHAPTER XII

1. See Instructions to Commissioners for Locations of Natives on Crown Lands, Pietermaritzburg, 31st March 1846, para. 23, and Despatch of Secretary to Government, Natal, to Secretary to Government, Cape, 7th May 1847.
2. Earl Grey to Sir Harry Smith, 30th November 1849.
3. For a very minor exception see Evidence of Sir J. Fraser before the S.A. Native Affairs Commission 1903-5. Vol. IV pp. 272-3. Schedule F to Proclamation R293 of 1962 makes provision for township grants in a Reserve but has been little acted upon.
4. *Vide* Section 147, South Africa Act.
5. Information in this paragraph from memorandum of Sir Michael Gallwey, Attorney-General of Natal, dated 12th April 1889 (Papers N.N.T. 32/1896).
6. From a copy in the Samuelson papers.
7. Report, para. 91, p. 39.
8. Report of Department of Native Affairs, 1913-18, p. 25.

9 Despatch of Sir Geo. Cathcart to the Duke of Newcastle dated 14th March 1854.
10 Report, para. 110, p. 40 and 112, p. 42.
11 Pretoria Convention, Article XXI.
12 Minutes of meeting of Commission, 22nd August 1883 (Archives G. 1234).
13 Article XIII.
14 *Tsewu* v. *Registrar of Deeds*.
15 Especially in the central and western Transvaal.
16 See Government Notice of 9th February 1849.
17 Despatch of Sir Harry Smith to Earl Grey dated 15th March 1849 (in Blue Book, Correspondence relative to State of Kaffir Tribes, 1850, p. 2).
18 Despatch of Sir Geo. Cathcart to the Duke of Newcastle dated 14th March 1854.
19 Report, para. 110 (9), p. 41.
20 Cape Native Blue Book 1882, p. 6.
21 The italics are the author's.
22 Report of W. Brownlee, R. M. Idutywa, Cape Native Blue Book 1896, pp. 88-9.
23 Report of R. W. Stanford, R. M. Butterworth, *ibid.*, p. 91.
24 Report of V. M. Watermeyer, R. M. Tsomo, *ibid.*, p. 95.
25 Report of W. C. Scully, R. M. Nqamakwe, *ibid.*, pp. 93-4.
26 Cape Native Blue Book 1896, p. 95.
27 Report, p. 2.
28 *Vide* Questions 178, 637 and 642, pp. 19 and 64.
29 Report, paras. 159-167, pp. 27-30.
30 Report of Native Affairs Commission 1921, pp. 16-17.
31 Cf. the following extract from a pamphlet: 'Some Notes on Java and its Administration by the Dutch' by Henry Scott Boys 'late Bengal Civil Service,' Allahabad, Pioneer Press, 1892:
'It was the intention (of Great Britain) to confer on the cultivators the full proprietary right in their holdings, involving the terribly doubtful privilege of alienating their fields, and the disastrous liability to be sold up, either by their civil creditors or by the Revenue authorities for default. By the return of the Island to Dutch rule, the Javans [sic] have escaped this fatal gift of absolute proprietary right, which has been the ruin of so many tens of thousands of the peasantry of India, and with which, while striving to bless, we have so effectually cursed the soil of India.
'The loss of all the many benefits which would incidentally have been conferred on Java by the substitution of English for Dutch rule, was not too high a price to have paid for escape from the many evils of unrestrained power to alienate landed property. The Javans are the most prosperous of Oriental peasantry, due mainly to one cause, their inability to raise one florin on the security of their fields, and the protection thus enjoyed against the money-lender and against themselves.'
32 *Vide* Report of Department of Native Affairs, 1913-18, p. 12.
33 Section 1, Act 14 of 1905 (Cape).
34 Despatch to Sir Harry Smith, dated 10th December 1847.

CHAPTER XIII

Agriculture

The major part of this chapter will be devoted to a careful account of the work done by the Cape Colony – the only part of South Africa to do anything very much – between 1830 and 1910 to develop African agriculture. Subsequent to Union, especially in recent years, much more has been done in this direction. There must be few aspects of African life where so much enlightened, unselfish and persevering work has been done by the Government and its servants. The results of this work are not proportionate to the care and labour put into it, and however qualified the agricultural experts are and however much they give themselves to their task, they will never transform farming in the African areas until two great difficulties have been overcome.

The first of these difficulties has been discussed in the previous chapter. It is the very general limitation of African farmers, on the 'one-man-one-plot' system, to approximately five morgen of dry-land farming. Unless greater areas can be allotted within the Reserves to Africans showing an interest in and aptitude for farming, or unless a more sympathetic policy is pursued about the acquisition of freehold land outside the reserves, no African farmer can provide adequately for his family from his agricultural activities. This means that he has to go out and work for wages in white areas, and this in turn means that the little land which he has, is not properly looked after in his absence.

Migrant labour is, indeed, the second difficulty in the way of a successful agricultural policy. In a fairly recent study of the Natal reserves[1] the masculinity rates of the various districts are shown to vary from 60 to 82 per 100 females.[2] The migrant labour system has a deleterious effect on health and is a cause of many social evils including the disruption of family life. It hinders the building up of settled and trained workers in industry and handicaps terribly the well-meaning and sincere efforts to improve African agriculture. It is almost universally condemned, but it goes on year after year and is bound to go on (a) while the African farmer has not enough land to provide adequately for his family out of his agricultural labours; (b) while he is not allowed to bring his wife and family into the industrial areas where he works, and where he is forced to work by sheer necessity. The absence of the majority of African heads of families means that even such land as there is available is neglected, and by a chain reaction the neglected and eroded land thus brought into being drives its occupier more and more into the towns to work.

We may well criticise the Government of the Republic for not facing the vital changes of general policy which alone can make good African agriculture a practical proposition. Today South Africa is increasingly an industrial country. Except for the gold and diamond mines, industry was in its infancy during the period (1830-1910) covered by this study, and so the earnest and laudable efforts of the Cape Colony to reform agriculture in its reserves (which is the main topic of this chapter) cannot be measured in terms of the unreality which hangs round similar efforts today.

The main successes of the early Cape administrators were three. Firstly they introduced the Africans to a wider range of subsistence crops, and thereby improved a diet preponderantly of cereals. Secondly, they introduced sheep farming among people accustomed only to horned cattle and goats. Thirdly, they introduced the plough.

But before Government officials stepped in, pioneer missionaries had already brought the plough to those among whom they laboured. In the Cape it was the *doyen* of Methodist missionary work in South Africa, the Rev. William Shaw, who was responsible for this.[3] In the Northern Transvaal the credit is due to the Rev. Ernest Creux and other missionaries of the Mission Suisse Romande.[4]

The drum-and-trumpet historian with his pen dipped deep in the crimson ink of wars and battles, with his 'purple patches' and his eloquent perorations, may perhaps scorn this little epic of progress – for it is an epic – among peasant cultivators in remote corners of Africa. It would not be difficult to write a picturesque history of the peoples of Southern Africa. Dingiswayo and Shaka, Mzilikazi and Moshoeshoe (Moshesh), Cetshwayo and Lobengula are not unworthy figures round which to build a history which would read like a romance. But the introduction of the plough into African life and farming is perhaps of more enduring importance, especially as it has spread to every tribe in South Africa.

It made slow progress at the beginning. After twenty years the progressive Mfengu had only sixty-six ploughs.[5] But with the burst of activity in African administration which marked the third quarter of the nineteenth century, matters moved apace. In 1874 Mr. J. Rose-Innes, Civil Commissioner of King William's Town, reported that in his district the number of ploughs represented one plough to every seventh man.[6] In the Idutywa district of the Territories 'every man that could afford it had a plough.'[7] Chief Kreli set the fine example of purchasing three.[8] At the same time magistrates in Natal were commenting on the great increase of ploughs in their districts.[9] In the Ixopo and Ipolela districts – not extraordinarily progressive areas – there were as many as 1 500 ploughs in the hands of Africans as early as 1878 and the hoe was beginning to be looked on by the Africans themselves as old-fashioned and out of date.[10] About the same time ploughs were introduced among the Shangaans of the Transvaal. A sum of £15 was paid for the first plough.[11]

At first the Africans simply scratched the land. But as early as 1893 Sir Henry Elliott considered that he could see an improvement, 'As good ploughing is now to be seen in many Native gardens as will be met with on a Colonial farm.'[12]

What was much more important than even the agricultural development was the change which the plough wrought in the status and general position of African women. Formerly all cultivation was done by the hoe. It was 'woman's work'. The more wives an African possessed the more land he could cultivate. His labour and implement expenses were practically nil. With the introduction of the plough the man had to set to work himself.[13] Compared with her former position the woman was virtually emancipated.[14] Few girls were willing to consent to marriage with a man who did not possess a plough[15].

Undoubtedly the plough has meant a blow to polygamy. Despite the absence of detailed statistics, it is certain that the increased use of the plough and the decrease of polygamy have proceeded simultaneously. They are clearly cause and effect. Additional wives were no longer needed for labour purposes: ploughs cost money and wives cattle. If additional wives were non-productive from the labour aspect, it is easy to see that monogamy would tend to win the day, even apart from the fact that the use of the plough began among Christian Africans.

Let us now turn to the introduction of new crops, and it may be best to begin by considering the condition of African farmers when they first came into contact with white farming. Their normal condition was that of herdsmen and small cultivators. Their chief wealth consisted of horned cattle and goats, though poultry were not unknown.[16] As regards crops, various varieties of millet ('kaffir-corn') with a few vegetables such as those later known as 'kaffir pumpkins' and 'kaffir beans' formed the whole range of their agricultural activities.[17]

At a very early stage, and before the people concerned came directly under European rule, maize was introduced from European – probably Portuguese – sources; and similarly mention of the horse begins to be made in African tradition under circumstances which lead us to believe that its introduction cannot be much earlier than the beginning of the nineteenth century. Zulu folklore shows it to have been unknown north of the Mzimvubu River a few years before the emergence of Shaka from obscurity.[18] It will be realised, however, that neither of these changes wrought any very violent revolution in African life. Maize and millet are in the same economic category; and the introduction of the horse at first tended to retard development instead of encouraging it, making the African more mobile and less inclined to settle down to agriculture proper than before. The tendency of European administrators has been to encourage the acquisition of less mobile stock, such as sheep, and the growth of crops affording a wider dietetic range than maize or millet and involving production for exchange, as well as for subsistence. Undoubtedly this policy has been sociologically sound, as merely accelerating natural development from pastoral-agricultural to more purely agricultural conditions.

This process began as early as 1825, when, under the paternal guidance of a government official, the Africans of Western Kaffraria were beginning to grow potatoes and green vegetables[19]. Under Sir Harry Smith and his successors this civilising process was accelerated. Sir George Cathcart appears to have been responsible for a successful endeavour to acquaint the tribes under Ngqika with the use of the spade and other implements.[20] Agricultural shows were instituted under the directions of the magistrate among the Mfengu and other tribes. The Government at Cape Town, apparently intoxicated by the loyal associations of the date, actually donated £25 for a show held in the Territories on the Queen's Birthday (May 24th) 1873.[21] Tree-planting was also encouraged and the Government offered prizes therefor in the Territories and also in Lesotho[22] – a practice which has unfortunately fallen into desuetude.

If the Government of the Cape Colony was somewhat niggardly in the matter of African agriculture, it was at least better than the remaining South African administrations which did nothing at all. This is particularly disappointing in Natal. It is significant that at the very time when the Cape Government was encouraging afforestation in Lesotho, the Natal Government was being appealed to in vain to encourage afforestation in Natal – in spite of the denudation of parts of the country by Africans who stripped the land and never replanted. After forty years of European rule in Natal it was possible to say, 'No attempt has been made to introduce any better mode of cultivating the soil, and if any among them have been led out of the beaten track it has been owing to the encouraging and directing efforts of private example.'[23] This appeal fell on deaf ears. In 1907 the commission appointed after the 'Rebellion' again emphasised the advisability of governmental training of the African population in agriculture, by means of demonstrations and the offering of prizes[24]. This was characterised as one of the definite objectives which should stamp the future policy of the Government[25]. Nothing was done before Union, although much has been done since.

In the last years before Union most encouraging departures had been made in the Cape. Since the grant of local autonomy which began with the Glen Grey Act of 1894, the Africans in the Transkeian Territories have – undoubtedly at magisterial instigation – done for themselves what no European administration has ever done for them. In each of the eighteen districts of the Territories was stationed an African demonstrator who was supplied with a plough, a harrow, a one-row planter and a cultivator, and who demonstrated to the people on their own plots how to grow maize according to up-to-date methods. These demonstrators were trained at the two agricultural schools at Tsolo and Teko (near Butterworth) both of which have had their accommodation taxed to the uttermost. These demonstrators undoubtedly exercised a great influence for good. Africans became convinced that their old methods were unprofitable and began to plant, harrow and cultivate their crops in the manner demonstrated to them. Farm demonstration work on a larger scale was urged by one of the most influential African leaders.[26]

The award of prizes by the Government, and the holding of agricultural shows are features of policy which have had a long and successful history in the reserves. The first instance of the award of prizes is to be found in the Smith-Calderwood location scheme of 1849. Prizes of £1, 10/- and 5/- were awarded for the best and largest quantity of cultivated ground, of 15/-, 10/- and 5/- for the best fencing, of £1, 10/- and 5/- for the best and largest quantity of wheat, barley and other 'European' produce, of £1 and 5/- for the best stock of poultry.[27] Presents of spades and hoes were first suggested by Colonel Hare, Acting Lieutenant-Governor, Eastern Districts, in a despatch dated Grahamstown, 10th October 1838; recommended (with the addition of ploughs) by Sir George Napier in a despatch dated Cape Town, 18th October 1838, and authorised by Lord Glenelg on the 24th January 1839. Little was done however until, as already mentioned, Sir George Cathcart introduced the spade amongst the people of Ngqika in 1853.[28]

The educative process was continued by Sir George Grey who presented a plough to Sandile, at the chief's own request, early in 1855.[29] The show movement which originated under Captain Blyth in 1873 was a success from the beginning. At the Mfengu show of 1875 Kreli himself was present and acted as a judge in the horse section. Over £66 was distributed in prizes.[30] In the following year a new departure was made by the creation of an Agricultural Society in Emigrant Tembuland (23rd December 1876). At its first meeting, 'certificates of improvements made' handed in to the Government Agent, Mr. C. J. Levey, showed that *inter alia* thirty-three members had, during the previous year, planted 6 495 trees. The encouragement of afforestation was extended to Lesotho, where prizes of £3 in each district and £6 for Lesotho as a whole were offered for the greatest number of trees planted during the year (1878). Mr. Levey's work continued so prosperously that in 1884 the people of the Cala district erected, at their own expense and without financial aid from the Government, a substantial hall costing about £400, to be used for agricultural society and other meetings.[31] Gradually the Agricultural Society movement has spread all over the Transkei. Its most striking feature has been its spontaneity. To take one example only, the Butterworth Native Agricultural Society formed in 1906 was, by the magistrate's own admission, the conception of the Africans and solely of the Africans.

The most encouraging developments in the years just before Union were the appointment of African demonstrators, already referred to, and the inauguration of the experimental farm of the Glen Grey (Native) District Council, founded in 1904 and finally approved in 1909[32].

Unfortunately this remarkable progress in the Transkeian Territories stood alone. Nothing like it was known in the Orange Free State, Transvaal or Natal.

The new crops which were introduced to the Africans with some measure of success included wheat, barley, oats, fruit and vegetables. Beginning with the Mfengu of the Victoria East and Peddie districts about 1865,[33] the cultivation of wheat soon spread throughout the Transkeian Territories,[34] a notable feature being the good example set by Chief Matuzana in St. Mark's district, who planted in 1885, as a pattern to his tribe, a fine field of twenty acres of wheat.[35] Ten years later in the Xalanga district – admittedly a progressive one – 4 000 bags of wheat were threshed by machinery.[36] The magistrate, Mr. C. J. Levey, says:[37] 'The prize wheat at last show was pronounced by competent judges to have been equal to the best grown in the Colony.' In Namaqualand, the Rhenish missionaries at Steinkopf, Richtersfeld and Kalkfontein had about the same time introduced the culture of wheat, oats and rye.[38] The oat crop first became large enough to be noticeable in 1875.[39] By 1903 it had become one of the most important exchange products of the Territories.[40] Orchards, now common in the Transkeian Territories, were first noticed in the year 1896[41] by that indefatigable observer, Mr. C. J. Levey, though he adds – what he could not say today – 'At the present time I don't know a Native in the district that can prune or graft a tree.'

Many attempts have been made to introduce other crops, suitable rather for exchange than for subsistence; but hitherto without any but the most limited success. The Cape Government in 1886 made a definite attempt to introduce the culture of tobacco, cotton and silk in the Territories. Every Transkeian magistrate was asked for his opinion as to the prospects of these crops. Their replies were unanimously in favour of tobacco, and unanimously against silk; as to cotton, opinion was divided.[42] By the generosity of Mr. Samuel Cawood,[43] experiments were carried out with some success in cotton-planting in the Albany division and in the districts of Mqanduli and Willowvale in the Transkeian Territories.[44] Unfortunately the first season was a bad one, and with the failure of the Government to respond to the Transkeian Chief Magistrate's suggestion of accepting the hut tax in cotton,[45] the experiment ignominiously fizzled out. A private trader by the name of Beattie introduced, about the same time, the silkworm in the Elliotdale district, where both kinds of mulberry grow luxuriantly, but with no permanent success.[46] Tobacco met with better luck. In 1886 and 1887 it was introduced widely, and fortunately many of the people were persuaded to grow it on enclosed ground,[47] thus avoiding the usual experience of progressive Africans – the destruction of any crops, which come above ground before the maize and millet crops, by their neighbours' unherded stock. Unfortunately, the Government had no marketing or rural economy service at that date and did little or nothing to assist Africans in the sphere of marketing. The crops were raised, but there was no remunerative market provided. The tobacco was bought by neighbouring traders at a low price, and even that low price had to be taken out in goods.[48] In these circumstances it is not surprising that, though tobacco-planting still continues in the Territories, it has at no time reached the dimensions of an industry.

Among the less successful agricultural experiments were indigo cultivation,[49] the collection of gum[50] and coffee-planting.[51]

On the eastern coast, sugar-planting began a modest existence. The Natal Africans have done their part correctly,[52] and are beginning to be integrated into the industry. Further north, in Portuguese East Africa, the cane is cultivated by Africans on a large scale. A few years ago one African, Ben Vumsen, had over two hundred men working for him in the season[53]. Where the mills are distant, or closed to the Africans, there is, however, a grave practical danger that their industry will be led into wrong channels. Instead of sugar, a delightful and insidious drink – *isishimiyana* – a kind of rum – is prepared and drunk with avidity.

It will be realised that, disappointments notwithstanding, real progress was made in African agriculture proper under European government. As regards stock, this has become much more noticeable. Unfortunately the attention of the Government has been directed mainly to sheep, instead of to the probably more generally suitable lines – poultry and pigs. Nevertheless the introduction of the sheep has resulted in a very marked difference in African life both in the Transkeian Territories and in Lesotho – a difference which is on the whole to the good.

As a result of inquiries made into missionary institutions in the Cape Colony in 1849, it was found that thirty-two mission stations, inhabited by 12 983 Africans, possessed 2 874 sheep. This probably represents more or less the total of African owned sheep in the Cape Colony at that date; for Government had done nothing, and the missions were obviously the centre of change from the old methods.

In 1879 the sheep possessed by the Mfengu alone were revealed by the census of that year as 211 174.[54] In 1888 the wool production of the Territories was estimated at 2 300 000 lbs.[55] In Lesotho the number of sheep rose to such an extent that complaints were made of the destruction of pasture by them, and large barren tracts of land are being created today owing to the excessive size of the flocks which have to be fed.

Our administrators were not slow to see the advantage of sheep-farming as against the exclusive production of horned cattle and goats. In a memorandum prepared for the High Commissioner, dated 3rd December 1864, Mr. Charles Brownlee points out that the sheep enables the African, by its wool, to pay his taxes without selling any of his livestock – a proceeding to which he is very averse. Moreover, by reason of the difficulty of conveying sheep rapidly from one part of the country to another, the possession of them by Africans formed one of the best guarantees of peace. As Government did not move in the matter, most of the progressive Africans among the people of Ngqika became flock-masters at Mr. Brownlee's personal risk.

A distinct impetus to sheep-farming in the Transkei was given by the movement of the Mfengu from Victoria East and Peddie into the Territories. The Mfengu are certainly one of the most progressive elements among the Africans. They have a shrewd eye for a bargain, and it is significant, therefore, to find them, in 1870, selling their cattle to buy sheep. Several Mfengu had at that date flocks of one to two thousand; and the value of their annual wool production was estimated by Captain Matthew Blyth, the Government Agent among them, at £60 000.[56] From them the practice spread rapidly to the Tambookies[57] and even to the Pondos.[58] Imported pedigree rams were purchased, privately, and the breeding of the African sheep much improved.[59] In Bomvanaland, at that date alleged to be the most backward of the Territories, sheep were introduced in 1888.[60] The practice of dipping was initiated in the same year.[61] Nor was this progress limited to the Cape, for gradually the practice spread northwards until today there is no Province where progressive Africans do not own sheep, though, unfortunately, their possession on a large scale by tribal Africans is still a feature of the Territories only.

Pig-farming has not been systematically encouraged. It can be traced to the Cape as early as 1849; it has spread to Natal and might have proved a success but for the fact that the bacon factories refused to accept the Africans' pigs. Poultry-farming can also be traced at an early date,[62] though it is comparatively recently that many Africans – the Zulus, for example – have succeeded in overcoming their aversion to poultry as food. Eggs are still not eaten in some parts of the country. The Natal Government made an effort (1909)to introduce donkeys for ploughing purposes, owing to the ravages played by East Coast Fever among the oxen, and upwards of five hundred of these animals were issued to approved applicants,[63] but the Union Government did nothing to push the scheme, and like so many other experiments, it has failed from want of perseverance.

The failure to manure has been a great defect of African agriculture. It was probably due in the first instance to the unlimited extent of acreage at the Africans' disposal which enabled them to select the most fertile spots and move about from place to place without regard to economy, dispensing with the necessity of manure. Almost all the African witnesses before the Natal Commission 1881-2 admitted that neither they nor their neighbours ever manured land. Even much later, when the African used ordinary kraal manure, as he did fairly frequently, it was very hard to induce him to adopt the application of artificial fertilisers, and a case was brought to the writer's notice where on one occasion, after the application of such a fertiliser, an African applied for some *muti* (medicine) to keep the weeds away!

Irrigation was never used by the Africans in their natural state. The demand for it seems to have arisen spontaneously by requests for watercourses addressed to Mr. Charles Brownlee in 1855 by Jobi, the father-in-law, and Tyali, the second councillor, of Chief Sandile.[64] In twenty years' time irrigation had become quite common.[65] In Natal, the Africans constructed watercourses on their own initiative, without magisterial advice.[66] There is still, however, room for improvement in this respect, especially when one remembers that Zululand and the Transkeian Territories abound in perennial streams.

In endeavouring to demonstrate the general progress which has taken place in African agriculture since the people first came under European government, it seems advisable to quote two documents *in extenso*. The first, written on the 22nd January 1825, describes what was then the most advanced African settlement in the Cape Colony:[67]

'The village contains . . . thirty houses or huts of two apartments each, constructed in the European fashion, with what is commonly called wattle and daub materials. These houses were erected entirely by the men (the rest of the people live in their usual round huts). One brick house has lately been commenced which will probably be followed by many more. To each house a small garden is attached, cultivated also by the men, in which, in addition to their usual crops, they rear a few potatoes and culinary vegetables. A few individuals have trained to the yoke and work their own oxen when necessary.'

The second document, fifty-five years later, drawn up by one man – Captain Matthew Blyth – to whom the Africans of the Transkei owe a deep debt of gratitude, and dealing with the work of another – Mr. C. J. Levey – to whom equal recognition is due, describes the progress of the Mfengu in the interval in words which make one forget for a moment that they form part of a Blue Book for they are in miniature an epic of all human progress – Hesiod, if not Homer. This document may well serve as a type of the many similar records extracted by the writer from original Archives:

'In 1835 the Fingos were brought down from the Gcalekas by the Government, and they were located in the colony at Peddie, Victoria East and Zitzikamma: many of the Fingos took service among the farmers, more particularly in the Somerset East district, where they obtained a knowledge of farming and the use of agricultural implements, and also the mode of irrigating crops, sowing wheat, etc. On their return to their homes they purchased ploughs; this was the first great advance made by them, thus enabling them to cultivate mealies and kafir-corn to a far greater extent than they had hitherto been able to do. They sold their surplus corn and purchased sheep with the proceeds; thus another great stride was taken.

'In 1865 the Government located a large number of Fingos in the Transkei; these brought with them the improved agricultural knowledge they had obtained in the Colony, also ploughs, wagons, etc. At this time there were but few ploughs amongst the Kafirs on this side of the Kei. They, however, soon saw the utility of them, and began to purchase ploughs and their use is now universal. At the present time there are 1 733 ploughs and 440 wagons in Fingoland alone. Many of the Fingos grow wheat, oathay, peas, beans, and owing to the late unfavourable season for growing mealies and kafir-corn the cultivation of wheat will be largely increased. This will lead to a certain change of living on the part of the Natives. They must make bread, and so another step in the stage of civilisation is taken. In growing wheat they must enclose their lands and irrigate; and would not be inclined to leave their lands upon which they had bestowed so much labour, and this, in process of time, will lead to better buildings being erected, gardens planted, etc.

'Sheep-farming is an important industry in Fingoland. When the census was taken at the end of last year, there were 211 174 sheep in that district alone. The sale of wool twice a year brings in a large sum of ready money annually into the pockets of the people, and leads to the increased trade and general prosperity of the people. A very large number of the Fingos are always employed on the public works or otherwise in the Colony, their savings are brought back into the district, and thus add to the general wealth.

'This state of things is not equalled among the neighbouring Kafirs, with the exception that perhaps amongst the Emigrant Tembookies, who grow a considerable quantity of wheat, and who, like the Fingos, gained their knowledge of agriculture in the Colony; they have also been encouraged by their magistrate, Mr. Levey.'[68]

From 1880, the date of the above report, to the present day, progress, while not so rapid as in the earlier period, has definitely continued. The use of the plough has become widely diffused. Sheep-farming is now usual in all parts of the Cape Province and Lesotho. Unfortunately the vast masses of tribal Africans in the Northern Transvaal and Natal still cling to maize, millet, horned cattle and goats. Pig and poultry farming is making slow progress in Natal, however.

In the latter part of 1903 Mr. E. E. Dower, Chief Clerk of the Cape Native Affairs Department, and subsequently Union Secretary for Native Affairs, gave the following description of the average Cape African:

'The average possessions of the ordinary Native consists of, say, from fifteen to twenty head of cattle, a flock of sheep and goats, a couple of horses and a plough. That is the usual possession of an ordinary Native peasant living in a communal Native Location . . . either in the Transkei or in the Cape Colony.[69]

This would be an incorrect description of the average African farmer in the other Provinces, inasmuch as he would have perhaps a few more cattle, some of which he would use for ploughing, no horses and no sheep.

To sum up, the benefits conferred on the African agriculturist up to 1910 owing directly to European influence, are as follows:

- (1) The granting of securer tenure than was possible under old conditions. Legally speaking, this applies to the Cape Province only; but practically speaking it holds good of the whole of

South Africa, for the African agriculturist no longer lives in constant fear of the depredations and inroads of other tribes. The European government keeps the peace for him.

(2) The extension of the range of crops grown to include wheat, oats, fruit and vegetables. On a large scale this is found in the Cape Province only.

(3) The introduction of less mobile forms of stock than cattle and goats – in particular of sheep, pigs and poultry. To some extent this change has affected all parts of South Africa, but only sheep-farming has reached really large dimensions, and that only in the Transkeian Territories of the Cape Province and in Lesotho.

(4) The introduction of better and less wasteful methods of agriculture, especially ploughing (all over South Africa) and latterly harrowing, manuring and irrigation, the last two chiefly in the Cape Province.

(5) The encouragement of afforestation (chiefly in the Cape Province) and the statutory restriction of the denudation of forests (chiefly Natal).

Except for its concluding chapter, this book does not purport to go beyond the year 1910. It would be positively misleading, however, not to mention the immense extension in all Provinces of African agricultural services and the loving enthusiasm put into this work by those responsible for it.

Unfortunately, however, the obstacles mentioned at the beginning of this chapter have increased even more rapidly than the enthusiasm and activity of the agricultural experts of the Bantu Affairs Department. The pressure of population in the limited reserves has made it even more difficult to provide larger areas for progressive and competent African farmers. The policy of apartheid with its hostility to freehold ownership by Africans outside the reserves has removed what might have been a valuable help in the situation. Finally, the rapid growth of industry since 1910 and with it of migrant labour for wages, has made agriculture relatively less important in African life.

The saga – and it is nothing less – of the great improvement of African farming in the Cape which is the subject of the greater part of this chapter has thus become somewhat 'dated'. No good work sincerely done is ever wholly lost, but the relative importance of the work is less than it used to be. Nevertheless, even under the different conditions of the present day, life in the reserves is happier and more productive than it would have been without the labours of the missionaries, magistrates and agricultural experts who have so well served Africa and the Africans.

NOTES TO CHAPTER XIII

1 Brookes, E. H. and Hurwitz, N.: 'The Native Reserves of Natal', Vol. VII, Natal Regional Survey (Oxford University Press, Cape Town, 1957).
2 *Op. cit.*, p. 99.
3 Report of Commons Committee on Aborigines (British Settlements) 1836, p. 58.
4 S.A. Native Affairs Commission 1903-5, Evidence Vol. IV, p. 64.
5 Special report of Rev. H. Calderwood on the Fingo Locations, dated 22nd January 1855.
6 Cape Native Blue Book 1874, p. 12.
7 *Ibid.*, p. 44.
8 Report of Rev. J. Ayliff, Agent with Kreli, Cape Native Blue Book 1874.
9 See, e.g. Natal Native Blue Book 1878, pp. 5 and 26.
10 *Ibid.*, p. 39.
11 S.A. Native Affairs Commission 1903-5, Evidence, Question 41762.
12 Cape Native Blue Book 1843, p. 44.
13 'The South African Natives: Their Progress and Recent Condition', edited by the S.A. Native Races Commission, London, pp. 10-11.
14 S.A. Native Affairs Commission 1903-5, Report, Vol. I, p. 52.
15 Sir Henry Elliott in Cape Native Blue Book 1893, p. 44.
16 Theal: History and Ethnography of South Africa before 1505, 2nd Edition (London, Geo. Allen & Unwin, 1919), p. 276.
17 *Ibid.*, p. 267.
18 Russell, R.: Natal: The land and it's story (Pietermaritzburg. P. Davis & Son 1904), pp. 180-1.
19 Letter from W. R. Thompson, Government Agent in Caffraria to the Commissioners of Colonial Inquiry upon the State of the Caffres, Ghonaques, etc. and upon the progress of missionary exertions among them, dated Chumie, 22nd January 1825.
20 Despatch to the Duke of Newcastle No. 47, dated Grahamstown, 15th October 1853.
21 Report of Capt. Matthew Blyth, Fingo Agent, dated Nqamakwe, Transkei, 4th March 1874 (Cape Native Blue Book 1874, p. 41).
22 Basutoland: Minutes of the Annual Pitso held at Maseru, 1st March 1877.
23 Natal Native Blue Book 1879, p. 6.
24 Natal Native Commission 1906-7, Report, para. 36, p. 34.
25 *Ibid.*, para. 53, pp. 19-20.
26 D. D. T. Jabavu, in 'The Black Problem', (Lovedale, The Lovedale Press 1921), p. 54.
27 Government Notice of 9th February 1849: Mr. Calderwood's Instructions and Regulations for Superintendents, dated Alice, 29th January 1849. The people concerned were Mfengu.
28 See his despatch No. 47 of 15th October 1853.
29 Report of Charles Brownlee, Gaika Commissioner, dated 30th May 1855.
30 Cape Native Blue Book 1876, p. 51.
31 Cape Native Blue Book 1884, p. 120.
32 Report of Cape Native Affairs Commission 1910, pp. 8-11.
33 Correspondence re Encouragement of Natives to engage in Agricultural and Other Pursuits, 1881, p. 21.
34 *Vide, inter alia*, Cape Native Blue Book 1886, pp. 33, 35, 53, 80.
35 *Ibid.*, p. 81.
36 Cape Native Blue Book 1895, p. 81.
37 *Ibid.*

38 Correspondence and Report relative to the Lands in Namaqualand, set apart for the occupation of Natives and others, 1889.
39 Cape Native Blue Book 1876, p. 88.
40 S.A. Native Affairs Commission 1903-5, Evidence of E. E. Dower, Chief Clerk, Cape Native Affairs Department, Vol. II, p. 2.
41 Cape Native Blue Book 1896, p. iii.
42 Cape Native Blue Book 1887, *passim*.
43 Cape Native Blue Book 1886, p. 5.
44 *Ibid.*, pp. 5, 55, 67, 78.
45 Cape Native Blue Book 1888, p. 33.
46 *Ibid.*, p. 58.
47 Cape Native Blue Book 1887, p. 63.
48 Cape Native Blue Book 1888, p. 103.
49 Correspondence respecting the affairs of Bechuanaland, 1887, C. 5363, p. 29.
50 Cape Native Blue Book 1889, p. 34.
51 Cape Native Blue Book 1893, p. 61.
52 Report of A. J. Shepstone, Secretary for Native Affairs, Natal, *vide* Natal Native Blue Book 1909, p. 5.
53 Information supplied by the late Rev. R. W. Loffhagen.
54 Correspondence on the encouragement of Natives to engage in agricultural and other pursuits, 1881, p. 21.
55 Cape Native Blue Book 1889, pp. 29, 37 and 47.
56 Papers on the Social and Political Conditions of the Fingo tribes located in the Transkeian Territory 1870.
57 Report of the Resident with Gangelezwe, Clarkebury, 28th May 1872.
58 Report of the Special Magistrate, St. John's Territory, 4th January 1877.
59 Cape Native Blue Book 1886, p. 63.
60 Cape Native Blue Book 1889, p. 37.
61 *Ibid.*, p. 33.
62 *Vide, inter alia*, despatch of Sir George Grey to Right Hon. H. Labouchere, No. 102, dated Cape Town, 18th October 1856.
63 Report of A. J. Shepstone, Secretary for Native Affairs, Natal, in Natal Native Blue Book 1909, p. 5.
64 Charles Brownlee to Sir George Grey, 30th May 1855.
65 Cape Native Blue Book 1876, p. 88.
66 Natal Native Blue Book 1878, p. 19.
67 Blue Book: Cape Native Tribes, 18th March 1836, p. 186.
68 Report of Capt. Matthew Blyth, Chief Magistrate, Transkei, dated 4th March 1880 (in Correspondence re encouragement of Natives to engage in agricultural and other pursuits, 1881, p. 21).
69 S.A. Native Affairs Commission 1903-5, Evidence, Vol. II, p. 3.

CHAPTER XIV

Industry

This book sets out to record Government policies affecting Africans from 1830 to 1910. Unless this limitation be borne in mind, the contents of the present chapter will be dismissed as jejune and superficial. Apart from gold and diamond mining, the large-scale industrial development of South Africa took place after 1910. All the immense problems of the post-1910 era such as competition between black and white labour, trade unions, wage regulation, strikes and industrial conciliation, are beyond the scope of this study. The strikes of 1913 and 1914, the attempted revolution of 1922,[1] the rise and decline of the Industrial and Commercial Workers' Union, the policy of job reservation, and much else, lie necessarily beyond the compass of this chapter. So much must be grasped before the chapter is dismissed as an unreal hovering on the periphery of South African industrial life.

What is here attempted is a survey of industrial pursuits among the Africans before the arrival of the white population, and of attempts by missionaries and others to give such industrial training as was suitable to a land without large capitalist enterprises. Following this we must study the rise of diamond and gold mining and the effect of this on African life and labour.

First among the 'kraal' or domestic industries of the Africans comes the basket-work group, with which must be associated the construction of the framework of their huts. The thatching of the huts was also a commonly-found art, carried out often with exquisite skill. Though the huts purported to be circular, the method of obtaining a circle by attaching a movable peg with string or its equivalent to a fixed peg does not appear to have been known to the builders until they were shown it by white men.[2] Yet much skill and artistic taste were employed in building huts, especially for the chief. The description of Dingane's hut at Mgungundlovu in Russell's 'Natal and its Story' (a book the MS of which was revised by Sir Theophilus Shepstone)[3] is of interest in this connection: 'It was twenty feet across and eight feet in height, and was supported by twenty-two pillars covered with beads of various colours. The floor shone like a mirror. The palace was surmounted by a crown, ingeniously contrived out of twisted mats.'

It will be noted that bead-work is mentioned here. This is a species of occupation which, though the materials were derived from European sources, is otherwise genuinely indigenous and is a valuable index

189

to African standards of art.

Domestic utensils were made out of wood or clay. Spoons and even pots were carved out of wood sometimes with great skill. The equivalent of a pillow – a carved piece of wood on which the *neck* rests – was one of the commonest of manufactures and continued long after 1910. Sticks were, and are, carved with great ingenuity and taste.

Other articles were modelled in clay. Most large pots were of this material. In clay-modelling Africans showed very great artistic skill. One early – perhaps rather naive – tribute to this is found in a report by Peter Paterson, Resident Magistrate of Estcourt, as early as 1878:[4] 'I have seen a wagon with wheels complete, and a span of oxen, very fairly modelled in clay by quite a young Native lad, and, among other things, a capital figure of his master on horseback modelled by a Native youth.'

The smelting of iron, and even of copper, and the forging of assegai blades was well-established before the beginning of our period;[5] and, if derived from external sources, must have been so derived at a date prior to the settlement of the present white inhabitants of South Africa. In some areas the smith's art became hereditary in a particular tribe. For example, in Natal, at the time of the Zulu War, nearly all assegais were manufactured by one tribe near Table Mountain, Pietermaritzburg, in which all the men, young and old, were trained to the work.[6] This is the nearest thing to a specialised industry of the European type which the writer has been able to trace among Africans apart from European influence. Of course iron work was not confined to the assegai, but extended also to hoes, knives and some rough picks and hatchets.

It was with this stock in hand – basketry, hut-building, thatching, mat-making, bead-work, wood-carving, pottery and smelting – that the Africans of South Africa came under European influence. That influence was by no means an unmixed blessing. Many of the early settlers were themselves below the standard of artistic taste of the Africans. Cheap metalware often replaced more attractive pottery. Who could blame the African women for preferring the use of a discarded paraffin tin to a clay pot for the carrying of water? Missionary training reflected the experience and capacity of the missionaries (and, indeed, could it have been otherwise?). A survey made in the Cape as early as 1849[7] showed that forty masons and builders were being trained, obviously to build on European lines, and the same may be said of the twenty-one carpenters. There were indeed twenty-seven thatchers, five basket-makers, one mat-maker and twenty blacksmiths, who can be said to represent the indigenous industries duly developed. But training as wagon-makers (fifteen), shoe-makers (thirty-one), tailors (ten), saddlers (three), and tanners (three) represent new, though admittedly very useful, skills.

A return made thirty-seven years later[8] shows that no less than forty-five per cent even of students at industrial schools were engaged on professional, semi-professional or clerical pursuits. Out of a total of 2 075 pupils, 580 had become teachers, 114 evangelists and catechists, 95 clerks and interpreters, 59 ministers of religion, 59 sewing-mistresses, 23 telegraph messengers, 10 law agents and 5 journalists. Only 504 – about twenty-five per cent – were employed on industrial work strictly so called.

This must not be construed as a criticism of either the missionaries or the Africans concerned. When Africans send their children for educational training they not unnaturally want to see them occupy a position in society better than that of their parents. This is the reason why schemes for the training of African domestic servants always fail. Nineteenth-century and even twentieth-century European standards tended to rate professional men higher than mechanics. In any event the statistics quoted show how slow and how limited African industrial progress would be if limited to home industries and self-employed builders or carpenters. It is only when big factories were opened that Africans began to *crowd* into industries and do very good work in them, leaving the management of the business to the white *entrepreneur*.

It is doubtful how far labour on roads and other public works should be considered in this chapter. It seems to have begun on a large scale in the Cape in 1855.[9] In the Cape the labourers were recruited under ordinary conditions. Forced labour on the roads (*isibhalo*) can be traced in Natal as early as November 1850. Thirty years later it was possible to claim that the Africans who were called up came quite cheerfully.[10] It continued in Natal, despite growing discontent, right up to the time of Union. One of the earliest actions of the Union Government was to abolish it.

A word should be said about the printing industry. A printing press was set up at Lovedale fairly early in the nineteenth century.[11] Skilled printers were found among Christian Africans in Natal as early as 1878, and in the same year a capable observer noted that the more advanced Africans were beginning to understand the uses of capital and the advantages of associated labour.[12] Other printing presses were set up as the years went by, of which perhaps the most famous were at Mariannhill (Natal) and Morija (Lesotho). Instances of self-help occurred as the years went on. In 1883 the people of the Cala district, Transkei, erected their own agricultural hall at a cost of £400.[13] A year earlier, the private enterprise of a progressive farmer, Mr. J. E. Methley of 'Newstead', Natal, had resulted in the Africans in his district building themselves five-roomed houses of dressed stone and brick and also the construction of a small church entirely by African labour.[14] In 1896 that indefatigable magistrate, C. J. Levey, introduced the osier willow in the Xalanaga district, with a view to a thorough establishment of a basket-making industry, recommending Government at the same time to introduce a few expert teachers of basketry from Europe.[15] But by the time his willows were grown the white races of South Africa were too busy cutting one another's throats to attend to basket-making.

All these trickles of activity were swamped by a raging torrent when diamonds were discovered in the northern Cape, from 1867 to 1871. Speaking of Kimberley in the latter year, Theal says:[16] 'In that little spot, thirty thousand men, white and black, were working at once.'

Thus began in a haphazard way, and without any settled policy or careful reflection, the large-scale employment of Africans in industry, the migrant labour system and the compound system. The effect of all this on African life has been incalculably great.

It does not seem to have occurred to any of those responsible to import white labourers for the more menial or laborious tasks of diamond-mining. Since the days of the Dutch East India Company and of slavery, white men in South Africa had come to rely on men of colour for arduous physical labour. On the African side no force was used or needed to secure labourers. They flocked to the diamond mines. This was partly the result of the pressure of increasing population on static reserves, partly the result of the *lobolo* custom, since it opened up an easy way of earning money for the *lobolo* cattle. Young men, eager for adventure and subsequent matrimony, left for Kimberley freely and gladly.

There was another reason for this inrush of labour. Guns were sold freely and publicly and it became the ambition of every young African to own one. The 'Gun War' in Basutoland and perhaps to some extent the Zulu War and the Ninth Frontier War were the results of this policy. White men and black were killed, that other white men might make profits. It is the gospel of Andrew Undershaft in Shaw's *Major Barbara*.

Be that as it may, young African men flocked to the diamond mines. And because they were mostly young and unmarried they were housed in compounds. It was not then foreseen that, a hundred years later, tens of thousands of married men would be working as migrant labourers and sometimes also housed in compounds. In this light-hearted way began the disruption of African family life.

Capitalists from Kimberley were among the first to develop gold mining on the Witwatersrand after the discovery of 1886 and, naturally enough, they too looked to the African population for underground labour and compounded it (though not so strictly as at Kimberley). No guns were sold but otherwise the attractions of the gold mines to young African men were much the same as those of the diamond mines. By 1899 there were approximately 97 000 Africans employed on the gold mines.[17] The majority of these, however, were not from the areas which now form the Republic. Half came from Mozambique and many of the rest from Rhodesia.[18] The Zulus in 1899 numbered 7 000[19]– a proportion which has not been kept up. Few Transvaal Africans presented themselves for employment.

When gold mining was resumed after the war of 1899-1902 there were only some 43 000 African workers, rising to 64 000 in 1903.[20] As Milner felt rapid recovery of the mining industry to be absolutely essential to his reconstruction policy he, with the approval of the mining industry, and even of the Transvaal Miners' Association, [21] brought in indentured Chinese labourers. Recruitment of these ceased in 1906 and from 1907 they were sent home as their indentures expired. In the first year after Union the number of Africans employed on the gold mines was 174 000.[22]

Since Union the *relative* importance of gold mining has declined owing to the extraordinary development of industries. But by the end of our period, secondary industry had made very little progress in the four South African Colonies. According to the census of 1911 only 62 000 Africans were employed in industries, and of these many thousands were employed on road and railway construction.[23]

The picture which emerges as we close this study of industry during the period 1830-1910 seems at first glance to have little to do with the prosperous industrial South Africa of the 1970's with its immense urban African population, absolutely indispensable as it is to the continuance of industrial prosperity. But the pre-1910 era left a legacy of migrant labour policy, which is being felt in the new industrial South Africa six decades later. What was all but inevitable in the diamond and gold mines, drawing their labour as they did from distant areas, has been allowed to form a precedent for the very different type of labour, composed to a considerable extent of married men drawn from reserves near to the industries concerned. What was a skilful improvisation in the 1870's and 1880's had by the 1970's become a rigid theory, destructive of family life, dangerous to agriculture and facing industrial employers with a constant turn-over of labour, because the labourer can never strike roots in the industrial area where he works.

NOTES TO CHAPTER XIV

1. For which see Herd, Norman: '1922' (Johannesburg, Blue Crane Books, 1966).
2. See R. W. Plant: 'The Zulu in Three Tenses'.
3. Which explains much in it.
4. Natal Native Blue Book 1878, p. 20.
5. *Vide, inter alia*, Evidence of Rev. Wm. Shaw before Commons Select Committee on Aborigines (British Settlements) 1835, p. 62.
6. Report of H. C. Campbell (later Judge of the Natal Native High Court) in Natal Native Blue Book 1879, p. 7.
7. White Book: Particulars of Missionary Institutions in this Colony, 1849.
8. Return of the extent to which African pupils after leaving Industrial Institutions were engaged in industrial pursuits among their own people or among Europeans, compiled in 1886 and published in a White Book dated 17th June 1887.
9. *Vide* speech of Sir George Grey in opening the second session of the first Cape Parliament, 15th March 1855.

10 Papers relating to the Supply by Native Chiefs of Native Labour in connection with the Public Works of the Colony, p. 10.
11 White Book: Report of the Lovedale Institution for 1860, p. 4.
12 Report of H. C. Campbell (later Judge) in Natal Native Blue Book 1878, p. 27.
13 Cape Native Blue Book 1884, p. 120.
14 See letter from J. E. Methley to J. P. Symons, Colonial Auditor, Natal dated 12th January 1882.
15 Cape Native Blue Book 1896, p. 112.
16 'History of South Africa since 1795', Vol. II, p. 333.
17 Van der Horst, Sheila T.: 'Native Labour in South Africa' (London, Frank Cass & Co., 1971), p. 156.
18 *Ibid.*
19 Stott, C. H.: 'The Boer Invasion of Natal', pp. 30-1.
20 Van der Horst, *op. cit.*, p. 115.
21 *Ibid.*, p. 171.
22 Horwitz, R.: 'The Political Economy of South Africa' (London, Weidenfeld & Nicolson, 1967), p. 215.
23 Van der Horst, *op. cit.*, p. 235.

CHAPTER XV

Religion and Education

Nothing has had a more profound effect on African life than the introduction of the Christian religion. This was the work of Christian missionaries, who have been subjected to unsparing criticism on the part of early colonists and now on the part of secularist radical thinkers. Before we attempt to deal with these criticisms we should be well-advised to look at the changes which missionary work has introduced.

Some of these were external – the wearing of European clothing and shoes, the building of houses rather than huts, with European furniture. It is easy for modern critics enjoying all these things themselves to sneer at the value of these changes, but it may be noted as a matter of simple experience, that no African who has made them ever permanently goes back to his previous mode of life.

The African languages were reduced to writing, and books, especially but not only religious books, were printed in them. This is one of the great steps in civilisation. Few differences, as the Great Cham of literature once said, are more important than the difference between the man who can read and the man who cannot.

Incidentally, in the nineteenth century it was almost exclusively the missionaries who preserved for posterity the unwritten literature of the Africans – proverbs, folk tales, praise songs and genealogies.

The missionaries were pioneers in medical work among the Africans. Untold agonies must have been suffered before their intervention. The fact that almost every missionary was called upon to be an amateur dentist speaks for itself.

Very important was the effect of Christian missionary work on the position of women and children. This has been the universal effect of Christianity: it is not only an African phenomenon. Many missionaries may have been unduly rigid about polygamists who desired baptism, but the establishment of monogamy as a norm has done great good.

It is, however, quite true that the transition from the old to the new life, and the abuse of their freedom by women, has led to a kind of sexual anarchy in many urban and peri-urban villages. This cannot be denied but perhaps it may be looked upon as a 'stumble upward' from the old tribal ways to a new life of disciplined freedom.

Every incursion of Christianity, whether under Constantine the Great, Ethelbert of Kent, or Khama of Botswana, has produced admirable Christians, converts whose lives have been really changed, and others whose 'conversion' has been much more superficial. Those who have met Christians of the former type and known them cannot doubt the great difference for good which has only to be known to be respected. But even those converts who are not saints have their points. An outstanding Zulu social anthropologist mentions that it is easy to see whether a worker coming home on leave is a heathen or a Christian. 'It is only the Christian men who worked with their wives in the fields over the weekends when they came back from the city.'[1]

The same Zulu writer,[2] quoting Williston Walker, says:[3] "Christians looked upon themselves as a separated people, a new race, the true Israel, whose citizenship was no longer in the Roman Empire, though they prayed for its welfare and that of its ruler, but in the heavenly Jerusalem." Change a few words as to place and national identity and you have the Zulu picture described accurately.

Here is a piece of true insight which many whites who have criticised the work of missions in South Africa have missed. The work of St. Boniface in Germany, St. Willebrord in the Netherlands, St. Imier and St. Gall in Switzerland, St. Remy in France, St. Augustine of Canterbury in England, may be usefully compared with that of John Philip, Henry Calderwood, Stephen Hofmeyr or Daniel Lindley in South Africa. The Dark Ages contain a mine of suggestive information for the study of missionary work in South Africa. Take France for example. Would humanity have been better served if Vercingetorix had never been conquered or Chlodovech had never been baptised? Would an additional Celtic or Teutonic literature have produced writers like Racine and Molière, Bossuet and Pascal? All history is a history of acculturation, and both the nineteenth-century farmers who complained that the Africans were being drawn away from working for minimal wages as farm labourers and the twentieth-century radicals who deplore missionary work as fighting against negritude, show in their arguments their ignorance of, or indifference to, the history of the first eight centuries of the Christian era.

For the missionary in the later nineteenth century is often depicted as the agent of 'colonialism' and 'imperialism', the servant of capitalistic trade, imbued with a spirit of superiority over the Africans, preaching provincial European customs rather than timeless truth. We in our study of the period 1830-1910 must examine whether and to what extent these devastating criticisms are true, and this we shall try to do as impartially as possible.

It is not possible to deny the imperialism of David Livingstone. He saw in British annexation and commerce the best and most effective remedy against the slave-traders who were ruining the life of Central Africa. Was he wrong in the conditions of the mid-nineteenth century? In the heyday of imperialism, the 1890s and 1900s, when imperial responsibility had come to be looked upon with an almost religious veneration, there were many missionaries, not so famous as Livingstone, and not as justified as he was by the existence of a slave traffic, who could fairly be classified as imperialists.

But what of the great missionary tribunes who fought against the local governments, and at times even against the Imperial authorities, for the rights of the Africans? Such a man was Dr. John Philip of the London Missionary Society, for long the *bête noire* of South African historians, but long since rehabilitated by Professor W. M. Macmillan's great trilogy.[4] Rightly described as 'the Wilberforce of Africa,'[5] he was ready to face any government in defence of the rights of the Coloured People and Africans whom he loved. In general, however, his appeal lay from the local Cape Government to authorities in England. John William Colenso, the heretical but valiant first Bishop of Natal, went further and severely criticised British policy in Zululand during the years 1873-83. The Zulus regarded him, and after nearly a century still regard him, as their champion and defender. One of his last letters was written in Cetshwayo's defence. He has left a noble and enduring reputation among the Zulus.[6]

A few years earlier his intervention in the notorious Langalibalele case[7] resulted in the recall of a Governor and the mitigation of the punishment inflicted on a 'rebel' chief. In taking the stand which he did on the Langalibalele affair he lost the friendship of Sir Theophilus Shepstone, his chief lay supporter in the great Church controversy in Natal. As Mrs. Audrey Brooke, no friendly critic, rightly said of him: 'When he had little left to lose he risked that little for the Africans' sakes.'[8] His latest biographer writes: 'His African people asked, "Is there any other man that will care for us as the Bishop has?"'[9]

Apart from the existence of such great missionary tribunes as these – and they were not the only ones – can it be seriously maintained that the American, German, French, Swiss, Norwegian and Swedish missionaries were agents of British imperialism, or that the extensive Dutch Reformed missions fall under this category?

The list of nationalities given above, and the even longer list of Christian denominations that could be given, show indeed a fault of missions in the Victorian era not much canvassed by modern radical critics. Nineteenth century missionary work in South Africa shows little trace of oecumenism. In this defect it mirrored the Christian world generally. In South Africa it had the particularly bad result that when secessions occurred, the African church showed such competitive and centrifugal characteristics that by 1910 there were a large number of 'independent' denominations and at the present day nearly 3 000.

There is some evidence to show[10] that the denominational differences gave heathen chiefs and others a reason, or at least a pretext, for not becoming Christians.

The 'superiority' of the missionary – one of the articles of charge against him – is sometimes shown in his insistence on the non-essential elements of a circumscribed provincial experience over the century-old traditions of the Africans. This would happen most often in the case of missionaries with a limited education, often (but not always) among the smaller missionary societies. Almost all, however, made the wearing of trousers one of the requisites of conversion, although St. Peter and St. Paul would both have considered them as essentially barbaric garments. Otherwise if the missionary insists on Africans conforming to the standards of Wigan or of Kansas City, the only defence that can be put up for this major solecism is that these are the best standards that he knows.

But there is another aspect of missionary superiority which goes deeper. Many highly educated and deeply spiritual missionaries have been ready to give to the limit, and this willingness is to be counted to them for righteousness, but have not even been aware that there is much for them to receive. There is here a lack of humility which has impoverished the missionary, his converts and the church generally. There have been notable and fairly numerous exceptions. Colenso is an outstanding example. Another during our period was the ex-Quaker medical missionary Callaway, later to become the saintly Bishop of St. John's. Just a little beyond our period comes H. A. Junod, author of 'The Story of a South African Tribe.'

Many others, not so famous, did have the spiritual gift of caring for and respecting the personality of their converts, including their traditions and even their animist religion, but it is only fair to say that a large number of able and respected missionaries saw in the African past much that was diabolical and looked on their converts as brands to be plucked from the burning.

In almost every case a missionary career in the nineteenth century, especially in the first half of it, demanded great self-sacrifice. The missionary was parted from his homeland for years, sometimes for ever. He lived usually in spots off the beaten track, reached by deplorable roads, and though he had enough to live on he was rarely if ever well paid. His wife and children shared his difficulties. (One missionary in the Northern Transvaal buried his wife and *all* his children.[11]) Moreover – a point which many people overlook – a man eloquent in English or French or Norwegian must spend his whole life addressing congregations in Xhosa or Sotho or Zulu, languages with a totally different structure from his own. That these disabilities were endured and conquered must lead us to honour and respect even mediocre missionaries who did their best in the love of God and man.

But any survey of the Christianisation of Africa which confined itself to the missionaries would be lamentably one-sided. The first African Christians needed immense courage to come out for the new doctrines and the new way of life. There were many who suffered; there were a few martyrs. As the years went by the Christian Africans built up a new society easily distinguishable from the traditional pagan society. As Absolom Vilakazi says: 'There is no westernized Zulu who is not a a Christian.'[12] And though there are those who under modern secularist and radical influence have virtually renounced their Christian faith, they have rarely, if ever, reverted to traditionalism. They are at least, to coin a term, sociological Christians if not believing Christians.

From the Christian group have come *all* the pioneers of thought, the political leaders, the professional men. The traditionalists remain in the past, passively resistant conservatives. In this sense we can really say, 'Vicisti, Galilaee!' Even those who are today in revolt and who criticise missionaries unmercifully are 'sociological Christians', whose ability to attack missionaries on western lines of argument and in the English language is the result of the education which missionaries pioneered.

For, apart from personal religion, the influence of the missionaries was most apparent in the sphere of education. It is true that the hospitalisation of Africans was their work, and that many missionaries were, like Father Bernard Huss, prominent workers for social and agricultural progress. The work of one of these, Rev. Henry Calderwood has been mentioned in some detail in earlier chapters. The Methodist missions, in addition to their outstanding educational work, were prominent in these practical activities.

But to come to the schools. In broad and general terms the education of the Africans was almost wholly left to the missions,[13] with or without grants-in-aid. The missions provided not only primary education but built up some of the most famous high schools in South Africa, and trained their own teachers. Let us examine these facts as they existed during our period somewhat more fully.

The very fact that Government control was minimal left scope for great diversity of syllabus and methods, and even the nationality of the missionaries left its mark. 'The stern German attitude to life has often found expression among these people in phrases like "NgiyiJalimane mina" or "Ubani uyiJalimane", i.e. "I am German-like in my ways" or "So-and-so is German-like in his manner", in connection with industriousness, strictness with wife and children, etc.'[14]

Undoubtedly schools run by Englishmen have subconsciously included a special preference for all things English, and by Americans for all things American. The writer once heard a Rhodesian student at Adams College praying to God to 'bless the whole wurrrld', and his natural guess that the lad had been trained by Scots Presbyterians was confirmed on investigation.

Yet despite national and denominational differences, these schools had many things in common. The writer has failed to find any primary school where the vernacular was not used as the medium of instruction in the lower classes, or any school where it was not replaced by English in the higher classes. All mission schools provided some work for the hands as well as for the brains. At the very beginning of our period good industrial training was going on in some schools, carpentry, building and domestic science being the most frequent subjects. In all schools there was some 'manual work', such as grass-cutting, sweeping, etc. Such 'manual work', inadequately supervised as it often was, and lacking in interest, often did more harm than good, especially when extra 'manual work' was imposed as a punishment for offences in class.

Boys often cut grass like Carlyle's stone-mason who, it will be remembered, 'broke the Ten Commandments with every stroke of his hammer.'

The extent to which European educational courses should be modified to recognise the African background and to meet African needs was a matter of dispute almost from the beginning, and was debated to the end, of our period (1910) and is still debated. But for most of the missionaries 'the sky was the limit' however slow or tortuous the course taken to reach it. Govan, the first, and Stewart, the second, Principal of Lovedale, concurred in the ideal, though differing in some of the methods. Stewart closed Govan's Greek and Latin classes, except for theological students.[15] Govan, for a time thought of as an unimaginative Scots classicist, has surprisingly found his ideals realised in the 'ethnic universities' established by the Nationalist Government, for, deplorably restricted though these are in student freedom and student practical interests, 'the sky's the limit' as regards their intellectual opportunities.

Stewart had no wish to restrict African intellectual opportunities and ideals, but was simply a practical man working for practical ends. His deep and sincere religion and his attractive personality kept him from any theories which could be exploited for the wrong ends, and indeed he himself was the first worker for African university education, though the first university institution was in fact situated, not as he wished at Lovedale, but as a separate institution next door to it at Fort Hare.[16]

Others were not so fortunate. At the very end of our period rose the star of Charles Templeman Loram[17] who served with great distinction as Inspector of Native Education in Natal and later, in 1920, on the Native Affairs Commission appointed by Geneeral Smuts. Loram's career was ambivalent. On the one hand he did more perhaps than any other man of his time to interest white South Africans in the Africans and their education. On the other hand his great interest in Booker T. Washington and Tuskegee, and in the works of Dr. Thomas Jesse Jones, led him to advance views on education which could easily lead to the attitude of the Eiselen Commission, the body responsible for the much-criticised 'Bantu Education' of the present day. Loram's influence – on the whole very much to the good – was marked in the lives of a great educationalist like A. E. Leroy of Amanzimtoti Institute (Adams College) and of a superb social worker such as J. D. Rheinallt Jones of the Institute of Race Relations. It was Loram who was mainly responsible for opening government schools in Natal from 1918 onwards. But this is to take us beyond our period.

Governments gave grants-in-aid and supplied inspectors, and this was all to the good. But the total of grants-in-aid from all the Provinces combined at the end of our period (1910) was only £340 000.

From all that has been said it will have been gathered that African education during our period (1830-1910) was essentially a missionary enterprise. There were no government schools for Africans in 1910. Whatever mistakes the missionaries may have made, the positive value of their work was very great. It was they who trained the stalwarts of the early years of Union, the men who founded the African National Congress in 1912, the men and women who became social and educational leaders, the founders of the African press, the pioneers of modern African literature. They served Africa well, and their denigration is neither justifiable nor even decent.

Yet once again we may say that it is the Africans themselves who deserve our highest meed of praise. For they responded magnificently to the work done for them and showed in many cases ability of a very high order. When Dr. Langham Dale, Superintendent of Education in the Cape Colony, visited Lovedale in 1864, he 'examined the most advanced scholar in a portion of a chapter of the Greek Testament, an ode of Anacreon, and a portion of the first book of the Aeneid, and put general questions on the parsing and derivation of words. He also demonstrated the 47th proposition of Euclid Book I, and a geometrical exercise connected with it.'[18]

Depending on one's point of view this may have been an excellent or a fantastic education, but one cannot doubt the mental ability of the man who did so well at it. And he was only one of many.

Advance, Africa!

NOTES TO CHAPTER XV

1 Vilakazi, Absolom: 'Zulu Transformations' (Pietermaritzburg, University of Natal Press, 1962), p. 138.
2 *Op. cit.*, p. 97.
3 Walker, Williston: 'A History of the Christian Church', (New York, Charles Scribner's Sons, 1918), p. 42.
4 'The Cape Colour Question', 'Bantu, Boer and Briton' and 'Complex South Africa'.
5 Davies, Horton and Shepherd, R. H. W.: 'South African Missions 1800-1950 (London, Nelson, 1954), p. 712.
6 Brookes, E. H. and Webb, C. de B.: 'A History of Natal', (Pietermaritzburg, University of Natal Press, 1965), p. 112.
7 For details of which, *vide op. cit.*, Ch. XII.
8 Brooke, Audrey: 'Robert Gray' (Cape Town, Oxford University Press, 1947), p. 95.
9 Hinchliff, Peter: 'John William Colenso' (London, Nelson, 1964), p. 195.
10 E.g. in Vilakazi's 'Zulu Transformations'.
11 There is a reference to this in du Plessis, J.: 'A History of Christian Missions in South Africa', (Cape Town, Struik, 1965), p. 333.
12 Vilakazi, *op. cit.*, p. 140.
13 There was one government school, the 'Zwaart Kop Industrial School' opened in 1885, and transferred to a mission in 1893 (unpublished thesis, O. E. Emanuelson, 'A History of Native Education in Natal between 1835 and 1927'.).
14 Vilakazi, *op. cit.*, p. 96.
15 Shepherd, R. H. W.: 'Lovedale, South Africa' (Lovedale, Lovedale Press, 1941), p. 173.
16 *Ibid.*, pp. 270-1.
17 Loram's main work was 'The Education of the South African Native', (London, Longmans, 1917).
18 Report of Supt. General of Education on Industrial Institutions and Schools, Cape Town, 1864, p. 10.

CHAPTER XVI

Addendum: South Africa since 1910

This book has so far tried to set out faithfully the way in which South African governments dealt with the Africans who came under their rule between 1830 and 1910. More than six decades have passed since 1910, and it would seem advisable to summarise briefly the trends of policy during that period, and especially to indicate the vast changes in human history and thought which render some of the finest state documents drawn up between 1830 and 1910 quaint or even ludicrous today.

This is not an easy task, for opinions on the issues of race and colour inside and outside South Africa are divided and held often with hot passion. An historian cannot avoid being also a citizen and a man, and the writer of this book would describe himself today as an ardent and committed liberal. It is right that he should warn his readers of this, even as he tries to discharge his task with impartiality, lest here and there some of his own convictions should peep through his sober recording of facts. These preliminaries stated, let us now press on to summarise the development of race and colour policies in South Africa since 1910.

The first period, which we may call the Botha period, covers the years 1910 to 1919. In matters of race and colour General Botha was a conservative, but he was in all things moderate, kindly and reasonable. In his Ministry's day by day administration of what were then called 'Native Affairs' there was no brutality, and no more injustice than is inherent in the rule of one race over another. Unfortunately, however, he was responsible for the introduction of the Natives Land Act of 1913. Piloted through Parliament by an old Cape Liberal, J. W. Sauer, it contained ingenious clauses which made it largely inoperative in the Cape Province. But it lay open to serious objections, and it was most unfortunate that it should have been the first major law of the Union of South Africa affecting race relations. It was open to criticism by liberals in that it divided ownership and even occupation of land in the country as a whole on lines of race and colour. It was liable to the further objection that while the restrictions it placed on freedom of purchase and lease became operative at once the compensation in the form of the provision of new areas for Africans was contingent only. It depended on the report of a commission appointed under the Act. This report was delayed by the outbreak of war in 1914. When at last

203

the report was available and its recommendations were put before Parliament in the Native Affairs Administration Bill of 1917, further delay ensued. As usually happens, those members who were in favour of 'segregation' coupled their support with the proviso that no new areas for Africans were to be demarcated in their own constituencies. The Report of the commission was referred to a number of local committees whose recommendations were also the subject of controversy. In the end an administrative arrangement was made which gave progressive Africans some relief, but they had to wait until 1936 before legislation was passed such as had been contemplated by the Act of 1913 and this compensation was inadequate.

The introduction of the Natives Land Act led to the formation by the Africans of their first National Congress at a meeting held in Bloemfontein in 1912, and thus to the channelling of constitutional African opposition to the white Government. It also caused one of the many appeals to England which Africans made until it was borne in on them that England would no longer interfere in the affairs of an autonomous South Africa and that the days of good Queen Victoria had gone.

From 1919 to 1924 General Smuts ruled South Africa. In this first Smuts period, as we may call it, the legislation mirrored faithfully the image of that great man who was at his best in international affairs and at his worst in dealing with the local race and colour problems of South Africa – eloquent, ambiguous, and in the end almost disastrous. The main piece of legislation carried out by him in this field was the Native Affairs Act of 1920. Under this Act the system of councils established in the Transkei was potentially extended to other parts of South Africa, and some councils were in fact brought into being, when the local officials did not oppose the change. General Smuts also introduced a system of Union-wide 'Native Conferences' which began to meet annually and which foreshadowed the Natives Representative Council of the Hertzog era. Here at least was a body which, though purely advisory, gave African leaders the chance to express their opinions constitutionally, at a national level. By the same Act was created a 'Native Affairs Commission' to advise the Government. It was purely white, but two of its three members were well acquainted with educated Africans and sympathetic to their views. The Commission has continued in existence up to the time of writing, but has become a purely political body reflecting the views of the governments which appointed it, and has not realised the high hopes which attended its inauguration in 1920.

But if the positive contributions of General Smuts to African freedom were not wonderful, he at least did not take any steps to restrict it. Indeed he exposed his person and his reputation to danger in quelling the Rand Revolution of 1922, which arose essentially from the opposition of white miners to the opening up of more worth-while jobs for Africans.

His person which he exposed with his usual dauntless courage escaped injury. The injury to his reputation brought down his government in 1924, and ushered in what we may call the Hertzog period (1924-39). General Hertzog and his Nationalist Party ruled, in alliance with the Labour Party, from 1924 to 1933. Thereafter he was forced by events into a coalition with General Smuts which led almost immediately to a fusion of the two Parties under Hertzog as Prime Minister and Smuts as Deputy Prime Minister. This lasted until the outbreak of war in 1939. During this whole period, later as well as earlier, it was Hertzog who moulded the race and colour policies of the Union, though admittedly Smuts was able to secure some modifications which made it less unacceptable to the Africans.

Hertzog was deeply committed to the policy which was afterwards called 'apartheid'. His enemies complained that he was a man in blinkers, but even they were constrained to admit that within his limited field of vision he tried to be fair and even kind. This much must be set to his credit. He was an upright man. Yet his record in questions of race and colour is very questionable. The first important Act on these matters which he succeeded in carrying through Parliament – the Native Administration Act of 1927 – did much to remove the benefits of the Rule of Law from Africans and to increase very markedly the power of officials over them. The last two important Acts for which he was responsible – the Land Act and the Representation of Natives Act of 1936 – call for more extensive comment. Up to a point both followed the recommendations of the South African Native Affairs Commission of 1903-5 set up by Lord Milner.

The Land Act went some way to meet the implied offers of the Land Act of 1913. On the other hand it helped to make more rigid the division of land ownership in South Africa on racial lines. When all the land indicated in the schedule to Hertzog's Land Act has been acquired, the Africans will have from 13 per cent to 15 per cent of the total area of South Africa and the other races (mainly the whites) from 85 per cent to 87 per cent. And this, so far as Hertzog's legislation goes, is to be looked upon as a final apportionment.

The Representation Act put an end to the non-racial franchise of the Cape. It is to be noted that Smuts and all his supporters in the Cabinet, with the single exception of J. H. Hofmeyr, voted for this revolutionary step. It may be that it was politically necessary, that fusion had to be maintained and that this was a condition of maintaining fusion. Yet it is characteristic of General Smuts that while he accepted this change to preserve fusion he broke fusion strongly and finally and without hesitation on a question of international politics – war with Hitler's Germany.

When the Representation Act was before the Cabinet it was Smuts and his followers who insisted that the Cape franchise should be preserved though on a separate roll, and that Cape African voters should return three white members to the House of Assembly. The enriching of the House of Assembly by members of the calibre of Margaret Ballinger and Donald Molteno is thus due to Smuts.

It may be noted that both white men sympathetic to African claims and Africans themselves were willing to take office in Hertzog's separatist institutions. A liberal like J. D. Rheinallt Jones, for example, was willing to sit in the Senate. Men like Z. K. Matthews, R. V. Selope Thema, John Dube, Paul Mosaka and Dr. Moroka were willing to sit in the Natives' Representative Council. Were the same opportunities to be offered today, they would probably be met by boycott. The abolition of the Cape non-racial franchise was hotly opposed, and yet some of its most vehement opponents took seats in the Hertzog institutions. Somehow a spirit of hope was in the air. The Representative Council began well. Its very able members worked skilfully but in an atmosphere of moderation. Its thoroughly capable and kindly chairman, Dr. D. L. Smit, handled the council well. But the various government departments to whom the resolutions of the Council went failed to act. Someone coined the phrase 'toy telephone'. It was too apt and too true a description to be forgotten. Before the end of the second Smuts period (1939-1948) the Council was in open revolt.

The second Smuts period was, like the first, one of somewhat ineffective goodwill. Expenditure on African education was very greatly increased. Some of the social pension benefits were extended – admittedly at very low rates – to Africans. African children were given free education, some free school books, and a free meal daily, all three of which benefits were withdrawn by the next government. It is noteworthy that all these changes were made within departments controlled by J. H. Hofmeyr. General Smuts used Africans in mainly non-combatant duties in the war, was always courteous and kindly, but never decisive in action. He met some of the members of the Representative Council for confidential discussions, and was about to introduce great changes in the life of the urban Africans, on the lines of what is known as the Fagan Report, when the tidal wave of 1948 swept him and his party out of office for decades.

From 1948 under a succession of Nationalist Prime Ministers, armed with constantly increasing majorities in Parliament, full opportunity was offered for the carrying out of the policy originally known as 'apartheid' and later designated by such terms as separate or differential development. Apart from legislation affecting the rights of individual citizens and the supremacy of the Rule of Law, the most important early action of the new Parliament under Dr. Malan's leadership was to separate African education (henceforth to be known as 'Bantu Education') completely from all other education, and to place it under the Department of Bantu Administration and Development. The Natives Representative Council was abolished in 1955. The representation of Africans in both the Senate and the House of Assembly was in its turn abolished by an Act of 1959.

Under J. G. Strydom, Dr. Malan's immediate successor, the policy of the Government was described as 'baasskap', the complete mastery of the whites over the blacks. But a great turn of fortune was at hand.

ADDENDUM: SOUTH AFRICA SINCE 1910

When Dr. H. F. Verwoerd succeeded to the premiership in 1958, the whole aspect of apartheid was changed. His surprise decision of 1959 to confer a measure of self-government on the Transkei, the most compact and homogeneous of African areas, may be described as a brilliant piece of 'window-dressing' or, perhaps more fairly, as an attempt to introduce morality into apartheid. Whether the conferring of autonomy on tribal areas was a fair exchange for the exclusion of Africans from all political rights in the rest of the country may be debated, but at least it was an attempt to provide some sort of *quid pro quo*. In the complex personality of Dr. Verwoerd it may have been considered a completely just equivalent. Be that as it may, it turned the current of South African politics into a new direction. It became the policy of Dr. Verwoerd's government and of that of his successor, B. J. Vorster, to create new Transkeis wherever this was geographically possible and even in areas like Zululand where it seemed geographically impossible. African leadership began to see in this 'homelands' policy an opportunity of immediate progress towards a final and perhaps different solution, and some white liberals began temporarily to sink their pleas for universal suffrage in favour of an effort to make the 'homelands' really free and to incorporate them into a future South African Federation.

But while these more political changes were taking place, quiet but equally important movements of thought were discernible among many young Afrikaners at Stellenbosch and elsewhere. In intellectual circles the policy of 'baasskap' was doomed, and even the policy of the 'homelands' was subjected to severe scrutiny. In the English-speaking universities also various degrees of liberalism and radicalism had a considerable following. The decisions of each parliamentary caucus were no longer a complete mirror of public opinion. The future is uncertain, but there is in it from the liberal point of view an element of hope.

In the early 1970s then the position is that, while Africans and other men of colour have been deprived of the parliamentary franchise and of all the political rights of South African citizenship, an attempt is being made to build up partly self-governing African communities, which may conceivably be one day wholly self-governing.

Any judgment of the changes here referred to, and any speculations as to the future of South Africa, must take account of the fact that South Africa lives in a changing Africa and a changing world. The main task of this book has been to study South African race problems from 1830 to 1910. If this study is to be of more than merely historical interest, it is important to note some of the ways in which the world of the 1970s differs from the world of 1910, and this we shall now proceed to do.

(1) The South Africa of 1910 was not in essentials an industrial country. Its gold mines, and to a lesser degree the diamond mines, were well-organised and very profitable financially, both to their share-

holders and to the Government, but apart from these South Africa was essentially an agricultural country. The South Africa of the 1970s is a thriving and prosperous industrial state. One of the effects of this is that South Africa is in a better position to resist external pressure. Another is the spectacular increase in the number of Africans living in urban areas, more than tenfold from 1910 to the present day. A policy based on independent 'homelands' is thus far less viable in the 1970s than it would have been in 1910.

(2) Communism as a theory had been in existence for over six decades in 1910. In 1870-71 the Paris Commune gave a first advance sketch of it in practice. But when the Union of South Africa came into being few South Africans took Communism seriously. The Russian Revolution of 1917-8, its extension to other European states, and the much later Chinese Revolution has made Communism a very living thing at the present day.

Its effects upon Africa have been various. Many independent African states have Russian or Chinese diplomats or technicians within their boundaries today. This does not mean that African states are 'going Communist'. Most African states do not subscribe to the full Communist programme. But Communism affects Africans in three ways.

Firstly, it has reduced American and British influence which would have been far greater than it is had there not been an alternative dispenser of grants-in-aid and expert assistance.

Secondly, it has set the sights of Africans higher. Since there is a sense in which Communism promises everything, reform movements, liberal or radical, must promise much more than would have seemed adequately attractive in 1910.

Thirdly, if few Africans are prepared to accept the full positive programme of Communism, many have fallen for its negative programme – denigration of the West and of even the best of the West's administrators, suspicion of reformers, repudiation of missionaries and enmity to Christianity.

Communism has affected large sections of white opinion in South Africa, though in a different way. The fear and hatred of Communism has become an obsession with many. Others are prepared to capitalise on this fear and hatred by labelling everything that they dislike and every serious attempt to alter the *status quo* as 'Communism'.

(3) A third great change between 1910 and the 1970s has been the virtual disappearance of the British Empire. Africans as late as 1912, and even later, looked to Britain, with a faith that seems almost pathetic today, to intervene on their behalf with the South African Government. The Nationalists who depict Botha and Smuts as South African Quislings have not been able to transport themselves back into the atmosphere of 1902-14 when the British Empire was the foremost fact of international politics. Smuts himself was mainly responsible for transforming it into a British Commonwealth of Nations (which incidentally meant that the Africans' approach to the British Government

was more remote and unreal than ever). The high hopes built by Smuts and others on this new conception have not been realised. The unreality of the new Commonwealth was illustrated by its component States voting in opposite directions during the Suez crisis and, in the case of India and Pakistan, going to war with each other. The greatly reduced power and prestige of Britain is part of the sacrifice she made in defying Hitler in 1940. Unfair and even regrettable as this may be, it has had to be reckoned with as a fact, and as one of the big differences of atmosphere between 1910 and the 1970s.

(4) Similarly to be recognised as a fact, without approval or disapproval, is the phenomenal growth of white Afrikaner nationalism since 1910. General Hertzog's revolt from Botha and Smuts in 1912 was a going out into the political wilderness. A little over three decades later, Hertzog himself was repudiated by the Nationalists of the Orange Free State for not being Nationalist enough. Though there are not wanting signs that the Nationalist movement has reached and is declining from its highest point of intensity, this has only happened after the essentials of the Nationalist movement have been accepted by white South Africa at large. Any survey of policy in South Africa of the 1970s must take account of the victories of Nationalism since 1910.

(5) But perhaps the biggest factor influencing African opinion in the Republic of South Africa has been the emergence of numerous independent African states. In 1910 there were only two independent African states – Liberia and Ethiopia – and no one took either of them very seriously. A few years before the Italian conquest of Ethiopia, that country was content to be represented in the Assembly of the League of Nations by a white man. Today African independent states are very conscious of both their Africanism and their independence. Collectively at any rate they are very powerful in the international world. Sometimes they are aggressive. They are utterly opposed to white domination in South Africa, and Africans in the Republic, who must be aware of the fact that they have a bigger proportion of African graduates than any other African state, cannot be satisfied that they are in so inferior a position compared with their fellow-Africans in Nigeria and Tanzania. This factor means that Africans in the Republic will never accept a policy of 'baasskap' and will only accept autonomy in the 'homelands' as a step towards full equality in the country as a whole.

(6) The influx of independent African nations into the United Nations General Assembly and the fact that they generally vote as a *bloc* and often have the support of the Asian powers has completely transformed the international situation for South Africa. This will best be seen by comparing the very mild criticism of the Permanent Mandates Commission and the League of Nations in the matter of the suppression of the Bondelswarts rising with the sharp action taken on lesser matters by the General Assembly of the United Nations and its Committees. Any policies put forward by South Africa must take account of the very changed international atmosphere.

(7) The evolution of the conception of 'negritude' in French West Africa, and, even more, the 'black consciousness' and 'black power' movements in the United States have had a very considerable effect on African opinion. It is specially the young and the intellectual classes who have been influenced, but their opinion cannot and must not be treated as unimportant. Chiefs, prosperous businessmen and illiterate workers may not have succumbed to any extent to this propaganda, but it is the thinking younger men whose opinion counts for most. Who can say how all this will work out in the future? We must certainly take account of it in the present.

It is a disconcerting phenomenon, especially when more young white men, many of them Afrikaans-speaking young men, are beginning to move towards and understand the African point of view, only to find it receding from them. The way out is not easy to see. The person in the greatest difficulty is the white liberal, now vigorously and very vocally repudiated by 'black consciousness' spokesmen. And yet no solution of our interracial difficulties in South Africa, unless it be a revolutionary one based on force, is possible unless thinking younger men, white and black, can meet and hammer out the basis of a new South Africa together.

Thus the situation in the 1970s is greatly different from the situation in 1910, on which the historical part of this book ends. Programmes which would have seemed fair and even generous in 1910 will not even be looked at in the 1970s. Whatever policies are ultimately adopted, South Africa must take full account of the immense changes elaborated in the seven sections above. There lies the challenge of life for the young South Africans of all races in the eighth decade of the twentieth century.

Index

Abakweta dances, 132
Abaninimizi, 134
Aberdeen, Lord (Secretary of State for the Colonies), 16, 29
Aborigines Protection Society, 24
Ackerman, J. W. (Member, Natal Native Commission, 1881-2), 61
Acts of Parliament:
  Basutoland Annexation Bill, 1871, 58, 74
  Burgers' Law 3 (Transvaal), 1876, 100
  Cape of Good Hope Constitution Ordinance, 1852, 10, 29
  Cape of Good Hope Constitution Ordinance Amendment Act, 1872, 29
  Disannexation Act (Lesotho), 1883, 78
  Disarmament Act (Lesotho), 1878, 76-7
  "Fiftieth Ordinance", 1828, 9, 73
  Glen Grey Act, 1894, 73, 82, 85, 104, 166-7, 171-3, 178
  Native Administration Act, 1927, 205
  Native Administration Act, (Natal), 1909, 67
  Native Administration Law (Natal), 1875, 147
  Native Affairs Act, 1920, 204
  Native Affairs Administration Bill, 1917, 204
  Native Labour Regulation Act, 1911, 105
  Native Locations Act (Cape), 1879, 166
  Native Successions Act (Cape), 1864, 130, 151
  Native Trust and Land Act, 1936, 101
  Natives (Urban Areas) Act, 1923, 157
  Natives' Land Act, 1913, 104-5, 165, 203-5
  Natives' Land Act, 1936, 205
  Port Elizabeth Native Strangers Location Bill, 1883, 166
  Representation of Natives Act, 1936, 205
  South Africa Act, 1909, 106, 173
  Squatters Law, 37, 98
Adams, Dr. (American Missionary, Natal), 43
Adams College, 199-200
Addison, Dr. (Member, Natal Native Commission, 1852-3), 53
Adultery, punishment of 114
African Customary Law: 111-128
  codification of, 21, 60, 61, 116, 121-3, 133-6, 139, 141-150
  exemption from, 55, 56, 58, 128, 135-140, 148
  recognition of: 111, 115
    British Kaffraria, 29, 129, 130, 143
    Cape, 113, 129-131, 142-4
    East Griqualand, 132
    Lesotho, 132, 144
    Natal, 50, 51, 113, 135, 136, 138, 139, 140, 141, 147-9
    Orange Free State, 113, 137
    Transkei, 80, 81, 113, 126, 131-6, 138, 140, 144, 147, 149
    Transvaal, 98, 99, 101, 102, 113, 115, 136
African independent states, 209
African languages, printing in, 195
African literature, 195, 201
African National Congress, 201, 204
African, educated, employment of, 69
Agar-Hamilton, Dr. J. A. I., 39, 108
Agricultural demonstration. *See* Demonstration, agricultural
Agricultural services, African, 185
Agricultural shows, 178-9
Agricultural societies, 179

Agriculture, 82, 89, 90, 91, 94, 95, 103, 117, 127, 160-2, 170, 175-187, 199, 208
Albany division, 180
Amadoda, 148
Amagwamba, 112
Amanzimtoti Institute, 199-200
Amapakati. *See* Counsellors of chiefs
Amatonga, 112
Amatuli tribe, 55, 164
Apartheid. *See* Segregation
Ayliff, Hon. J., 80, 143, 147
Ayliff, Rev. J., 186

"Baasskap", 206-7, 209
Bagshaw, W. (Member, Commons Select Committee, 1836-7), 19
Baines, T. (Member, Commons Select Committee, 1836-7), 19
Ballinger, Margaret, 205
Bantu Administration and Development, department of, 157
"Bantu authorities", 83
Barkly, Sir Henry (Governor, Cape of Good Hope), 108
Barnett, L. (Assistant Commissioner, Quthing, Basutoland), 128
Barry, Hon. Sir J. D., 80, 144
Barter, Chas. (Author of "Stray Memories of Natal and Zululand"), 46, 48, 53, 140
Basket-work, 189-91
Basutoland. *See* Lesotho
Basutoland Annexation Bill, 1871, 58, 74
Battle of Blood River, 36
Bead-work, 189-90
Beattie, — (Native Trader), 180
Beaumont, Hon. Sir Wm. (Administrator of Natal, etc.), 66, 67, 149
Berry, Sir W. Bisset, 80
"Bhunga", 93
Binns, Rt. Hon. Sir Henry, (Prime Minister of Natal), 63
Bird, John, C.M.G., 39, 53
Birkenstock, Hon. C. J. (Member, Natal Native Commission, 1906-7), 66
Black Mfolozi River, 36
"Black spots", 160
Blyth, E. (Assistant Commissioner, Berea, Basutoland), 77, 128
Blyth, Capt. Matthew (Chief Magistrate, Transkei, etc.), 78-9, 81, 87, 146, 166, 179, 182-3, 186-7
Blythswood Industrial Institution, 81

Boards, village management, 172
Bogadi. *See* Lobolo
Bohadi. *See* Lobolo
Bomvanaland, 182
Bondelswarts' rising, 209
Boshoff, Hon. H. G. (Judge President, Natal Native High Court), 149
Boshoff, Hon. J. N. (President, Orange Free State), 53
Botha, Gen. the Rt. Hon. Louis (Prime Minister of the Union), 11, 203, 208-9
Botha, P. R. (Member, Natal Native Commission, 1881-2), 61
Bowker, J. H. (Governor's Agent, Basutoland), 85
Boys, Henry Scott, 174
Bridgman, Rev. F. B., D.D., 90
British Kaffraria, 21, 23, 24, 27, 51 annexation of 1866, 28, 74
British Kaffraria. *See also* Ciskei
Brooke, Audrey, 197, 201
Brookes, Edgar H., 39, 58, 71, 186, 201
Brownlee, Hon. Chas. (Secretary for Native Affairs, Cape of Good Hope, etc.), 21, 39, 46, 74, 78-80, 83, 85, 143, 181-2, 186-7
Brownlee, W. T. (Magistrate, Butterworth), 89, 93, 132, 174
Buffalo River, boundary of Zululand, 31, 41
Bulwer, Sir Henry (Governor, Natal), 11
Burgers, Rev. Thomas Francois (President, S.A. Republic), 98, 101
Burgers' Law (Transvaal), 1876, 100
Bushmen, 9
Butterworth, 82, 89, 92, 93, 167, 174
Butterworth Native Agricultural Society, 179
Buxton, Fowell (Chairman, Commons Select Committee, 1836-7), 19

Cala district, 179, 181
Calderwood, Rev. Henry, 23, 29, 129, 166, 186, 196, 199
Callaway, Rt. Rev. H. (Bishop of St. John's, Kaffraria), 198
Campbell, Hon. H. C., I.S.O. (Judge President, Natal Native High Court), 66, 126, 193-4
Campbell, Hon. Marshall (Member, S.A. Native Affairs Commission, 1903-5), 103, 109

INDEX

Campbell, W. H. (Member, Natal Native Commission, 1881-2), 61
Campbell, W. Y., 148
Canham, A., 66
Cape African dependencies, proposal of abandoning to U.K. government, 77-8
Cape Native Affairs Commission, 1910, 87-8, 128, 151, 186
Cape Native Blue Books, 11, 58, 81, 85, 95, 146, 151-2, 174, 186-7, 194
Cape Native Laws and Customs Commission, 1883-5, 11, 29, 71, 75, 80, 81, 87, 118, 123, 128, 131-3, 143-4, 146, 150-2, 165-6
Cape of Good Hope, grant of responsible government to, 10, 29, 74
Cape of Good Hope Constitution Ordinance, 1852, 10, 29
Cape of Good Hope Constitution Ordinance Amendment Act, 1872, 29
Carnarvon, Lord (Secretary of State for the Colonies), 29, 47
Cathcart, Sir George (Governor, Cape of Good Hope), 24, 25, 29, 51, 151, 174, 178-9
Cato, G. C. (Member, Natal Native Commissions, 1852-3 and 1881-2), 53, 61
Cawood, Samuel, 180
Cetshwayo (Zulu Chief), 58, 60, 85, 176, 197
Chadwick, Hon. J. (Judge, Natal Native High Court), 69
Chalmers, W. B. (Member, Cape Native Laws and Customs Commission, 1883), 80
Chiefs and headmen, 111, 113-5, 153-4, 161-2, 194, 210
  British Kaffraria, 129
  Cape, 16, 20, 21, 24-8, 129, 146, 153
  Natal, 44, 51, 59, 136, 148, 153, 163-4
  Transkei, 74-7, 133, 144, 149, 167
  Transvaal, 101-2, 109, 156
Chinese labourers, 193
Christianity, conversion to. *See* Missionaries
Christians, African, 198-9, 201
Ciskei, 28, 73, 87
Ciskei. *See also* British Kaffraria
Civil Law, 113-4, 133, 136, 144, 147, 148
Clarke, Col. Sir Marshall (Resident Commissioner, Basutoland), 78

Cloete, Dr. Henry (H.M. Special Commissioner in Natal), 31, 38, 50, 151
Code of Native Law, Natal. *See* Natal Code of Native Law
Codification of law, 61, 149, 150
Cole, Sir Lowry (Governor, Cape of Good Hope), 15
Colenso, Rt. Rev. J. W. (Bishop of Natal), 57, 61, 197-8
Colley, Sir George Pomeroy (Governor of Natal), 141, 152
Colonial Law, 28, 118, 129, 130, 131, 141-2, 144-5
Commerce, Native, 103, 109
Commissioners of African Affairs, 153
  Cape, 21, 23, 129, 165
  Natal, 60, 66-8, 155, 164, 173
  Transvaal, 100, 102, 109, 129, 156
Commissions and Parliamentary Select Committees:
  Cape Native Affairs Commission, 1910, 87-8, 128, 151, 186
  Cape Native Laws and Customs Commission, 1883-5, 11, 29, 71, 75, 80-1, 87, 118, 123, 128, 131-3, 143-4, 146, 150-2, 165-6
  Commons Select Committee on Aborigines (British Settlements), 1836-7, 11, 18, 19, 24, 29, 58, 186, 193
  Eiselen Commission, 1951, 200
  Intercolonial Commission, 1903-5, 49, 56, 64, 80, 83, 89, 118, 120, 127, 141-2, 148-9, 168
  Location Commission, Transvaal, 1881-6, 100, 101, 109, 165, 174
  Natal Commission, 1887, 122
  Natal Native Affairs Commission, 1906-7, 11, 66, 68-9, 139-40, 149, 151, 152, 164, 178, 186
  Natal Native Commission, 1846-7, 11, 42-5, 53-4, 58, 135, 163, 170
  Natal Native Commission, 1852-3, 11, 39, 42-4, 53-4, 58, 121
  Natal Native Commission, 1881-2, 11, 42, 61, 117-8, 121, 126, 128, 141, 152, 182
  Native Affairs Commission, 1920 82, 94-5, 174, 200, 204
  Select Committee of the Cape House of Assembly . . . Grey Act, 1898, 88, 151

213

South African Native Affairs Commission, 1903-5, 11, 85, 103-7, 109, 128, 136, 151-2, 158, 171, 173, 186-7, 205
South African Native Races Commission, 186
Survey Commission, 1920, 168
Zululand Delimitations Commission, 1902-4, 69
Commonage, 168, 170-2
Commons Select Committee on Aborigines (British Settlements), 1836-7, 11, 18, 19, 24, 29, 58, 186, 193
Communal locations, 170
Communal responsibility, 114, 129, 133-6, 144-5, 148
Communism, 208
Compound system, 192
Connor, the Hon. Sir Henry (Chief Justice, Natal), 61
Contract, law of, 115
Council system, 83, 204, 206
  Natal, 66-8, 163-4
  Pondoland, 153
  Transkei, 79-83, 87-95, 167, 179, 204
Counsellors of chiefs, 111, 113, 115, 133, 146, 149, 161
Courts of Law. *See* Law Courts
Creux, Rev. Ernest (Mission Suisse Romande), 176
Crimes, punishment in African Customary Law, 51, 52, 112, 114
Criminal Law, 27, 51-2, 112-4, 135, 144-5, 147
Crops, agricultural, 177-181, 183-5
Currie, Sir Walter, 29, 143-4, 151

Dale, Sir Langham, 201
Dances, 132
Davies, Horton, 201
Death penalty, 51, 52, 114
De la Harpe, J. B. (Member, S.A. Native Affairs Commission, 1903-5), 103
Demonstration, agricultural, 178-9
Denominations, "independent", 197
Diamonds, discovery of, 1867-71, 192
Dickson, Capt. Quayle (Member, S.A. Native Affairs Commission, 1903-5), 103
Dingane (Zulu Chief), 31, 36, 42, 189
Dingiswayo (Abatetwa Chief), 176
Dipping, 182
Disannexation Act (Lesotho), 1883, 78

Disarmament Act (Lesotho), 1878, 76-7
Dohne, Rev. C. L., 58
Donkin, Sir Rufane (Member Commons Select Committee, 1836-7), 19
Dower, E. E. (Union Secretary for Native Affairs), 83, 168, 171, 184
Du Plessis, Rev. Dr. J., 201
Dube, John, 206
Dugmore, Rev. H. H., 22, 143
Dunn, John (Zulu Chief), 47
D'Urban, Sir Benjamin (Governor, Cape of Good Hope), 16, 17, 18, 21, 29, 30, 42, 142-3
Dyke, Rev. R. M., 120, 122

East Griqualand, 78-80, 145-6, 159
"Eating up", 75, 129
Education, 69, 91, 95, 105, 170, 191, 199-201, 206
  agricultural, 54, 90, 91, 94, 178
  industrial, 43, 54, 90-2, 94, 105, 189-90, 193, 199, 201
Eiselen Commission, 1951, 200
Elliotdale, 146, 180
Elliott, Major Sir Henry (Chief Magistrate, Transkei), 79, 146, 186
Emanuelson, O. E., 201
Emphyteusis, 168
Engcobo, 146
English Common Law, 111, 162, 164
Escombe, Rt. Hon. Harry (Prime Minister, Natal), 152, 164
Evans, Maurice S., C.M.G., 66
Experimental farm, Glen Grey, 179

Faku (Pondo Chief), 20, 38
Faku, Chief (Witness before Natal Native Commission, 1881-2), 62
Family life, disruption of, 175, 192-3
Fannin, J. E. (Member, Natal Native Commission, 1881-2), 61
Farm labour, 37-8, 53-4, 97, 104, 183, 196
Females, position of, 114, 126, 127, 177, 195-6
Fertilisers, use of, 82
"Fiftieth Ordinance", 1828, 9, 73
Fines. *See* Taxation and fines
Fingo. *See* Mfengu
Fitzgerald, Dr. J. P., 28
Fort Beaufort, 164
Fort Hare, 200
Foxon, C. C. (British Resident, Maputaland), 128

214

INDEX

Franchise, 207
  Cape, 10, 73, 106, 151, 205-6
  Natal, 56, 62
  Transkei, 73, 81-2, 138, 170
  Transvaal, 106-7
Fraser, Sir John George, Kt., 173
Frere, Sir Bartle (Governor, Cape of Good Hope), 48, 49, 60
Frontier Wars:
  6th, 16, 17, 42
  7th (War of the Axe), 21, 23
  8th, 24
  9th, 78, 192
Frost, John, C.M.G., M.L.A., 167
Fynn, A. F., 53, 121, 122, 128

Gallwey, the Hon. Sir Michael H., (Chief Justice, Natal), 58, 173
Gangelezwe, 187
Gcalekaland, 183
  annexation of, 1885, 78
Gibbs, Lieut C. J. (Member, Natal Native Commission, 1846-7), 43
Gibson, J. Y., 149
Gladstone, Rt. Hon. W. E., 19
Glen Grey, 87, 154
Glen Grey Act, 1894, 73, 82, 85, 104, 166-7, 171-3, 178
Glen Grey Experimental Farm. *See* Experimental Farm, Glen Grey
Glen Grey System, 79, 82, 83, 87, 88, 94, 105, 151, 154, 166-173, 179
Glenelg, Lord (Secretary of State for the Colonies), 16-20, 24, 142, 143, 179
Glynn, C. R., 69
Godley, Lieut-Col. G. A., 103
Gold, discovery of, 1886, 192
Goodenough, Rev. H. D., 69
Goodwood, Wm., 85
Gordon, General Charles George, 77
Gordon, Dr. Ruth, 58
Great Trek, 17, 19, 35, 36
  causes of, 35, 36
Green, Dean (Member, Natal Native Commission, 1881-2), 61, 118, 121, 140
Green, R. A. (Member, Natal Native Commission, 1881-2), 61
Grey, Earl (Secretary of State for the Colonies), 24, 29, 43-4, 52, 58, 135, 159, 170, 173-4
Grey, Sir George, Bart. (Secretary of State for the Colonies), 25

Grey, Sir George (Governor, Cape of Good Hope), 19, 25-9, 80, 83, 143, 179, 187, 193
Griffith, Col. C. D., C.M.G. (Governor's Agent, Basutoland), 58, 74, 77, 82, 158
Grout, Rev. Lewis, 58
Gumede, P. J., 90
"Gun War", Basutoland, 192
Guns, selling of, to Africans, 108, 192

Hamilton, J. A. (Member, S.A. Native Affairs Commission, 1903-5), 103
Harding, Hon. W. (Member, Natal Native Commission, 1852-3), 53
Hardy, W. (Member, Commons Select Committee, 1836-7), 19
Hare, Col. (Lieut.-Governor, Eastern Districts, Cape of Good Hope), 179
Hawes, C. (Member, Commons Select Committee, 1836-7), 19
Headmen. *See* Chiefs and headmen
Henderson, J. (Member, Natal Native Commission, 1852-3), 53
Herd, Norman, 193
Herschel, 130, 154
Hertzog, Gen. the Hon. J. B. M. (Union Prime Minister), 101, 204-6, 209
Hicks-Beach, Sir Michael, 49
Hinchliff, Peter, 201
Hindley, T. (Member, Commons Select Committee, 1836-7), 19
Hlubi tribe, 57
Hofmeyr, the Rt. Hon. J. H. (Deputy Prime Minister of the Union), 205, 206
Hofmeyr, Stephen, 196
Holland, B. H. (Civil Commissioner, King William's Town), 167
Holland, W. (Member, Commons Select Committee, 1836-7), 19
"Holmen", 42, 58
"Homelands", 83, 157, 160, 207-9
Hook, D. B. (Magistrate, Herschel), 130-1
"Horse tax", 27
Horses, 177, 179
Horwitz, R., 194
Hospitals, 28, 90, 199
Hottentots, 9, 10, 73
Houses, building of. *See* Huts and houses, building of
Hrayi, Lot, 28
Hudson, George (British Resident, Transvaal), 101

Hulett, the Hon. Sir J. L., Kt., 66
Hurwitz, N., 186
Hut Tax, 23, 27, 54, 65, 76, 98, 100, 103, 162, 180
Huts and houses, building of, 189-91, 195

Idutywa, 82, 89, 167, 174, 176
Ikazi. *See* Lobolo
Impapala Native Mission, 69
Inanda, 126
"Independent" denominations, 197
Indian Penal Code, 145
Industrial labour, 175, 191-4, 204, 208
Industrial state, South Africa as, 207-8
Industries, African domestic. *See* "Kraal" industries
Inheritance, 50, 98, 118, 129, 131, 136, 142
Integration, 73, 157
Intercolonial Commission, 1903-5, 49, 56, 64, 80, 83, 89, 118, 120, 127, 141-2, 148-9, 168
Intonjane dances, 132
Ipolela, 176
Irrigation, 182
Isandhlwana, 76
Isanusi, 145
Isibhalo. *See* Letsima
Isishimeyana, 181
Ixopo, 176
Izinsizwa, 148
Izizi, 144

Jabavu, Prof. D. D. T., 95, 152, 186
Jameson, Sir Leander Starr (Prime Minister, Cape of Good Hope), 47
Jervis, Captain, 42
Jobi, 182
Johnston, W. H. (Member, Commons Select Committee, 1836-7), 19
Jokweni, 20
Jones, J. D. Rheinallt, 200, 206
Jorissen, Dr. E. J. P. (Attorney-General, S.A. Republic), 47, 58
Junod, H. A., 198
Jus Naturale, 50, 101, 112, 116, 121, 127, 135, 137
Justice, department of, Cape, 154-5
Natal, 154-5
Transvaal, 155
Justinian, code of, 112
"Kaffir Express", 123

Kaffir Wars. *See* Frontier Wars
"Kaffir-farming", 37, 103
"Kafir Laws and Customs". *See* "Maclean's Compendium of Native Law"
Kaffraria, British. *See* British Kaffraria
Kaffraria, Western, 178
Kama, Chief, 26, 27
Kei River, boundary of Transkeian districts, 17
Keiskama and Kei Rivers, boundaries of British territory, 17, 21, 24
Kentani, 83
Ketchwayo (Zulu Chief). *See* Cetshwayo
Kimberley, Earl of (Secretary of State for the Colonies), 152
Kimberley, 192
Kimberley diamond fields, annexation of, 20
King William's Town, 18, 19, 131, 154, 172, 176
King William's Town Hospital, 28
Kirkman, Hon. J., M.L.C., 31, 32
Kok, Adam (Griqua Captain), 20
Kona (Xosa Chief), 22
Kornet Spruit, 85
"Kraal", head of. *See* Umninimizi
"Kraal" industries, 189-191
Kreli (Xosa Chief), 20, 176, 179, 186
Krogh, Senator the Hon. J. C., 103
Kropf, Rev. A., 123
Kruger, His Honour S. J. P. (President, S.A. Republic), 101

Labouchère, Rt. Hon. H. (Secretary of State for the Colonies), 29, 187
Labour, 65, 69, 103-5, 108, 159, 160, 184, 185, 189, 191; farm, 37, 38, 53, 54, 97, 104, 183, 196; industrial, 175, 191-4, 204, 208
Labour, migrant. *See* Migrant labour
Labuschagne, C. (Member, Natal Native Commission, 1852-3), 53
Lagden, Sir Godfrey (Resident Commissioner, Basutoland), 95, 103
Land, African leasing of, 109; expropriation of, 160; location and reserve, 55, 101, 109, 160-73, 205; mission, 163, 166; vested in Crown or State, 163-6, 170, 173
Land, trusteeship of. *See* Trusteeship of land

Land tenure, individual, 159-161, 175, 184, 203; Cape, 159, 166; Ciskei, 87, 88; Natal, 54, 61, 159, 162-3, 166; South-West Africa, 165; Transkei, 82, 83, 90, 93, 94, 168-73; Transvaal, 98, 100, 103-5, 107, 159, 165; statutory conditions, 168-73
Landman, C. (Member, Natal Native Commission, 1852-3), 53
Langalibalele (Chief of the Hlubi tribe), 57, 197
Lanyon, Sir Owen (Administrator, Transvaal), 99, 108
Laurence, T. E., 128
Law:
  African Customary Law
  Civil Law
  Colonial Law
  Contract, law of
  Criminal Law
  English Common Law
  Martial Law
  Persons, law of
  Property, law of
  Roman Law
  Roman-Dutch Law
  "Spoor Laws"
  For details *see* individual headings
Law Courts, "Native", 27, 60, 68, 99, 100, 126, 127, 129-31, 136, 137, 140, 147, 156
Law Courts, of chiefs and counsellors, 111
Laws, Parliamentary. *See* Acts of Parliament
Leary, W. P., 83, 90, 128
Leroy, A. E., 200
Lesotho, 112, 153
  boundaries, 1843, 32
  annexation by Cape, 20, 24, 28-9, 58, 73-4
  Cape rule, 73-4, 79-80, 83
  disannexation, 77-8
  British rule, 78, 97
  Wars with Orange Free State, 97
  Pitsos, 76-8, 85, 186
Letsie (Basuto Chief), 78
Letsima, 75, 191
Levey, C. J. (Magistrate, Xalanga, etc), 133, 179-80, 183-4, 191
Leyds, Dr. W. J. (State Secretary, S.A. Republic), 108
Liberalism, 203, 206-8, 210
Libode, 94

Lindley, Rev. D., 43, 196
Livingstone, David, 196
Lobengula (Matabele Chief), 176
Lobolo, 61-2, 75, 102, 112-3, 115-123, 126-130, 132, 136, 142, 148, 150, 157, 192; comparison with custom in other nations, 123-5
Location Boards, 87, 170, 172
Location Commission, Transvaal, 1881-6, 100, 101, 109, 165, 174
Locations, communal. *See* Communal locations
Locations, surveying of. *See* Surveying, location
Locations and reserves, 153, 157, 160-2, 204
  Cape, 23, 29, 83, 131, 144, 159, 166, 176
  Ciskei, 87
  Natal, 43-5, 53-5, 63, 65, 69, 155, 159, 161, 163-4, 173, 175
  Orange Free State, 161
  Transkei, 161, 166-173, 176, 186
  Transvaal, 100, 101, 105, 109, 159, 161, 165
Loch, Sir H. B. (Governor, Cape of Good Hope), 78
Loffhagen, Rev. R. W., 187
London Convention, 1884, 101
Loram, Dr. C. T., LL.B., Ph.D. (Member, Union permanent Native Affairs Commission), 200, 201
Lovedale, 80, 191, 194, 200, 201
Lushington, Dr. (Member, Commons Select Committee, 1836-7), 19
Luthuli, Martin L. 9
Lydenburg, Republic of, 36, 97
Mabille, Rev. L., 120, 122
Macfarlane, W. (Member, Natal Native Commission, 1852-3), 53
Mackinnon, Col., 151
Maclean, Col. (Commissioner for British Kaffraria), 21, 27, 80, 143
"Maclean's Compendium of Native Law", 80, 143
Maclear, 160
Macmillan, W. M., 12, 196
Magisterial system, 153, 154, 157, 185
  Cape, 21, 24-7, 130, 132, 133, 144, 146, 154, 155, 162
  Natal, 43, 53, 60, 61, 63, 68-70, 143, 147, 149, 154, 155, 167

217

Transkei, 74-7, 79-81, 83, 87, 89, 90, 92-5, 126, 131, 133, 134, 136, 144, 154, 166, 169, 170, 172, 178, 180
Transvaal, 155, 156
Magistrates (District Resident):
Butterworth, 89, 93
Elliotdale, 146
Engcobo, 146
Glen Grey, 87, 154
Herschel, 130, 154
Idutywa, 89, 167, 174
Inanda, 126
Ipolela, 176
Ixopo, 176
King William's Town, 154
Kornet Spruit, 85
Mount Ayliff, 146
Mount Frere, 128
Mqanduli, 146
Nqamakwe, 89
Pietermaritzburg, 121
St. Mark's, 146
Tsolo, 146
Tsomo, 85, 89, 167
Umtata, 146
Umzimkulu, 146
Xalanga, 146, 180, 191
Magistrates, original reports of, 11
Maine, H. S., 128, 152
Maitland, Sir Peregrine (Governor, Cape of Good Hope), 24
Maize, 177, 180, 184
Makanya, Plant, 69
Makulula, 62
Malan, Rt. Hon. F. S., 73, 206
Mamaree, 108
"Mandated territory", 161, 163
Manu, Code of, 149
Manuring. See Fertilisers, use of
Mapasa (Emigrant Tembu Chief), 20
Mariannhill, 191
Maritz, S. (Member, Natal Native Commission, 1852-3), 53
Marketing of agricultural produce, 180-1
Marriage, 50, 56, 61-2, 75, 98, 102, 111-32, 136-8, 140-2, 148, 177, 192
Martial law, 21, 51, 130, 132, 142-3
Martineau, J., 58, 71
Marzolff, Rev. H., 120, 122
Matatiele, 160
Matthews, Z. K., 206
Matuzana, Chief, 180
Medical treatment, for Africans, 28, 90, 195, 199

Merriman, Rt. Hon. John X. (Prime Minister, Cape of Good Hope), 45, 49, 74, 77
Methley, J. E., 191, 194
Methodist mission, 199
Mfengu, 23, 79, 143, 151-2, 166-7, 176, 178-84, 186-7
Mgungundlovu, 189
Migrant labour, 175, 185, 192-3
Millet, 177, 180, 184
Milner, Rt. Hon. Viscount (High Commissioner in South Africa), 101, 103, 107, 192, 205
Milner, H. (Member, Natal Native Commission, 1852-3), 53
Mining, 189, 192-3, 204, 207
Mission land. See Land, mission
Mission Suisse Romande, 176
Missionaries, 18, 22, 30, 36, 43, 55, 73, 78, 81, 84, 91, 117-20, 122, 165, 176, 180-1, 185, 189-91, 193, 195-201, 208
Molesworth, Sir Wm. (Secretary of State for the Colonies), 29
Molteno, Donald, 205
Moreland, J. (Member, Natal Native Commission, 1852-3), 53
Morewood, E. (Member, Natal Native Commission, 1852-3), 53
Morija, 191
Moroka, Dr., 206
Mosaka, Paul, 206
Moselekatse (Matabele Chief), 20, 30, 176
Moshesh (Basuto Chief), 20, 24, 30, 32, 33, 176
Moshoeshoe. See Moshesh
Mount Ayliff, 146
Mount Currie, 160
Mount Frere, 128
Mpande (Zulu Chief), 20, 30, 31, 32, 36, 47
Mqanduli, 146, 180
Mtamvuma River, 36
Mti, Peter, 120
Murder, 51, 52, 99, 112, 114, 133, 145
Murray, Sir George (Secretary of State for the Colonies), 15
Murray, Hon. Sir T. K., 66
Mzimvubu River, 36, 177

Namaqualand, 180, 187
Nambula, 62
Napier, Sir George (Governor, Cape of Good Hope), 24, 33, 179

218

INDEX

Natal: annexation by British, 1843, 36, 38; responsible government, 1893, 60, 64
Natal African tribes, control of by Natal Parliament, 64
Natal Code of Native Law, 60, 61, 68-70, 80, 114, 122-3, 125-6, 135-6, 139, 142, 145, 147-9
Natal Commission, 1887, 122
Natal Gazette, 128
Natal Native Administration, proposals of self-contained constitution for, 66
Natal Native Affairs Commission, 1905-7, 11, 66, 68, 69, 139-40, 149, 151, 152, 164, 178, 186
Natal Native Blue Books, 11, 58, 128, 151-2, 186-7, 193
Natal Native Commission, 1846-7, 11, 42-5, 53, 54, 58, 135, 163, 170
Natal Native Commission, 1852-3, 11, 39, 42-4, 53-4, 58, 121
Natal Native Commission, 1881-2, 11, 42, 61, 117-8, 121, 126, 128, 141, 152, 182
Natal Native Rebellion, 1906, 65, 178
Natal Native Trust, 55, 69, 162-4
Natalia, Republic of, relations with Africans, 36-9, 44, 53
National Convention, 1908-9, 73, 106
Nationalism, Afrikaner, 206, 208-9
Native Administration, Board of (Natal), 147
Native Administration Act, 1927, 205
Native Administration Act (Natal), 1909, 67
Native Administration Law (Natal), 1875, 147
Native Affairs Act, 1920, 204
Native Affairs Administration Bill, 1917, 204
Native Affairs Commission, 1920, 82, 94-5, 174, 200, 204
Native Affairs Department: Cape, 79-80, 84, 154-5; Natal, 64, 66, 69, 155, 163; Transvaal, 155-6
Native Labour Regulation Act, 1911, 105
Native Law. See African Customary Law.
Native Locations Act (Cape), 1879, 166
Native Succession Act (Cape), 1864, 130, 151

Native Trust and Land Act, 1936, 101
Natives' Land Act, 1913, 104-5, 165, 203-5
Natives' Land Act, 1936, 205
Natives' Representative Council, 204, 206
Natives (Urban Areas) Act, 1923, 157
Nel, T. (Member, Natal Native Commission, 1852-3), 53
Newcastle, Duke of (Secretary of State for the Colonies), 29, 58, 174, 186
Ngqeleni, 94
Ngqika, 178-9, 181
Ngqobela v. Sihele, 131
Noble, John, 80
Nongqase, 27
Nqamakwe, 82, 89, 167, 174

Oecumenism, 197
One-man-one-lot tenure, 82, 161, 162, 169, 173, 175
Orange Free State, relations with Africans, 36, 39, 97
Orpen, J. M., 76, 77, 79, 85
Otto, P. A. R. (Member, Natal Native Commission, 1852-3 and 1881-2), 53, 61

Pakington, Sir G. A., Bart. (Secretary of State for the Colonies), 29, 151
Panda. See Mpande
Passes, 9, 29, 69, 101, 102, 111
Patterson, Sheila, 12
Pease, C. (Member, Commons Select Committee, 1836-7), 19
Peddie district, 180, 182-3
Penal Code, Transkeian. See Transkeian Penal Code
Persons, law of, 114-5
Philip, Rev. John, D.D., 18, 33, 196-7
Philipps, Thomas, 58
Pietermaritzburg, 121
Pine, Sir Benjamin, 57
Plakkers Wet. See Squatters Law
Plant, R. W., 193
Plough, use of, 117, 176-9, 183-5
Plumptre, E. H. (Member Commons Select Committee, 1836-7), 19
Poll tax, 65
Polygamy, 50, 56, 61, 114-8, 129, 136, 141-2, 177, 195
Pondoland, 83, 153, 182
 annexation of, 1894, 78, 82

219

Pondoland, Western, 94, 153
Pondoland General Council, 94
"Poor White" question, 103-4, 107
Port Elizabeth Native Strangers Location Bill, 1883, 166
Port St. John's, 94, 160
annexation of, 1884, 78
Potgieter, E. (Member, Natal Native Commission, 1852-3), 53
Pottery, 190
Pottinger, Sir Henry (Governor, Cape of Good Hope), 58
Press, African, 201
Pretoria Convention, 1881, 100, 101, 165, 174
Pretorius, A. W. J., 39, 97
Primogeniture, 50, 114, 129, 142, 172
Printing industry, 191, 195
Prizes for agriculture, 178-9
Property, law of, 115, 169
"Putili" Trust, 164

Queen Adelaide, Province of, 17, 19, 21
Queen's Town, 131, 164
Quit-rent, 23, 82, 83, 161-2, 166-73

Race policies, 203-5, 207, 210
Rand Revolution, 1922, 204
Rawson, Col. H. E. (Member, Natal Native Commission, 1906-7), 66
"Red Kaffir", 93
Reeve, Capt. J., 26
Relationship amongst Africans, 114
Religion, Christian. *See* Missionaries
Representation of Natives Act, 1936, 205
Reserves. *See* Locations and reserves
Responsibility, communal. *See* Communal responsibility
Responsible Government: Cape of Good Hope, 10, 29, 74; Natal, 60, 64
Retief, Piet, 36
Reynolds, T. (Member, Natal Native Commission, 1881-2), 61
Rhenish missionaries, 180
Rhodes, Rt. Hon. Cecil John (Prime Minister, Cape of Good Hope), 79, 166
Rhodesia, Southern, adoption of Shepstone system, 59
Robinson, Rt. Hon. Sir John (Prime Minister, Natal), 63

Rolland, Emile S. (Member, Cape Native Laws and Customs Commission, 1882), 80
Roman Law, 115
Roman-Dutch Law, 50-1, 55, 98, 111, 129, 136, 141-2, 164, 168
Rose-Innes, J. (Civil Commissioner, King William's Town), 176
Rose-Innes, Sir James, 73
Rudolph, G. M. (Member, Natal Native Commission, 1881-2), 61
Russell, R., 58, 186, 189
Ryley, R. R. (Member, Natal Native Commission, 1852-3), 53

St. Mark's, 146, 180
Samuelson, S. O. (Under-Secretary for Native Affairs, Natal), 11, 64, 65, 67, 68, 70, 103, 109, 128, 136, 139, 151, 173
Sandile (Xhosa Chief), 22, 179, 183
Sauer, Hon. J. W. (Union Minister for Native Affairs), 76, 77-8, 203
Saunders, Sir Charles (Chief Magistrate, Zululand), 69, 152
Saunders, Dr. Christopher, 85
Scanlen, Hon. Sir T. C. (Prime Minister, Cape of Good Hope), 76, 79, 103
Scheepers, F. (Member, Natal Native Commission, 1852-3), 53
Schoeman, H. J. (Native Commissioner, Pretoria and Heidelberg), 101
Schreiner, W. P., 73
Scott, J. H., 83, 90
Scott, Rev. James (Member, Natal Native Commission, 1906-7), 66
Scott, Sir John (Lieut.-Governor, Natal), 58
Scully, W. C., 89, 174
Segregation, 157, 159, 160, 185, 204, 206, 207; Cape, 24, 73; Natal, 24, 37, 38, 43, 45
Sekelini *v.* Sekelini, 151
Sekukuni, Chief, 98-9, 108
Select Committee of the Cape House of Assembly ... Grey Act, 1898, 88, 151
Separation. *See* Segregation
Shaka (Zulu Chief), 41, 153, 176-7
Shangaans, 176
Shaw, Rev. Wm., 176, 193
Shepherd, R. H. W., 201
Shepstone, A. J., C.M.G. (Secretary for Native Affairs, Natal), 67, 187

Shepstone, Henrique, C., C.M.G. (Secretary for Native Affairs, Transvaal and Natal), 10, 59, 99-100, 147, 149, 156
Shepstone, John W., C.M.G. (Secretary for Native Affairs, Natal), 56, 59, 141
Shepstone, Sir Theophilus (Somtseu), 10, 23-5, 37, 39, 42-5, 50-9, 61-7, 70, 80-1, 85, 87, 128, 135, 144, 147, 150-1, 153, 159, 189, 197;
early years, 41-2
Administrator of Transvaal, 47-50, 59-60, 98-101, 107-8;
character, 45-50
Shepstone, Theophilus, Jnr., C.M.G., 120, 128
Shepstone, Rev. Wm., 41
Sigcolo v. Mokau, 136
Slavery, 38, 107
Slaves, emancipation of, 10, 35
Sloley, Sir Herbert (Resident Commissioner, Basutoland), 103
Smelting, 190
Smit, Dr. D. L., 206
Smith, Sir Harry (Governor, Cape of Good Hope), 16, 19, 20-25, 29, 82, 142-3, 151-2, 166, 173-4, 178
Smith, Major T., 38, 41
Smith-Calderwood Location Scheme, 1849, 23, 29, 83, 166, 170, 179
Smuts, Gen. the Rt. Hon. J. C. (Union Prime Minister), 48, 204-6, 208-9
Sohm, R., 152
Solomon, Sir Richard, 80
Somtseu. See Sir Theophilus Shepstone
South Africa Act, 1909, 106, 173
South African Native Affairs Commission, 1903-5, 11, 85, 103-7, 109, 128, 136, 151-2, 158, 171, 173, 186-7, 205
South African Native Races Commission, 186
South African Native Trust, 55
South African Republic. See Transvaal.
South African War, 1899-1902, 64, 103, 105, 192
Spies, A. (Member, Natal Native Commission, 1852-3), 53
"Spoor laws", 114, 129, 133
Sprigg, Hon. Sir J. Gordon (Prime Minister, Cape of Good Hope), 76-7

Squatters Law 37, 98
Squatting, 37, 45, 65, 98, 103-5, 109, 159, 171
Stainbank, D. L. W. (Member, Natal Native Commission, 1881-2), 61, 62
Stanford, R. W. (Magistrate, Butterworth), 174
Stanford, Senator the Hon. Sir Walter ("Ndabeni"), 79-80, 103, 109, 134, 146
Stanger, Dr. (Member, Natal Native Commission, 1846-7), 43
Stewart, Dr. James, 80, 200
Stock, agricultural, 177, 181-2, 184-5
Stockenström, Sir Andries, Bart., 19
Stott, C. H., 194
Strachey, Lytton, 77, 85
Struben, Capt. (Member, Natal Native Commission, 1852-3), 53
Strydom, the Rt. Hon. J. G. (Prime Minister of the Union), 206
Stuart, J., 66
Succession, 114, 118, 129, 130, 132, 136, 138, 142, 169, 172-3
"Supreme Chief": 51, 52, 57, 60, 99, 148, 163
Supreme Court: Cape, 131, 132, 144, 171; Natal, 60; Transvaal, 100, 156, 165
Surmon, W. A. (Magistrate, Kornet Spruit), 85
Survey Commission, 1920, 168
Surveying, location, 168-9, 171, 173
Sweeney, C. J. (Magistrate, Glen Grey), 87
Symons, J. P., 194

Taberer, H. M., 103
Tambookies, 182, 184
Tatham, E., 53
Taxation and fines, 23, 25-7, 54, 62, 65, 76, 78, 83, 87, 93, 98, 100, 101, 103, 105-6, 114, 144, 162, 166, 180
Taylor, Rev. J. D., 69
Teko, 178
Tembuland, 80, 82, 146, 179;
annexation of, 1885 78
Teteluku, Chief, 62, 117
Thaba Nchu, 97, 137
Thatching, 189
Theal, Dr. Geo. McCall, 19, 21, 76, 77, 81, 85, 186, 192
Theft, punishment of, 114, 129, 133-5
Thema, R. V. Selope, 206

221

Thompson, Col. (Member, Commons Select Committee, 1836-7), 19
Thompson, "Matabele" (Member, S.A. Native Affairs Commission 1903-5), 103
Thompson, Newton O., 132
Thompson, W. R. (Government Agent, Kaffraria), 186
Thukela River, boundary of Zululand, 31, 36, 41
Title deeds, 168-9, 173
"Togt" labour, 65
Tooke, Hammond, 80
Transkeian marriage regulations, 1879, 118
Transkeian Penal Code, 80, 81, 133, 142, 144-5, 147
Transkeian Territories, 29, 73-95, 160, 167, 207
Transkeian Territories General Council, 88-95
Transvaal:
 annexation, 1877, 46-7, 49, 60, 98, 108
 administration, 1877-81, 47, 49, 50, 59-60, 98-101, 107-8, 156
 disannexation, 1881, 48-50, 99-100, 165
 policy towards Africans, 36, 39, 97-109
 Pitso, 1881, 100
 annexation, 1900, 165
Transvaal Miners' Association, 193
Treaty policy, 16-17, 19-22, 30-3, 36, 38
Tree-planting, 178-9, 185
Trials, African tribal, 113, 133, 149
Tribal system, 113, 115, 144, 153, 161, 162
 Cape, 28
 Natal, 37-8, 44, 49, 53, 59, 64, 70, 163
 Transkei, 161
 Transvaal, 165
Trust system: Cape, 164-5
 Natal, 55, 69, 162-5
Trusteeship of land, 55, 69, 161-6
Tsewu v. Registrar of Deeds, 100, 174
Tshaka (Zulu Chief). See Shaka (Zulu Chief)
Tsiko, 129
Tsolo, 91, 146
Tsomo, 82, 85, 89, 167, 174
Tugela River. See Thukela River.
Turner, G. (Member, Natal Native Commission, 1881-2), 61

Twelve Tables, code of, 149-50
Tyali, 183
Ukungena, 133
Ulundi, 76
Umgudhlwa, 134-5
Umhlambiso, 20
Umlobokazi, 121
Umnini Trust, 55, 164
Umninimizi, 133
Umtata, 146
Umzilikazi. See Moselekatse
Umzimkulu, 92, 146
Umzimvubu River. See Mzimvubu River
Universities, African, 200
Upington, Sir Thos., 80
Uys, Dirk (Member, Natal Native Commission, 1882-3), 53

van Aswegen, Dr. H. J., 108, 158
van der Horst, Sheila T., 194
van Rensburg, W. H. Janse, M.L.A., 167
Vereeniging, Treaty of, 106
Verwoerd, the Rt. Hon. J. F. (Prime Minister of the Republic of S.A.), 95, 206
Victoria, H.M. Queen, 28, 31, 32, 48, 204
Victoria East, magisterial division of, 23, 129, 164, 166, 180, 182-3
Vilakazi, Absolom, 198, 201
Village Management Boards. See Boards, village management
Voortrekkers, policy of, 21, 35, 36-9, 159
Vorster, the Rt. Hon. B. J. (Prime Minister of the Republic of S.A.), 207
Vumsen, Ben, 181

Walker, Williston, 201
Walton, J.V. (Member, Natal Native Commission, 1881-2), 61
War of the Axe. See Frontier War, 7th
Warner, J. C., 143
Waterboer, Andries (Griqua Captain), 16
Watermeyer, V. M. (Magistrate, Tsomo), 89, 174
Webb, C. de B., 39, 58, 71, 201
Welsh, David, 71
West, Martin (Lieut.-Governor, Natal), 42, 43, 44, 58

Wheelwright, C. A. (Chief Native Commissioner, Natal), 123
Willowvale, 180
Wilson, A. (Member, Commons Select Committee, 1836-7), 19
Witchcraft, 22, 24, 52, 112, 114, 132, 135, 144-5
Witwatersrand, 192
Witsieshoek, 97
Wodehouse, Sir Philip (Governor, Cape of Good Hope), 151
Wolseley, Field-Marshal Lord (High Commissioner in South Africa), 60
Women. *See* Females
Wood-carving, 190
Wyndham, W. (Secretary for Native Affairs, Transvaal), 109

Xalanga, 146, 180, 191
Xesibe territory, 133
annexation of, 1886, 78

Yonge, C., M.L.A., 63

Zietsman, P. H., 39
Zikali, Mahlati, 28
Zulu War, 1879, 60, 192
Zululand, annexation of, 1897, 148
Zululand, "homelands" policy regarding, 207
Zululand and Natal, boundaries of, 31, 36, 41
Zululand Delimitation Commission, 1902-4, 69
Zululand Trust, 164
Zwaart Kop Industrial School, 201